MODERN
AUTOMATION

MODERN
AUTOMATION

BY

DAVID FOSTER

LONDON
SIR ISAAC PITMAN & SONS LTD.
in association with
ROWSE MUIR PUBLICATIONS LTD.

First published 1963

SIR ISAAC PITMAN & SONS, Ltd.
PITMAN HOUSE, PARKER STREET, KINGSWAY, LONDON, W.C.2
THE PITMAN PRESS, BATH
PITMAN HOUSE, BOUVERIE STREET, CARLTON, MELBOURNE
22–25 BECKETT'S BUILDINGS, PRESIDENT STREET, JOHANNESBURG

ASSOCIATED COMPANIES
PITMAN MEDICAL PUBLISHING COMPANY, Ltd.
46 CHARLOTTE STREET, LONDON, W.1
PITMAN PUBLISHING CORPORATION
20 EAST 46TH STREET, NEW YORK, 17
SIR ISAAC PITMAN & SONS (CANADA), Ltd.
(INCORPORATING THE COMMERCIAL TEXT BOOK COMPANY)
PITMAN HOUSE, 381–383 CHURCH STREET, TORONTO

ROWSE MUIR PUBLICATIONS LTD.
THE ROWSE MUIR BUILDING, 77-79 CHARLOTTE STREET,
LONDON, W.1

Made and printed in Great Britain
by Bookprint Limited
Kingswood, Surrey
F3 – (T. 947)

TO

MY WIFE

MIN

PREFACE

THE general idea of automation as a new technique dates from just after the war; it originated in the conviction of a few people that remarkable wartime developments, such as computer-controlled gun-laying and automatic aerial navigation, would make a major impact on post-war industrial processes. The interest of these possibilities was enhanced by parallel developments in scientific electronic computers, backed financially in Britain by the National Research Development Corporation, and also philosophically by the establishment of a new science called *cybernetics*. Now cybernetics means *the art of the steersman*, but the technical implication is that, in the future, robot electronic brains will direct (or steer) all physical industrial processes towards perfection, whilst mere humans will concentrate on solving the problems of excess leisure.

Such attractive ideas were not lost on the world's press. Between 1945 and 1955 very considerable enthusiasm was generated for the Golden Age of Cybernetics, and the more pronounceable word *automation* was revived to classify the practical aspects of the concept. The impact of these ideas was really considerable. Trade unions set their research workers to study the potential effects on labour, international technical bodies were founded, Russia adopted automation as a main economic policy; and Britain, as usual, formed a committee. Even our Institution of Production Engineers held a momentous conference.

After ten years of automation talk, electronics in most factories was nevertheless conspicuous by its absence. My own serious interest in automation dates from 1957, by which time the first wave of enthusiasm in the national press, and the general starry-eyed optimism, were beginning to wane; the word "automation" was nearly in disgrace. Towards the end of 1957, however, I became increasingly impressed by the extraordinary potentialities of electronics as a technique for the control of fast and difficult processes. I was led to a personal conclusion that industrial electronics *really had* a tremendous part to play in future industry, but that the time needed for its actualization might be far longer than people had supposed. Nor, indeed, was I at all sure at that time exactly what the word "automation" meant, although I was prepared to accept provisionally the current notion that it was something to do with running industries with computers or robot brains. Anyway, I found myself so increasingly interested in the subject, and by the bewildering number of opinions expressed about it, that I felt obliged to make the search for clarification a full-time occupation.

Right from the start I decided to have nothing, or pretty well nothing, to do with pure talk or theory. Instead I resolved that, whenever I heard a rumour or report about existing automation, I would pack my bags and go and look at it. Thus, over the last five years, I have done a great deal of looking into automation rumours and automation actualities, and—whether the rumour emanated from Moscow, Munich or Minnesota—if it sounded interesting, I went.

In retrospect I am inclined to think that this method was the best, and I suppose that I have now visited something over half the world's best automation rumours. But one thing I would make like to clear, and that is that I *never* saw the ultimate magic, a *process being controlled by a computer*, although the Los Angeles road-traffic control system might just qualify. I often got very near to the mirage, but when I finally knocked on the gates and said "I have come to see your process run by a computer," it always turned out to be, like the report of Mark Twain's death, grossly exaggerated.

On the other hand, as is the common experience on any voyage of discovery, I came across the unexpected, in this case some of the most fascinating pieces of automation equipment, outstandingly in the U.S.A., and the four visits I have made to that country since 1958 have always been amply repaid with exciting experiences which have pointed the way clearly into the future.

Thus, if I were to be asked now, in 1962, 'Is there really such a thing as automation?' I would certainly have to reply "Yes, automation does exist, though it takes a bit of finding. But one day these techniques will become pretty universal, and all this will cause a profound change in industry." I would have to add that the shortest time-interval in which an onlooker might observe significant changes in industry at large would probably be about a decade.

Towards the end of 1960 I had discussions with the editor of the British journal *Control* and the technical editor of Pitman's. As a result I undertook to write a book on the subject of "Modern Automation," and I was happy to do this for the following reasons.

About a year after I had commenced these explorations I began to get a glimmer of a simple theory about automation, a theory which had little do with computers as these devices are usually understood, and I began to try out this theory at various technical and industrial meetings which I was occasionally asked to address. This theory constitutes the first four chapters of this book, and has sometimes been described as "Automation without Tears." It is entirely non-mathematical, and is based on a simple analogy with human nervous and mental operations, combined with a simple analysis of different sorts of industrial process to which these mental operations can be applied in robot form. Thus I see automation as the subject concerned with the control of processes by electronic and similar devices which simulate human nervous and brain functions. In general I would confirm the popular belief that industry is moving towards the state in which it will be controlled by robot brains.

This does not necessarily imply the use of enormously expensive electronic computers, since even the simplest piece of electronic gadgetry usually has a correspondence with a specific human mental or nervous function. Furthermore, the higher flights of automation in the future will, I am convinced, follow this same pattern, and we may expect to see all sorts of electronic devices which will simulate the higher human mental functions of judgement and decision.

This book is divided into three sections—

1. A group of four chapters, dealing with the general approach to automation and its understanding by analogy with human mental and nervous functions.

2. The middle set of about fifteen chapters, which deal with practical examples of automation taken from various parts of the world. I have chosen those examples which are of particular interest and which in totality cover almost all possible techniques.

3. A final group of six chapters, which deal with general aspects, culminating in the last chapter with a discussion on the future of automation in Britain.

At the risk of anticipating the final conclusions of this book I would say that we in Britain could lead the world in automation if we only *applied* ourselves to it. There is little doubt that our backroom boys are some of the best in the world, but we are shockingly slow in getting down to the job of applying these new techniques in industry.

This book is not written for the British electronics industry, whose personnel are capable of reproducing any of the techniques described here without difficulty. It is aimed at general British industry, and perhaps particularly at those members of its management—at all levels—who do not realize the new wonders which are available for their exploitation. At present, in 1962, there is a tremendous gulf in Britain between the electronics industry and general industry, and it is my hope that these chapters will help a little to bridge it.

My thanks are due to very many people for assistance on parts of this book, but I would particularly like to thank Mr. H. A. V. Bulleid of British Nylon Spinners Ltd. He most conscientiously undertook the role of critic as the chapters successively rolled off the typewriter, and made many valuable suggestions towards greater clarity.

White House,   DAVID FOSTER
Sunninghill Road,
Windlesham, Surrey

CONTENTS

CHAPTER 1

PHILOSOPHY OF AUTOMATION

THERE is a great deal of controversy about the exact meaning of the word *automation*. One school of thought takes the simple view that it means making processes progressively more automatic. Others consider that the essential feature is represented by the enigmatic expression "closing the feedback loop," whilst a third viewpoint is that automation means "process control," and preferably controlling the process with some sort of computer.

As one might expect, each of these viewpoints contains some piece of truth. But if you accept any one of the above definitions then you exclude much that is genuine automation. It is necessary to find a definition which is both exact and comprehensive. The definition which I prefer, and which I have found to stand the test of time, both practically and theoretically, is—

automation = development into data-controlled process

The essential feature of this definition is its implication that, somewhere in a physical process or its control system, there exist *data* which are playing a vital role. Such a definition therefore embraces all feedback systems where data are extracted from the process for correcting process performance. It also covers *programmed* processes, a very important automation group, in which there may be no feedback element; and it even includes simple instrumental systems as *partial automation*, where data are picked up from a process and presented to an operator for his better information.

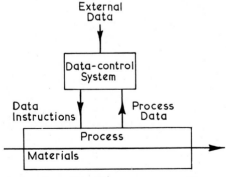

FIG. 1.1.   AUTOMATION GIVES DATA-CONTROLLED PROCESS

1

Our definition is illustrated graphically in Fig. 1.1. All processes involve some manipulation of materials, whether we refer to manufacturing or chemical processes, or even to such processes as transport systems, where the materials may be goods or passengers. Furthermore, there will always be, in principle, three sorts of data involved in linking a data-control system with the process. Most obviously, there have to be two links to provide an interchange of data between the process and the control system, so that the control system can give instructions to the process and receive responses from it. In addition, there has to be some sort of data link between the whole process (including its control aspects) and the external environment, even if this consists only of a "start" button which has to be pressed every five years. By no means all automated systems have all three sorts of data link fully established and fully automatic, and many worth-while systems of "automation" are really examples of *partial* automation.

A further merit of our definition is that it is historically correct— the seeds of automation were sown as techniques of process-instrumental measurement, i.e. data-gathering devices. You will also note that a key word in the definition is "process," and this is because in some systems one cannot clearly separate the control function from the process itself: indeed, any control system is itself a process— a "data process." Furthermore, the definition is at home as much in physical automation, applying to a manufacturing or chemical process, as it is in clerical automation, where the end product may be a piece of printed paper.

At this point let me state that this book is essentially concerned with physical automation, as applied to the processes of manufacture and distribution, and I shall only bring in clerical automation where its techniques make an integral part of a physically automated system.

AUTOMATION IS NOT MECHANIZATION

Whilst our definition is broad, it is also specific: it excludes that process which may be described as pure mechanization, since the data involved in pure mechanization exists only in the head of the original designer. In true automation the data-control aspect can normally be specifically recognized as such. It also is a fair working rule to say that *automation commences where mechanization leaves off*.

If automation starts essentially where mechanization leaves off, we should have a clear idea of the inherent limits of mechanization. These limits are set by the laws of mechanics. The basic materials used in the construction of machines are rigid materials such as steel and other metals, and the most we can do in applying engineering design to these materials is to produce useful structures of a mechanical or chemical engineering nature which, at best, can be made sufficiently automatic in their operation to go on repeating the same sort of *cyclic* mechanical actions. It is true, that in earlier days, mechanisms were designed as data-handling devices, and, in the last century, Babbage (the inventor of computers) designed a computer entirely based on gear-wheels, levers and chains, but this was very cumbersome and very slow in operation.

The fact is that the materials used in machines and mechanization are too heavy and too clumsy, *in principle*, for the rapid operations required in data control; so we have to turn to the lightest material known, the electron, to achieve data-handling speed, and this is why electronics is the prime technique in the evolution of automation.

Thus it is philosophically correct, and a fact of experience, that pure machines are essentially unintelligent and unadaptable in their nature, and are only fit for the transmission of force and power. No matter how complicated we make them, or how much we integrate them together in the transfer lines of the motor industry, they nevertheless retain a basic sort of blindness, stupidity and lack of adaptability.

From the production point of view, perhaps the major defect of this inherent blindness of mechanical processes is that the *quality* of production must always progressively deteriorate, and this is because a pure machine does not have built-in properties to detect the quality of the work it is producing. Thus complete mechanization can only ensure that the process mechanized will produce an adequate *quantity* of work, but it can never ensure that the process will produce adequate *quality*.

The classical philosopher would explain all this by pointing out that Newton's laws of mechanics, upon which mechanization is based, are rigid causal laws which have no connexion with nervous sensitivity, or psychological activities like observation and comparison, or intelligence, or thinking, which are essential requirements for a controller of quality. In the most general sense, therefore, we can describe a machine as a device which simply does not know what it is doing; its effectiveness depends entirely upon the brain of its original designer, and any deterioration in the tune of the machine will reflect in deterioration of its performance and in the quality of the article produced. Thus, for mechanization to be effective, materials of construction must be durable enough, and they must possess sufficient resistance to change of dimension by the natural processes of wear and tear. At best, mechanization may be economically adequate for a particular series of products, but even then its products will always be stupid and unadaptable without considerable human intervention.

MECHANIZATION AND HUMAN BEINGS

So machines and mechanized processes can only be made effective by the injection of considerable and repeated doses of intelligence emanating from human supervisors. We call these people machine-setters, operators, maintenance men, supervisors, etc., and they are all living testimony to the fact that machines cannot be left to look after themselves. The general arrangement of human beings controlling a physical process is as shown in Fig. 1.2, and this can be directly compared with the automated version of Fig. 1.1.

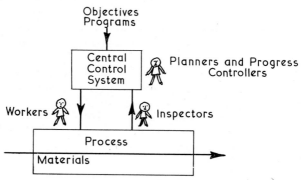

FIG. 1.2. HUMAN CONTROL OF PROCESS

Now what are the essential psychological properties possessed by these human supervisors, whose intelligence is required to keep machines and mechanized processes up to scratch?

First and foremost, the human attending a machine has to be aware of the *object* of the process concerned: he must be aware of what the machine is *intended* to do and to produce, concerning which the machine itself is totally unaware. So, first and foremost, the human machine-minder has product specifications and quality standards in mind, and he is constantly watching and adjusting the machine or process to ensure that these standards are maintained.

THE HUMAN PSYCHIC FUNCTIONS

In order to observe successfully, the human has to use various senses, and he may also require various measuring devices to enable him to inspect accurately whatever is being made. In addition he must know exactly the ideal standards to which the process *ought* to work, and he must also have the experience, intelligence and ability to readjust the process in the correct manner if it is tending to produce an incorrect product. At the very least, therefore, the human requires—

Senses for observation.
Ability to recognize what he observes.
Knowledge of correct standards of performance.
Intelligence.

These are a minimum requirement for effective process supervision, and if the process being worked is complicated, he may be called upon to perform further nervous and mental functions, including calculating. If the situation is still beyond his own ability, he must have the sense to call upon the more extensive experience of his foreman or boss.

Let us call all these human attributes, which are required by good process supervisors, the human *psychic functions*. We are then ready to expand our earlier definition of automation to—

Automation is the application to established industrial processes of artificial devices which can simulate the human psychic functions (senses, memory, standards, intelligence) in order that these processes may acquire characteristics of adaptability and self-optimization.

RELATION BETWEEN DATA CONTROL AND PSYCHIC FUNCTIONS

In our original definition of automation we used the expression *data-controlled process*. In the definition above we have related automation to the artificial simulation of the human psychic functions. What is the relationship and where the equivalence of these two definitions?

The human psychic functions are simulated by so-called data-processing devices of (principally) light electrical and electronic kinds. Thus the human ear performs a *human psychic function* but a microphone is a *data-processing device*. The two definitions are thus reconcilable by a change in language as we cross over from psychology to physics and engineering.

WHY ELECTRONICS IS BASIC TO AUTOMATION

It is common, if somewhat vague, knowledge that modern automation is closely associated with electronics. Thus every two years, in London, there is an exhibition called the Instruments, Electronics and Automation Exhibition. Why is there this close association between the two subjects? The reader may well ask this question, especially if he has been round a modern "automated" motor-car factory and seen almost no electronics.

Part of the answer is that most mass-producing factories are at present based almost entirely on pure mechanization, and not on automation in the way we have described it. Secondly, in a truly data-controlled plant you will not see very much *evidence* of the data-controlling operations because data-controlling equipment is very small and compact compared with the process it is controlling. Thus one of the most advanced data-controlled processes in existence is the traffic-light system in Los Angeles, which is controlled by a central computer. But this device is tucked away in a corner of the traffic manager's office at the Los Angeles City Hall, and unless you knew of its existence you would never notice it.

But this still has not answered the question, exactly why is electronics fundamental to automation?

Let us give the answer first, and then try to explain it.

Answer
Data control means knowledge control.
Knowledge is expressed by language.
Language consists of wave-forms.
Electronics is the easiest way of producing wave-forms.
Hence electronics is the easiest technique of data control. Q.E.D.

We will now take this a little more slowly.

Data Control Means Knowledge Control

This is simply a question of Latin versus English. My edition of the Oxford Dictionary gives "Datum: Thing known or granted," and "Knowledge: Person's range of information." Perhaps the best argument that *data* means *knowledge* is that they are both "something you can put into a memory."

Knowledge is Expressed by Language

If the test for data or knowledge is that they can be put into a memory, what do we mean by this? The fact is that the only thing you can *really* put into a memory is language, which is the *form* of data or knowledge. Take the piece of knowledge: *That is the pen of my aunt*. This can exist as an expression in my memory as language, but it means something to me as knowledge because I can refer it to the actual pen of my aunt, which I have seen. A Frenchman can have the same knowledge, but his memory will store the expression *C'est la plume de ma tante:* same knowledge but different language. Thus what is *actually* stored in the memory is language, which is the *form* of knowledge.

Language Consists of Wave-form

Language is physical: the form of knowledge. All language is expressible in wave-forms. The spoken word is a wave-form in space-time created by our vocal chords. Written language is a wave-form in space, and we read it by scanning it, making a space-time wave-form by the movement of our eyes. All coded languages, such as Morse or the digital codes of computers, are wave-forms. A simple proof of this statement is that all language forms can be transmitted over radio or television, and the ether can transmit *only* wave-forms.

Electronics is the Easiest Way of Producing Wave-forms

We have thus reduced the problem of data and data control to the problem of wave-forms and wave-form control. What is the easiest way to produce wave-forms? What indeed is a wave-form?

A wave-form is the pattern made by something which moves. But if you, reading this book, wanted to make a wave-form, what would you do? You could pick up a chair and wave it around and describe a wave-form: but you would soon drop the chair and pick up a pencil, and then you would be able to describe wave-forms in the air much more quickly and with far less trouble. If now you tried to express the same amount of knowledge, such as "my cat is black," *as fast as possible* by: (*a*) waving a chair about; (*b*) waving a pencil in writing, you would find that Chair Writing would take you about twenty-five seconds and Pencil Writing about six seconds. From this you conclude: "The speed required for making wave-form language is related to the heaviness of the device used—the lighter the faster."

But the lightest thing known to man is the electron, and this means that *electronic wave-forms provide the fastest language known.* Not only is the electron the most suitable thing for embodying the wave-forms of language and knowledge; it is also about the most common entity in the universe, and intrinsically the cheapest.

I hope that the reader will consider the case proven; data control and data processing must almost certainly involve electrons and electronics. Thus the futures of automation and electronics are sure to be increasingly interwoven. There are, of course, simple forms of data handling in which it may be adequate to use those knowledge and language wave-forms more commonly described as gear-wheels, cams, etc., but you will soon forgo these if your problem is complex or if you are in a hurry.

THE FOUR KINDS OF ELECTRONIC LANGUAGE

In order to have a very fast language for data processing, then, we shall use electronic wave-forms for words and figures. There are four principal varieties of electronic wave-form language, as illustrated in Fig. 1.3. They are as follows:—

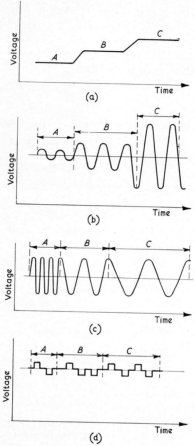

FIG. 1.3.   FOUR ELECTRONIC WAVE-FORM LANGUAGES
                   (a) D.C. analogue; (b) A.C. analogue; (c) Frequency change;
                   (d) Digits or pulses.

D.C. (DIRECT CURRENT) ANALOGUE LANGUAGE is shown in
Fig. 1.3 (a), and the basis of it is that the strength of an electric
current or voltage, shown by the height of the graph above the
baseline, forms a code. We could, for example, represent the
alphabet by twenty-six different strengths of current.

A.C. (ALTERNATING CURRENT) ANALOGUE LANGUAGE uses an
alternating current or voltage of varying amplitude. The variations
can form a code, as shown in Fig. 1.3 (b). This is the language used
on ordinary ("amplitude-modulated") radio sets.

FREQUENCY-CHANGE LANGUAGE employs an alternating current

as shown in Fig. 1.3 (c), and the code is expressed by the change in the frequency of oscillation of the current. Thus the letter A could be represented by a frequency of 10,000 vibrations a second, the letter B by a frequency of 10,100 vibrations a second, and so on. This is the sort of electronic language used on f.m. ("frequency-modulated") radio sets.

DIGITAL OR PULSE LANGUAGE. As shown in Fig. 1.3 (d) positive and negative current pulses form patterns which can carry information. For binary numbers, which are expressed in terms of the digits 0 and 1 only, a positive pulse is used to represent 1, and a negative pulse (or no pulse at all) to represent 0. This system is virtually an up-to-date version of the Morse code.

CHAPTER 2

WORKING OF THE MIND IN PROCESS CONTROL

As I have already said, the word *cybernetics* (lit: "the art of the steersman") was coined to cover the science of process control. The science of cybernetics is an attempt to amalgamate two allied fields (*a*) *human cybernetics*, the study of how the human mind works, and (*b*) *robot cybernetics*, the study of electronic computers or robot thinking. These two aspects of cybernetics are very close to each other, for research into pyschology throws light on the theory of computers, particularly in the common field of "logic," whilst developments in computer technology are often very suggestive in explaining how the human mind works. Many words such as "memory," "logical functions," etc., have been borrowed from the corresponding psychological field.

Now the essence of advanced automation is the robot brain for controlling industrial processes. A rough familiarity with human cybernetics therefore serves as a broad foundation for understanding robot cybernetics. The robot gadgets used in automation will be largely attempts to imitate the human mind and nervous system.

In this chapter we shall study the working of psychology in relationship to process-control situations, and in the next chapter we shall consider how the various psychological and nervous functions can be imitated by electronic devices.

THE TWO PRINCIPAL HUMAN CAPABILITIES
FOR PROCESS CONTROL

The process-control problems facing human beings can be divided into two main groups:—

Corrective control in which a process is already operating and a supervising human is expected to keep it operating correctly.

Planned control is which a person is given a general order from a higher level and is expected to control a process to put the order into effect.

We shall later see that all practical automation can be related to simulating the above two sorts of human control function by means of appropriate robot functions.

Corrective Control by Reflex Skill

The simplest form of human process-control makes use of reflex skill. If you are driving your car and a tyre bursts, you almost immedi-

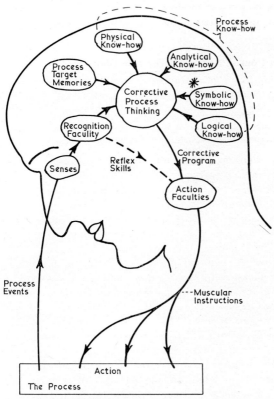

FIG. 2.1.   CORRECTIVE PROCESS CONTROL
*Includes mathematics, diagrams, words

ately begin to stop the car. The elements of this sort of control skill
are shown in the lower part of Fig. 2.1. They are (1) recognition of
something wrong with the process, (2) immediate coupling of recognition with automatic corrective reactions, and (3) action faculties.
This form of reaction is based on the well-known nervous reflex arc,
in which no thinking is involved, and which is as well developed in
lower animals as in humans. In automated systems it corresponds to
all immediate-reaction devices, such as direct-acting thermostats,
centrifugal governors, lavatory ballcocks, etc., in which there is an
immediate connexion between a disturbing cause and a counter
effect.

   In general this form of process-control reflex skill can only deal
with immediate and obvious situations, and is too elementary to be
considered an important part of the modern automation concept.

Indeed, the concern of modern automation is how to fulfil corrective control functions more complex than those corresponding to human reflex skills.

Corrective Control by Considered Know-how

Let us consider a more sophisticated example of corrective control, beyond the level of what is effectively a reflex skill reaction.

> *Example.* The pilot of an aeroplane suddenly notices that one of the fifty dials in front of him shows an unusual reading and indicates that one of the four engines has low oil-pressure. What does he do next?

Such a situation clearly calls for action decision, but if the oil pressure is not disastrously low the first decision is to *do nothing* except "figure it out." This is the essence of complex corrective control, and the good operator is the one who comes to the correct control decision in the shortest time. In the upper part of Fig. 2.1 are shown the elements essential in coming to a *considered* control decision. These involve—

Senses and Recognition Faculty. Clearly the process controller must have faculties for seeing that something is wrong, and these will involve one or more of his senses and his power of recognizing the facts that he observes.

Process-target Memory. The controller requires a clear picture of the objectives, with which he can compare the results of the faulty operation. Note that, in the example of the aeroplane pilot, the process target is not necessarily to have the engine oil-pressure normal, but is to make a flight safely and on schedule. It is partly this sort of complex relationship between process faults and process targets which makes simple reflex skills ineffective in such a situation.

Process Know-how. Any complex corrective problem has to be referred back to process know-how before a controller can come to his decisions. This know-how is the sum of all the controller's past experience, and all his mental skills in understanding how the process is intended to work and how it does work. This total process know-how may be conveniently divided into four main categories—

1. *Physical Process Know-how.* This is the controller's "picture" of his physical experience of the process. It includes all memories of past happenings in the process, both normal and abnormal, and it includes a great number of mental images of what goes on inside the process under normal and abnormal conditions. The mental model of a process is probably the most valuable part of human control know-how, but if you asked a controller to describe his mental model he would probably be largely unable to do so. This valuable aspect of manual control is usually greatly under-

rated, because of its relative vagueness and incompleteness if expressed on paper; it is closely related to the human capacity for imagining.

2. *Analytical Know-how*. The human mind can take a complex situation and sort it out. This is not the same thing as problem-solving, but it may often be a necessary preparatory step. "Getting the facts straight" is preparation for progressive logical thinking, and works by sorting things into *like* and *unlike* categories.

3. *Symbolic Know-how*. This is the theoretical counterpart of physical process know-how, an abstract representation of a physical process by such means as graphical flow-sheets or mathematical formulae. Facts are represented by symbols and the factual process is represented by mathematical processing of symbols.

4. *Logical Know-how*. When you hear a person say "That simply does not make sense," you are witnessing the operation of his logical faculty. Logic is defined in the Oxford Dictionary as "The Science of Reasoning." Its end-point is a decision as to whether a statement is true or false. Logic is particularly concerned with rules for deciding whether one stage of a reasoned progressive argument has been correctly derived from the previous stage. Thus logic will decide that the statement "All cats are animals" is true, but that the statement "All animals are cats" is false. All human fault-diagnosing skills must be applied according to logical rules. In a comparable way, all the data processing in a computer must also be based on correct logical relationships; otherwise the answer is either meaningless or misleading.

WHAT DO WE MEAN BY THINKING?

So far, in considering how human beings control external processes in a corrective way, I have suggested that first there must be process-fact recognition and knowledge of process targets, and that then these must be referred to human know-how consisting of physical, symbolic, analytical and logical components. We now have to consider how all these may work together to solve corrective control problems, and this total operation we shall call "process thinking."

In Fig. 2.2 is a suggested model of how process thinking may work. It starts with the two inputs: the observed current facts of process behaviour, and the general aims or targets. The main line of thinking proceeds from analysis of the facts towards mathematical or symbolic solution of the problem, which in turn will lead to a program of corrective action. At the side of this main line of solution are arranged the logical mental functions to check that thinking procedures are not breaking logical rules. Also, as a side aspect, there are the physical

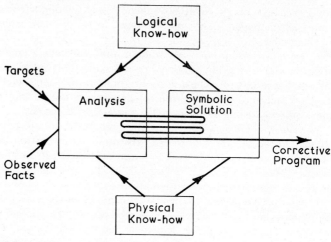

FIG. 2.2.   CORRECTIVE THINKING

know-how and experiential background, which must also be taken into account; it is no use suggesting solutions which do not agree with past experience. Also shown on the diagram is the progressive step-by-step procedure between analysis and the symbolic solution. This procedure vacillates between the two until the proposed solution is entirely satisfactory. With the above in mind we can now formally define process-control problem-solving as follows—

> Thinking for solving process-correction problems commences with an analysis of observed facts of the process and of process targets, and moves progressively towards a symbolic solution in mathematics, words or diagrams, whilst the correctness of the solution is checked at each stage against logical and experiential factors. The end solution is the corrective program.

Nature of Action Decisions

If process thinking has been correct and has been embodied in a corrective program, there still remains the problem of putting such a solution into effect, and this raises two issues: how does a human being *decide to act* after he knows *how* to act? And after he has decided to act, how does he *convey* his actions to the process?

From a psychological point of view the first problem is a tricky matter, and could involve such issues as free-will versus determinism. Yet it is a fact that one may sometimes have a solution to a problem and not put it into effect, and sometimes one may simply be slow about it. What is the *decisive* element? In the particular circumstances we are considering it is probably simply "a sense of professional duty."

If one did not act decisively when the circumstances required it, one would suffer disapproval from one's fellows.

Action Faculties

Actions, when a man knows how to act and has decided to act, are initiated by his motor centre. This is located in the cerebellum and spinal chord. It appears to have a great deal of knowledge in its own right; if you say to yourself, "I will hit that nail with this hammer" your motor centre has all the knowledge needed to make the action go correctly.

HUMAN CAPACITY FOR PLANNED PROCESS CONTROL

At the beginning of this chapter human process-control abilities were divided into two classes: first, ability to *correct* the operation of a process, and second, the control of a process by planning. So far we have dealt with only the first of these, but in doing so we have established much, in connexion with language and methods, which is related to the second category, *planned action*.

The essential difference between corrective and planned action is that the former commences with observation of a deviation or error whilst the latter commences with a request or instruction to operate. Thus planned action in a process may commence with such an instruction as "today make 200 tons of sulphuric acid of 95 per cent purity." From this starting point a great deal of planning will result in the creation of detailed process-operation programs and ultimate operation.

The general scheme of such planned action on the part of human beings is given in Fig. 2.3, and has the following features—

An Input Order or Instruction, which has merely to be understood, will normally be expressed in writing, possibly illustrated by drawings if the process is one of manufacture. This input originates outside the mental sphere of the process-controlling individual.

Analytical Capacity must exist in a human process-supervisor, who has to sort the general instruction into its component parts. He must assess material requirements and consider the processing of these materials. The result of his analytical work is a great number of smaller instructions which, when added together, are virtually equal to the original simple instruction but with much more detail. There has been a transition from a broad indication of what is wanted to an exact and detailed analysis of it.

Planning Ability. The analysis of detailed process targets or "wants" must next be converted into a corresponding range of detailed action programs. This "planning thinking" is different from the thinking

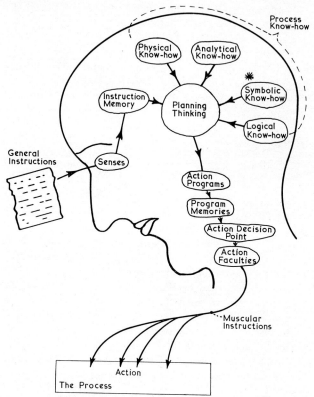

FIG. 2.3.　　PLANNED PROCESS CONTROL
*Includes mathematics, diagrams, words

required for process-corrective action. The latter is concerned with facts and devising a single corrective program, whereas planning thinking is concerned with a simple, general, incoming instruction and breaking it down into many detailed programs.

Action Decisions for Planned Action. Decisions for planned action are basically different from those involved in corrective action. In both cases, at the end of the process thinking phase, there are detailed programs for action, but in the corrective case such programs are usually for immediate action. With planned action, the decision to put the plan into effect has to wait on the *correct time* to do it, and this has usually to be referred back to a more general timing plan which involves such considerations as programming the factory for an even production rate and taking into account the requirements of other programs which may use the same resources.

Such considerations imply that there must be means for storing action programs until wanted.

THE TOTAL HUMAN PSYCHIC SYSTEM FOR PROCESS CONTROL

We can now take into account the psychic requirements for both corrective and planned process control. These are as shown in Fig. 2.4. The main faculties and requirements will be—

Senses
Recognition
Target or instruction memory
Thinking, with analytical, logical, physical, mathematical and symbolic know-how

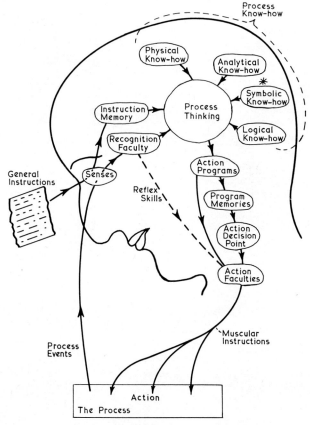

FIG. 2.4.   TOTAL HUMAN PSYCHE FOR PROCESS CONTROL
*Includes Mathematics, diagrams, words

Program memory
Action decision centre
Motor muscular control centre or action faculties.

Thinking will involve the four constituent faculties in a rather different fashion in corrective and planned process control. In all faculties there will be some aspect of factual knowledge and some aspect of procedural know-how, the two aspects having a relationship which we shall see later corresponds to *data* and to *data processing* respectively.

CHAPTER 3

ELECTRONIC SIMULATION OF PSYCHIC FUNCTIONS

BY the end of the previous chapter we had established a group of human factors required for human supervision of planned and corrective process control. How can such faculties and functions be simulated by electrical and electronic techniques? The differences between corrective and planned control functions need not be considered here, since the co-ordination of various parts for effective automation of systems will be dealt with in the following chapter. Our immediate concerns are the senses and sensing, recognition, program memories, process know-how, decision, and action.

SIMULATION OF SENSE ORGANS: SENSING

Sensing is not the same as recognition. You may look out of the window at your garden and your head will be filled with impressions of brightness, colour and form: this is sensing. But if out of the scene you select a particular rose-bush and concentrate on it, then you may be involved in the further function of recognition. In the simulation of human sensing, therefore, a channel of transmission has merely to be established between a process and its control system.

Now, whilst one may divide the human senses into the five crude groups of sight, hearing, touch, smell and taste (corresponding to the five sense-organs concerned), these categories have many important subdivisions such as—

Sight	Smell and Taste	Touch	Hearing
Movement	Qualitative (many)	Contact	Loudness
Position		Force	Pitch
Size		Heat	Harmony
Warning of approach		Wetness	Rhythm
Number		Texture	Direction
Colour			
Brightness			
Texture			
Translucency			
Form			

Many of the above varieties have sensing and recognition mixed together, and to eliminate pure recognition we should probably require to know the pure powers of sensing of a new-born child. For example, in relationship to sight we may expect that a new-born child is sensitive to both brightness and colour, but that "form," "number" and "size" may be categories of recognition acquired by experience.

In sensing we are concerned with the transmission of information from matter to mind, from physical process to data handler. In general this may be called "data gathering," and an essential requirement is that an artificial sensor shall pick up the same *essential, total, wanted information* as the human sense. I emphasize the expression "total information" because the information may be mixed up and complex, but the important thing is not how clear it is but that it should all be there. It is always feasible to unscramble an information complex and reject unwanted information, but one is lost if the *required* information is simply not present in the sensed signal.

Physical or Amplitude Sensors

Physical sensors are to some extent the equivalents of the three human organs of hearing, touch, and sight. In general they can give information related to the world of mechanics and energy. In almost all cases they put out an electrical signal proportional to the strength of the stimulus (see Fig. 3.1). There is a great variety of physical sensors, but there are four examples of outstanding importance—

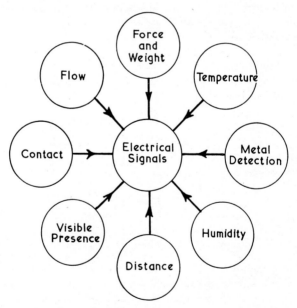

FIG. 3.1.   SOME PHYSICAL SENSORS

1. The *thermocouple*, which senses temperature, and puts out a proportional electric signal.

2. The *strain gauge*, which senses physical strain (and hence force) and puts out a proportional electrical signal.

3. The *photocell*, which senses a light beam and puts out a proportional signal; this corresponds to brightness sensitivity in sight.

4. The *limit* or *proximity switch*, which puts out a signal when it is touched (or nearly touched).

Chemical or Analysing Sensors

The senses of taste and smell, and of colour distinction in sight, are essentially chemical senses since they detect certain molecular properties of materials. This is obvious in relation to taste and smell, because one can taste and smell so many chemicals. The colour aspect of sight as a chemical detector may not be so obvious, but colour is always related to the electronic configurations of the atoms from which the light emanates, and this is the province of chemistry ("molecular spectrometry").

Physical sensors are usually amplitude or strength sensors, whereas chemical sensors are mainly *qualitative*. The devising of chemical sensors involves problems of *pattern* rather than force, and this is basic, because chemicals are patterns of atoms. A chemical sensor must have some form of analytic device to sort out the pattern in the incoming signal. A device to "sense red colour" can use a photocell responsive to white light, but must have associated with it a red colour filter so that it responds only to red and not to blue or green light. Similarly, to sense "aluminium in steel" an X-ray spectrograph bombards the metals with X-rays but analyses out those reflected rays which are characteristic of aluminium. Chemical sensors are essentially analysing sensors, just as smell, taste and colour vision are analysing senses, We shall, therefore, call chemical sensors *analysing sensors* to distinguish them from the purely *amplitude sensors*, which are generally adequate for physical sensing in the world of mechanics and gross objects. This is not to say that there is not also an amplitude requirement in analysing sensors, since one may not only require to know whether there is *some* aluminium in the steel but also *how much* aluminium there is in the steel. Some typical chemical analysing sensors are given in Fig. 3.2.

I have related artificial sensors to human sensing, but the development of technique now enables men to sense, artificially, many process properties which the human senses cannot detect, e.g. many chemical differences, and very high and very low pressures and temperatures. On the other hand, human senses can detect differences which cannot yet be found artificially, notably subtleties of taste and smell. In colour and texture matching, too, the eye is still supreme.

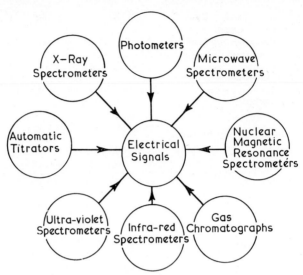

FIG. 3.2.   SOME ANALYSING CHEMICAL SENSORS

The technique involved in the construction of sensors is so varied that one cannot generalize, except to say that the natural physico-electrical or chemico-electrical properties of materials are exploited to produce an electrical signal in the right sort of wave-form language for further artificial manipulation.

SIMULATION OF RECOGNITION AND CLASS MEMORIES

We have touched on the fact that sensing and recognition are not the same things. Let us see how the human being recognizes, as in the example shown in Fig. 3.3.

Imagine that "My Auntie" is coming towards me in the street. At first I am looking only in her general direction and she is part of the general scene—I am merely sensing. Later, as she comes nearer, I focus my eyes on "This Lady" and unfocus on the rest of the view. As she gets even nearer something clicks in my brain and I say, "That Lady is My Auntie," and this is *recognition*.

There are four elements involved in human recognition as listed on the left-hand side of the table below. The automated equivalent is shown on the right-hand side.

Human Recognition	Robot Recognition
1. General sensing	Sensing by sensors
2. Sense focusing	Data classifying
3. A memory of "My Auntie"	Class memory
4. Recognition by comparison of 2 and 3	Class comparator

Fig. 3.3 shows the two forms of recognition, human and robot. The data classifier eliminates unwanted information from the output of the sensor. In an automated system the strength of red signals could be recognized by a sensor consisting of a photocell, and the data classifier would be a glass filter which eliminated all colours except red. Note that the data classifier does not itself recognize, but it eliminates confusing signals and prepares the way for recognition.

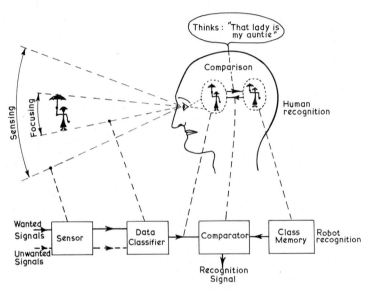

FIG. 3.3.   HUMAN AND ROBOT RECOGNITION

The class memory is a prearranged series of electrical wave-forms, each of which corresponds to one item or class memory. The type of wave-form stored in the class memory will vary considerably, according to the sort of thing one wishes to recognize. In general, there will be two groups: amplitude recognition and quality recognition.

Amplitude Recognition

Amplitude Class Memories. These will be used mainly with physical sensors for recognizing "force," "weight," "temperature," "humidity," etc., where the sensor's electrical output can only vary in amplitude. The amplitude class memory will normally consist of a series of preselected voltages which are equal to the sensor voltages at the required recognition points. For example, if a temperature of

85°C corresponds to an electrical output of (say) 3·2 volts from the sensor, the corresponding amplitude class memory is an electrical potentiometer voltage of 3·2 volts: when a temperature of 85°C is reached the two voltages are the same and this coincidence is detected in the class comparator.

Amplitude Class Comparators. This is the real recognition device, since it is arranged to put out a signal when sensor voltage and memory voltage are the same. The usual arrangement is to detect voltage balance in an electrical "bridge" circuit which is, in effect, a pair of electrical scales. As an example, one may cite a commercial unit which combines the functions of nine amplitude class memories and an amplitude class comparator. This system can be used to recognize different amplitude signals from one sensor and a typical application is for dimensional inspection of a product which has to be graded into size ranges.

Quality Recognition

The problem of robot recognition becomes much more complex when *qualities*, or general classes of things, are to be recognized. There is almost no limit to the depth of these quality-recognition problems. Many are still unsolved, particularly in the recognition of chemicals. One approach is an expansion of the previous description of amplitude recognition.

Suppose it is required to recognize the presence of a certain chemical, and the colour of light transmitted when it is present is known to be ten per cent red, fifty per cent yellow, and forty per cent blue. The method is shown in Fig. 3.4. A white light is shone through the chemical and an optical prism splits the emergent beam into red, yellow and blue. The prism thus acts as the data classifier. The three coloured beams are sensed by three separate photocells and taken to three amplitude comparators. Corresponding electrical amplitude memories V_1, V_2, and V_3 are set up in the recognition ratios 10, 50 and 40, and these are also taken to the three amplitude comparators. As it stands, however, the system will not recognize the required chemical because, although the *ratios* of the memory voltages are correct, their amplitudes may be quite incorrect. The next thing is to bring the memory voltages to the correct amplitudes whilst still maintaining the correct ratios. This is done by adding together the voltages from the three photocells (S_1, S_2 and S_3) and comparing these with the addition of the memory voltages (V_1, V_2 and V_3) in a voltage balancer whose function is to readjust the common voltage supply, V, to the three amplitude memories until the sum of the photocell voltages and the sum of the memory voltages are the same. When this is done, recognition can take place on coincidence of correct ratios in the three amplitude comparators. This coincidence can be detected by a simple logic box of a sort which will be described later. Such a system will not only recognize the particular chemical but also measure its quantity. Quantity is measured by the degree of adjustment required in the voltage balancer to bring the added memory voltages to a total which is the same as the sensor voltages.

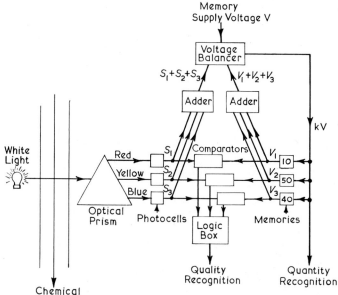

Fig. 3.4.   QUALITY RECOGNITION

From the above *simple* example the reader will realize that quality recognition can be very complex. The main present effort on quality recognition is in the chemical field, and much progress has been made in the development of self-contained analysers which can recognize certain chemicals both qualitatively and quantitatively .

SIMULATION OF PROGRAM MEMORIES

All physical processes require some statement of targets. Consider a few that are applied in industry.

> Railway: "Run the trains to the timetable."
> Motor-car factory: "Make 1,500 cars tomorrow."
> Postal sorting office: "Finish all the sorting by 9.30 p.m."
> Chemical factory: "Make 250 tons of sulphuric acid today."

These are the most general instructions or targets which an industrial system must obey, and an automated system must respond to this sort of general command. Such instructions may be called a *command program*, and they correspond to the instructions which permeate down from management until they become effective on the shop floor.

It is clear that a command will have to be considered in detail between its bald announcement by a managing director ("Make 1,500 cars tomorrow") and its actualization on the shop floor. As observed in the previous chapter, it must be split into many sub-command programs, and in an automated system this analysis is the job of intermediate data-processing, or "automated planning."

Four Main Forms of Program Memory

A program is the starting point for operation of a process, the initial instruction. There are four main forms of command program—

End-point Programs simply specify the result wanted at the end of the operation. Such end-point programs do not tell one *how* to achieve the desired result and they are, as it were, policies or general programs. They are the most important programs of all, for they can determine the activity of a whole industrial undertaking.

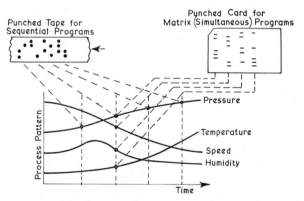

Fig. 3.5.   Sequential or Matrix Programs

Sequential Programs result from breaking down an end-point program into consecutive steps in time. Sequential programs can operate automated systems directly if they contain all required detailed instructions. A typical sequential command program will carry detailed information equivalent to instructions such as: (1) carry out operation A; (2) wait for ten minutes; (3) carry out operation B until product quality is satisfactory; (4) carry out operation C for two minutes; and so on.

This is probably the most common form of program in automated systems, and the program memory may be a punched paper tape or a magnetic tape. In these cases the length of the tape provides the sequential time axis (*see* Fig. 3.5) and the breadth of the tape is punched or otherwise coded for the particular operation to be carried out at the particular time.

Matrix Programs are required for processes operated in parallel. It is unfortunate that the term "program" is usually taken to imply only a sequence of events, and there is not a good word to describe a parallel or simultaneous set of events. The term "simultaneous program" might suffice, but it is rather a mouthful. The word "matrix" in mathematics, which describes a notation taking account of several factors *at the same time*, is not available. But we can use the term "matrix program" to describe a set of simultaneous command instructions which have to be performed *together*. The term "program" is quite legitimately used in this context, since nothing can stop the passage of time, and this also applies to simultaneous or matrix events. In Fig. 3.5 is shown the general form of a matrix program as applied to a four-variable system. This gives simultaneous instructions to all four variables. Practical examples of matrix programs and instructions are—

Airport landing system: "All aircraft stacked at 10,000, 12,000 and 14,000 ft altitude, drop to next stacking altitude 2,000 ft below."

Weighing system in chemical industry: "Add 200 gal of water, 2 lb of salt and 10 lb of sulphuric acid *together* into mixer."

Police patrol system: "Erect roadblocks on all roads leading to Aldermaston."

Oil refinery: "Reset distillation column to 200° F, 500 gal/min, and 75 per cent yield of 70-octane gasoline."

A typical device to memorize a matrix program is a punched card. This can hold a great deal of data recorded in its hole-code, and the holes can be "read" simultaneously by a punched-card reader.

Sequential-matrix Programs are needed in the many automated systems that require a combination of sequential and simultaneous instructions. This is really a recipe for good cookery (all cooks have to do some operations in sequence and others simultaneously: they have to keep their eye on the soup whilst preparing the pudding). This form of programming, which is potentially the most important for automation, is shown diagrammatically in Fig. 3.6. A typical device for memorizing a sequential-matrix program is a multi-track magnetic tape which holds parallel and serial data at the same time.

In summary, program memorizing will be simulated by data-handling devices such as punched tapes and cards, or magnetic

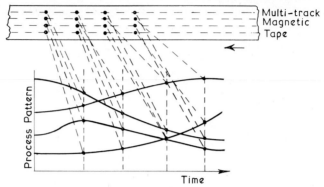

FIG. 3.6.   SEQUENTIAL-MATRIX PROGRAMS

tapes, which can remember data in correct order and which can also, if required, remember several sets of data at the same time.

SIMULATION OF PROCESS KNOW-HOW

A man has tremendous resources on which to fall back when faced by difficult problems. This unseen background can be called either *experience* or *know-how*, but it is mainly knowledge of *how processes should work*. There are four aspects of such know-how—physical, analytical, logical and symbolic.

One of the main problems in automation is how to reconstruct such know-how in a robot, and with particular reference to complex processes.

The generally accepted approach is to try to make a mathematical model of the process and then to convert the model into an electronic one. This is the task of electronic computers and simulators, which must be able to answer such questions as, "what should be happening now?" or, "if I make a change in the process, what will be the effect in four hours' time?"

The know-how memory may be compared with a really good motoring map, which shows where one has come from, where one is now, and where one will go if one chooses a particular route. Thus it is a sort of navigational aid, and human experience and know-how are used in just this way. In most cases the simulating robot cannot simply be a static aid like a map; it has to contain an element of time. Try to devise an electronic robot which can play tennis: it will not be too difficult to construct one that can hit a ball thrown in its direction, but tennis players have to do much more than this! They have to know when to change ends, and when to anticipate where the returned ball will come. In other words, they have to know the rules of the game and to anticipate all likely reactions before they come to an action decision. The first characteristic of a process-know-how simulator is embodiment of the "rules of the game"—the rules of the process—and ideally this means that the simulator must embody all the causal laws affecting the process under all practical conditions. This is no mean requirement.

DIFFERENCE BETWEEN A PROCESS MEMORY AND A PROGRAM

What is the essential difference between a process memory and a program such as a punched tape? A program only contains *instructions to the process;* it does not contain knowledge of the likely reaction of the process to the instructions. Thus a process memory has to know *how to modify* programs based on the process reactions, and is a much more intelligent device than a program.

LIMITATIONS OF ELECTRONICS IN SIMULATING PHYSICAL PROCESS KNOW-HOW

It would be very desirable for physical process memories to be simulated electronically, but although efforts are being made in this direction, the techniques are still primitive. The main reason is that physical memories involve a great deal of *co-ordination* of space-time functions whereas electronics deals best with sequential functions.

At the end of the last chapter it appeared that know-how memories in the human being fall into four categories—

1. Direct, physical, process memories, mainly mind's-eye memories, of the sort required to play a game of tennis or file a casting.
2. Analytical know-how, mainly concerned with classification and sorting facts.
3. Symbolic and verbal memories, incorporating mathematical skills and experience.
4. Logical process memories, mainly for deciding whether propositions are true or false, or in coming to conditional decisions.

There are a few cases where a physical process memory can be simulated mechanically. The simplest is a clock, which is a time-process memory.

Process know-how problems, when they involve consideration of "what will happen if," demand *calculation,* and process simulators have to be mathematical in form, in other words computers.

COMPUTER SIMULATION OF PROCESS KNOW-HOW
AND PROCESS THINKING

There are normally two basic ways in which to use mathematical calculations: the way of proportions and the way of numbers. These lead to "graphical solution" or "numerical solution." Simulation of these techniques leads to "analogue computing" and "digital computing" respectively.

Analogue Computing

Graphical solution of problems involves making lengths equal to numerical values. A value of ten units is represented by a line ten inches long. In electronic analogue computing, the magnitude of an electrical voltage represents other magnitudes; ten volts might represent ten inches.

But the representation of magnitudes by voltages is only the starting point; the values require adding and subtracting, multiplying and dividing, integration, differentiation, trigonometrical operations, logarithmic operations, squaring and square-rooting, etc.

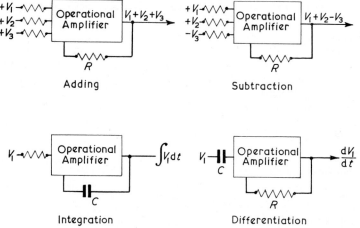

FIG. 3.7.   ANALOGUE COMPUTING

All these can be done by means of assemblies of standard boxes which go to make up analogue computers. The central device used is the "operational amplifier." This is a highly stabilized amplifier, and Fig. 3.7 shows how resistors and capacitors connected to the amplifier enable it to subtract, integrate and differentiate respectively.

It is not my intention in this chapter to give a lengthy account of the possibilities of analogue computing, but the following two points may be worth remembering: (*i*) almost all normally-encountered mathematical operations may be carried out by analogue computing units to an accuracy of about one per cent in the answer; (*ii*) if a process simulation problem involves such analogue computer units, there is no need to buy a general-purpose analogue computer with many standard units in a splendid rack, but just to buy and employ such units as may be required to solve the problem.

Digital Computing

An ordinary electrical switch has two positions, "on" and "off." It is not difficult to see that one may represent the number 1 by the presence of an electrical current (switch "on") and represent the number 0 by the absence of an electrical current (switch "off").

A computer can be made entirely of "on-off" switches that do a form of arithmetic which only uses the numbers 0 and 1. This kind of arithmetic was invented many years ago, and consists of counting from 0 to 1 and then saying "carry one." This "binary" system is equivalent to a decimal system in which the number 9 has been replaced by the number 1 and leads to the following arithmetical language—

Ordinary Number	Binary Number
0	0
1	1
2	10
3	11
4	100
10, etc.	1010, etc.

Thus the value of a "1" in the successive columns (from right to left) represents the values 1, 2, 4, 8, 16, etc., a progressive doubling instead of multiplying by ten as in the decimal system.

Two sorts of switches are required in a computer, those that go "on" when pressed but go "off" when released, and those that stay put in whichever way you leave them, "on" or "off." The former are usually transistors and are used for the active calculating in digital computers. The latter are usually magnetic devices ("flip-flops"), which will stay in either the magnetized or the demagnetized position until further notice, and act as memories.

The digital pulses in a computer can be manipulated in "logical switching circuits" (*see* later in this chapter) to perform the normal calculations of adding, subtracting, multiplying and dividing, and these four are the main calculations which a digital computer can do. Almost all mathematical calculations can be reduced to these four basic forms, though this may entail a long series of operations; calculations of such qualities as logarithms, trigonometrical functions, etc., can all be expressed in a mathematical series. A digital computer may have to perform a hundred arithmetical operations to find such a simple value as sin 60°, but as it works very fast, often at tens of thousands of operations a second, it can do all these calculations very quickly indeed. Furthermore, the routines to solve complex mathematical equations are now largely standardized on punched or magnetic tapes, and if such a tape is put into the computer together with particular numerical values, then the answer is forthcoming very quickly.

So, to simulate human know-how, one must first express the experience in mathematical and logical laws, and then embody these laws in a mathematical robot such as an analogue or digital computer, which is then the process-know-how simulator.

DIFFICULTIES WITH MATHEMATICAL MODELS

Do not imagine that the simulation of process know-how by analogue and digital computers is an easy matter. In the first place someone has to be able to write down all the relevant causal laws in mathematical form. Now a process is a dynamic state of affairs—if you want to control the making of sulphuric acid by adding hydrochloric acid to a sulphate it is no good writing down the chemistry-textbook equation for this and putting it into a computer. The process mathematics start with such an equation but they must go on to include all the effects of temperature, pressure, time, and reaction kinetics in general.

Furthermore, such mathematical studies having been done, the result probably will not correspond to practice. When chemicals are treated in bulk, all sorts of different things go on in different parts of the containing vessel, and the result is mathematical chaos. At present, in 1962, we are still at the beginning of the subject, and time alone will tell whether complex chemical processes will yield to mathematical analysis.

With physical processes, the problem of mathematical simulation by computers is not so difficult. The most advanced examples are flight-training simulators, which are remarkable mathematical models of the process of flying an aircraft. One of the most interesting problems being tackled at the present time is the mathematical simulation of many aircraft approaching an airport, so that warning is immediately given of any danger of collision.

SIMULATION OF LOGIC AND ABILITY TO DECIDE

The characteristic *result* of a decision is an unambiguous action, and the most popular device for this is some sort of electrical switch. There is nothing quite so definite in its effect as a switch. But how can one simulate the process of choosing whether to operate the decisive switch? It is just this "whether" which is at the core of decision.

How does one arrive at a decision in normal life? As I write, it is one o'clock in the morning, and I am faced with the question, "Shall I stop writing this chapter and go to bed?" I hear my wife still playing the piano in another room, and I say to myself, "I will go to bed when she stops playing." In other words, my decision is *conditioned* by a factor outside my control.

This is characteristic of concrete examples of what we choose to call decision—they are usually conditioned by indirect factors: "I will do this *if* that occurs," "I will buy some shares on Tuesday *if* the Wall Street prices rise on Monday," and so on. It is the essence of a correct decision that all these conditional factors are taken into account.

Now exactly similar factors are relevant to decision in an automated system. Thus a London underground train will continue to move *if* the signal is at green. On the other hand, some main-line trains should only decide to move *if* the next signal is at green, *and if* the signal after that is *either* at green *or* yellow, *but not if* it is at red.

The problem of decision in automation is therefore solved by—

(*i*) taking into account the automated measurement of the prime contributory factors: whether signals are green or red; whether conveyors are full or empty; whether boilers are hot or cold, etc.;

(*ii*) providing automatic "logical" devices which will simulate such words as *if, or, and, not, only, either, both*, etc., i.e. conditional logic functions; and

(*iii*) providing a set of relevant process rules (or logic) linking the conditional logical functions of (*ii*) with the measured factors of (*i*).

Now the first of the above problems is a matter for the sensors and recognition devices discussed earlier. The provision of conditional logic functions is a matter for complex switching procedures (*see* Fig. 3.8). These circuits have been highly developed, and are usually combinations of transistors acting as relays. Rules must be formulated, according to which the switching networks will arrange the sensing signals. The formulation of the rules follows from study of the process and translation of the results into logical terms. The problem may be simple, as in traffic-signal problems, where the rules are of a yes-no kind, but may become very complicated if continuous variables have to be taken into account together with awkward time-lags and other obscurities.

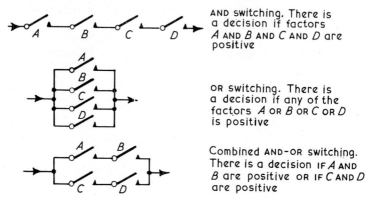

AND switching. There is a decision if factors *A* AND *B* AND *C* AND *D* are positive

OR switching. There is a decision if any of the factors *A* OR *B* OR *C* OR *D* is positive

Combined AND–OR switching. There is a decision IF *A* AND *B* are positive OR IF *C* AND *D* are positive

FIG. 3.8.   LOGICAL SWITCHING AND CONDITIONAL DECISION

SIMULATION OF ABILITY TO TAKE ACTION

Human ability to act as the result of some inner thinking and deciding usually takes one of two forms: (i) *unambiguous action* (chop the tree down, press the self-starter, put the cat out); (ii) *measured action*

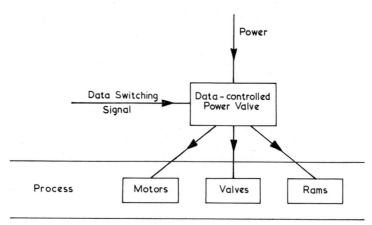

FIG. 3.9.   TWO-STATE DECISION ACTUATION

(saw off *twelve inches* of wood, pour *half a cup* of water, go for a *fortnight's* holiday).

Correspondingly, when a logical decision has been made in a data-handling process as described in the last section, the means of action will either be some sort of "on-off" switch, in which "on" represents action, or it will be the increase or decrease of a signal demanding a proportionate increase or decrease of physical response. The devices to carry the action into effect will be either switching actuators or analogue (variable) actuators.

Typical of the first group is the power transistor (*see* Fig. 3.9), or a relay electrical contactor, which will accept a light-current signal and control a high-power electrical circuit, or operate pneumatic or hydraulic valves for controlling processes working at a higher power-level.

Typical of the second group is the light-current servo-mechanism (*see* Fig. 3.10) which sets the target for a power device that moves itself to the target.

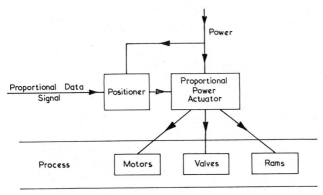

FIG. 3.10.   PROPORTIONAL DECISION ACTUATION

THE TOTAL ROBOT

In this chapter we have dealt with the simulation of the following main human psychic functions—

Sensing and Recognition.
Target and Action Programs.
Process Know-how.
Decision.
Physical Control.

It now remains to synthesize these functions to create a complete equivalent of the human mind and nervous system. This equivalent

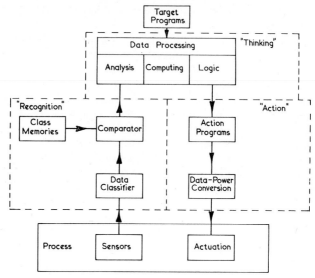

FIG. 3.11.   THE TOTAL ROBOT: DETAILED SCHEME

is shown in the diagram in Fig. 3.11, which can be compared with the human version shown in Fig. 2.4. The robot contains five main parts—

1. A programming system, to receive instructions from outside and set the main process objectives.

2. A sensing and recognition system which extracts data from the process and presents them to the central "brain" or data-processing centre.

3. A data-processing centre, which "knows" all about how the process should work, and may have functions of data analysing, data computing (including process simulation) and logical decision. This data-processing centre may be a single electronic computer.

4. Action program for process instruction.

5. Devices to convert action programs into power for process actuation and operation.

Note that the simplified diagram for all this, Fig. 3.12, is identical with the original diagram of Fig. 1.1 in Chapter 1, where automation was described as development into data-controlled process. Whilst this description covers all automated systems, the way of working will vary greatly according to the requirement of the particular process, and many truly automated systems have some of these functions only in embryo form—or even not at all, if the process is very simple or very well behaved.

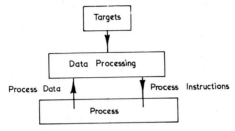

FIG. 3.12.   THE TOTAL ROBOT: SIMPLIFIED SCHEME

Having assembled the structure common to all automated systems, we shall in the next chapter consider some of the sorts of physical process that may require control, so that we can prepare the way for a description of practical automated systems.

CHAPTER 4

THE NINE AUTOMATION SYSTEMS

THE previous chapter was intended to give a broad description of some of the principles involved in simulating the human psychic functions for the purpose of constructing electronic controlling robots. In Chapter 1 automation was described as "development into data-controlled process," but intermediate chapters have concentrated on some of the techniques involved in "data control" and said very little about the "process."

THE THREE MODES OF AUTOMATION

Material processes vary greatly in their natural characteristics. Consider the following three examples: (*i*) a metal-shearing guillotine; (*ii*) a coal-fired domestic water heater; and (*iii*) a postal sorting office. Each of these represents a radically different physical process, and the imposition of data control would require a fundamentally different approach in each case. Let us examine their basic characteristics.

The Metal-shearing Guillotine. The task of this machine (the "process") is to cut sheet metal, and it does so by means of a descending blade. The only variation required from the process is adjustment of the length of metal cut off. This is obtained by adjusting a back-stop to which the metal is pushed before the blade is allowed to descend (*see* Fig. 4.1). All that is required to automate such a process is mechanical handling of the metal up to the back-stop, but the latter must be self-setting. A variable-program device, such as a

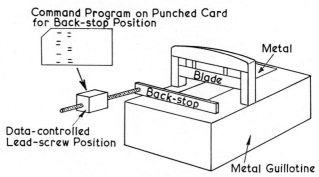

FIG. 4.1.   COMMAND (PRE-PROGRAMMED) AUTOMATION FOR OBEDIENT PROCESSES

set of dials or a punched card, will answer the purpose. Such a system requires very little "automatic recognition," except perhaps for a simple limit switch to detect that the metal is up against the back-stop and in the correct position for the blade to descend and cut. The central feature here is the data-controlled back-stop positioning. This can be arranged by means of a punched card controlling the number of revolutions of an electric motor turning a leadscrew attached to the back-stop. Such a straightforward process can be described as being *very obedient* to a command program, and one can be pretty sure that whatever positional instructions are put into the punched card, they will be obeyed. Furthermore, such a system as applied to a guillotine will normally only require to be accurate to 0·005 in., and this is well within the design limits of a simple automatic positioning system.

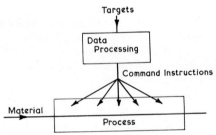

Fig. 4.2.　　General Scheme of Command Programmed Processes

The essence of this type of automated process is that a simple result is produced by a simple cause. As shown in Fig. 4.2, it is an instance of *command programmed automation for obedient processes*. Note that in principle no return of information is wanted from the process—it is just told what to do and then performs satisfactorily.

The Coal-fired Domestic Water Heater. The purpose of this process is to provide water at some predetermined temperature, usually about 160°F. But those who have such a boiler under manual control know that the water temperature is rarely at its required value, and that these heaters are highly temperamental, depending on the air settings, the amount and type of coal in the boiler, and the state of the clinker. Thus hand-fired coal boilers are basically *unstable and badly behaved*, and to automate them one has to install the system shown in Fig. 4.3. This will consist of a dial with which we set the desired water-temperature (the command program), a device for measuring the actual water-temperature, and a device which compares the actual with the desired temperature, measures the difference, and acts to reduce it, usually by altering the air-draught settings.

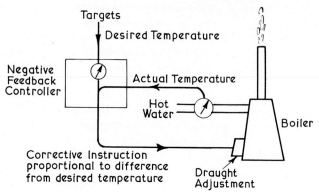

FIG. 4.3.   NEGATIVE FEEDBACK AUTOMATION FOR CORRECTING UNSTABLE PROCESSES

This type of improvement is called *negative-feedback-corrective automation*, the word "negative" implying that the correction signal opposes the error signal. If the water temperature is *below* the desired value, then the control system will *increase* the air draught, and conversely. The expression "feedback" implies that the measurement of the actual temperature takes place further on in the process, after the stage at which the incorrect temperature is caused, and that the corrective signal related to the effect is fed *back* to that stage, as shown in Fig. 4.4.

It will be clear that negative-feedback control is more complicated than simple command-control, and consists of command control (the desired-state specification) plus extra corrective action because the process is inherently unstable. *Unstable processes require negative-feedback corrective automation.*

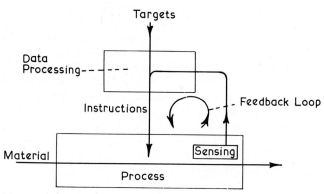

FIG. 4.4.   GENERAL SCHEME OF NEGATIVE FEEDBACK CONTROL

A Postal Sorting Office. The activity characteristic of a postal sorting office is receipt of a miscellaneous input of letters and parcels and their sorting by destination. The essence of the problem is that the input to the system is *random,* and the command or objectives program can only be a general statement of aim, "send this mail to the places marked thereon." A random-input process of this type has to commence with the sensing and identifying of the input (the marking on the mail). The second phase is to ascertain what action to take after identification. This will involve sorting into like-destination groups, as shown in Fig. 4.5. The type of thing is illustrated

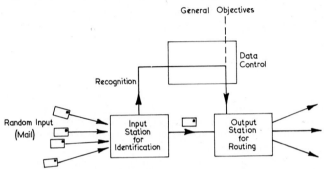

FIG. 4.5.   SORTING (FEEDFORWARD) AUTOMATION FOR CORRECTING RANDOM INPUT PROCESSES

generally in Fig. 4.6, and is an instance of a *feedforward* system—the result of recognition only affects *later* consequences, such as rerouting. It is, nevertheless, a corrective system of control. *Sorting automation is used for the control of random-input processes.*

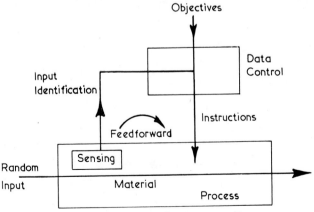

FIG. 4.6.   GENERAL SCHEMATIC OF FEEDFORWARD CONTROL

Thus there are three principal modes of automation—

1. *Command or programmed automation* for stable or obedient processes.

2. *Negative-feedback-corrective automation* for unstable processes.

3. *Sorting automation* for processes with a random input.

INTEGRATED AUTOMATION

Although the above three modes of automation each apply particularly to the three stated aspects of processes, there are often occasions when two modes of automation may be used together, and even all three modes may be combined. This is shown diagrammatically in Fig. 4.7. Applied to a chemical process, the combination might be—

Sorting automation applied to the analysis of input materials, so that the results of examination of random variations in input quality can be used to modify command programs

plus *Command automation* applied to the sequence control of subsequent batch processing

plus *Feedback automation* applied to quality control of the products, and resulting in modification of command instructions.

The diagram in Fig. 4.7 may be considered as the *master diagram of automation*, since it expresses all automation possibilities in the simplest possible form.

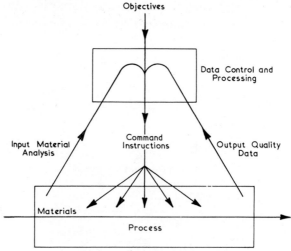

Fig. 4.7.   The Master Diagram of Automation

THE THREE MATERIAL PROCESSES

All processes consist of subjecting some *material* to a procedure, and the nature of that material determines the nature of the process. Examination of all physical processes in manufacturing and distributive industry shows that they can be divided into three classes (Fig. 4.8)—

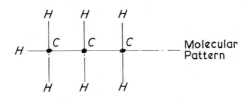

Molecular Pattern

1. Process of Chemistry

— Item Pattern

2. Process of Shaping

Assembly Pattern

3 Process of Position

FIG. 4.8.   THREE MAJOR FORMS OF PROCESS

1. Process on the atomic and molecular scale, i.e. the processes of *chemistry*.

2. Processes on a visible scale, concerned with the *form* or *shape* of the material.

3. Processes on a visible scale, concerned with the relationship of one material to another material, i.e. processes of relative *position*.

Let us check this threefold classification by fitting some well-known processes into it.

Process	Process Type
Transport system	Position
Heat-treatment furnace	Chemistry
Manufacturing assembly	Position
Machine tools	Shape
Postal sorting office	Position
Blast furnace	Chemistry
Extrusion press	Shape

All these are really the same process, in that they are all processes of *pattern*; only the pattern occurs on three different scales, molecular, single-object and many-object. Automation is, in fact, concerned with the automatic control of patterns on different scales, with the moulding of patterns in molecules, objects, and the relationship between objects. To complete the picture one could add a fourth category, on the smallest material scale. This is the electron. One could then say that data processing is the art of organizing patterns in electricity.

THE NINE PRACTICAL AUTOMATION SYSTEMS

So there are three basic modes of automation—

1. Command automation for stable processes.
2. Feedback automation for unstable processes.
3. Sorting automation for random-input processes.

And there are three forms of process as revealed by the nature of the materials employed—

(i) Chemical processes.
(ii) Shaping processes.
(iii) Positional processes.

The next problem is to consider how the three modes of automation relate to the three forms of material process. It would be convenient if there were direct correspondence, and, indeed, there is some significant correspondence between command automation and the stable processes of mechanical engineering. There is also some correspondence between feedback automation and chemical processes, which are usually unstable, and there is often a sorting requirement for positional processes. But a more detailed study reveals that all three modes of automation can be applied to all three forms of material process, and so we find that the permutations and combinations lead to nine principal automation systems, thus—

1. Command automation of chemical processes.
2. Feedback automation of chemical processes
3. Sorting automation of chemical processes.
4. Command automation of shaping processes.
5. Feedback automation of shaping processes.
6. Sorting automation of shaping processes.
7. Command automation of positional processes.
8. Feedback automation of positional processes.
9. Sorting automation of positional processes.

The remainder of this chapter will be devoted to considering the main practical applications of the above nine automation systems.

GROUP 1. COMMAND AUTOMATION OF CHEMICAL PROCESSES

This group has four major applications.

Sequentially-controlled Batch Processes

A batch chemical process is one in which the process pattern has to be moved progressively with respect to a relatively stationary material. This illustrated in Fig. 4.9, which represents a chemical process in which a material is processed through successive stages of (i) temperature and (ii) pressure. Some kind of program controller is required to govern the predetermined changes of pressure and temperature. This type of system is usually described as batch sequence control. It is described in detail in Chapter 5.

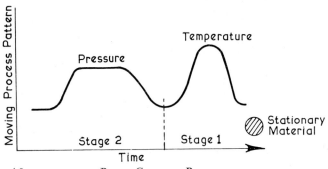

Fig. 4.9.   BATCH CHEMICAL PROCESS

Material-dispensing for Batch Processes

Most batch processes have to commence with the dispensing of the required quantities of material. If these can be entirely predetermined, command programming is the ideal way of dealing with the situation. This is described in Chapter 6.

Starting-up of Continuous Processes

Continuous chemical processes usually need to be started up according to a carefully planned routine, until they come to the point where they can be taken over by (usually) feedback control. Command automation is often convenient for this starting-up procedure.

Continuous Chemical Processes

The detailed regulation of continuous chemical processes is normally a matter for feedback control, since such processes tend to be unstable. In continuous chemical processes (Fig. 4.10) the material moves through a constant process pattern, and the important points in this pattern are usually kept at constant values by individual feedback controllers, as shown at X_1, X_2, etc., in Fig. 4.10.

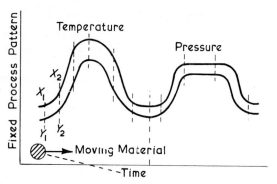

FIG. 4.10.   CONTINUOUS CHEMICAL PROCESS

It may well be that all the set points of these feedback controllers should be changed together (*see* points Y_1, Y_2, etc.) to suit some changing requirement for, say, throughput level or input material, and this can be done by command automation using a matrix-program change of the sort illustrated in Fig. 3.5. This type of scheme will be described in Chapter 8 under the heading *The Logical Juke-box Computer*.

GROUP 2. FEEDBACK AUTOMATION OF CHEMICAL PROCESSES

Because the data devices used in electronic automation are essentially *physical*, they are unable to speak the exact language of chemical reactions, so only the *operations* of a chemical plant can enjoy command automation. The user has to hope that physical operations will control the chemical reactions. This is very rarely the case, and most chemical reactions can only be very inexactly controlled by regulating plant conditions. For good control it is necessary to check how the chemical reaction is proceeding, and, if necessary, make corrective changes. Thus in many chemical processes, particularly continuous ones, it is necessary to employ negative-feedback control. Feedback may be obtained from sensing of physical conditions such as temperature and pressure, or from chemical quality-analysers of the sort shown in Fig. 3.2. In the latter case some sort of computer is required to comprehend the relationship between quality changes and their causes. This subject will be dealt with in Chapter 8.

A further use of feedback control is in connexion with batch processes, when it can be employed jointly with procedural command control to determine the correct end-point of a reaction stage. Command-sequence control may be exercised over a certain number of procedures, but a particular stage (such as *Boil until a temperature of* 110°C *is reached and then keep unchanged for ten minutes*) may require a feedback controller (to hold the conditions constant during the ten minutes).

GROUP 3. SORTING AUTOMATION FOR CHEMICAL PROCESSES

You will recall that sorting automation is applicable to random-input processes. The main random input to chemical processes is variation in the quality of the raw materials. This is a very severe practical factor in chemical processes using natural materials such as organic matter and natural minerals. In a process such as cement making, the main control problem is to know the exact nature of the input materials and to be able to process them accordingly. Thus practical sorting automation of chemical industry involves mainly the introduction of automatic analysis of input material followed by modification of the process program. Such procedure may be necessary not only to ensure that the product is generally correct, but also to ensure that too high and uneconomic a quality is not attained. This particularly applies to such processes as animal-foodstuff manufacture, where very expensive additives of varying quality may be used, and it would apply equally to such processes as rare-metal alloying.

Sorting automation is also applicable in principle to all chemical separation processes, sieving, distillation, etc., where the input analysis gives the data required to determine the possibilities of the subsequent process.

GROUP 4. COMMAND AUTOMATION FOR SHAPING PROCESSES

In general, shaping processes are rather obedient ones, if too fine dimensional limits are not required, and command automation is a natural solution. Command automation of shaping processes is normally the province of tape-controlled machine tools, as described in some detail in Chapters 9 and 10.

GROUP 5. FEEDBACK AUTOMATION FOR SHAPING PROCESSES

Feedback control of shaping processes has three major subdivisions—

Single-operation Machine Tools

A typical machine tool is the grinder. Here a finished dimension is data-programmed into a controller, and the grinding wheel advances until the dimension is reached, the final fine cuts being slowed because the error-signal diminishes as the target dimension is approached. This group also includes "in-process" inspection systems (discussed in Chapter 11) in which the inspection information is fed back to earlier stages in the process to improve the process.

Data-programmed Machine Tools with Feedback Control

As you will see in Chapter 9, data-controlled machine tools are of two types, those with command programming alone, and those with additional feedback control. The latter usually aim at an *absolute* dimensional target, so backlash, and sometimes also cutter wear, are compensated automatically.

Plastics Manufactures

Plastics substances, such as heated aluminium, steel, or thermo-plastic synthetics, are rather badly behaved and unstable in their response to shaping by processes such as rolling or extrusion. In such cases it is often necessary continuously to measure the dimension of the product and to feed the information back to correct the action of the machinery. This form of control is well developed in sheet-metal rolling, and we may shortly expect to see corresponding developments in the extrusion of steel.

GROUP 6. SORTING AUTOMATION FOR SHAPING PROCESSES

Sorting automation of shaping processes involves particularly the dimensional grading of piece parts, and especially before selective assembly (*see* Chapter 11 on automatic inspection machines). This is a very important form of automation. It is considered to be economic in the American automobile industry, which accepts random input variation in piece parts and secures fine-limit fits by selective assembly.

GROUP 7. COMMAND AUTOMATION FOR POSITIONAL PROCESSES

Command automation of positional processes involves predetermined physical arranging. In general, this is the field of automated mechanical handling and automated traffic control. There are many practical applications of this form of automation, as follows—

Self-routing Conveyor

A common mechanical-handling conveyor system can be used for routing articles to different destinations. For details see Chapter 15.

Automatic Stores

Goods can be mechanically consigned into and out of stores by systems operating off punched cards as described in Chapter 13.

Automated Cranes

Cranes can be sent to predetermined stations.

Lifts

Perhaps the most common example of command automation of a positional process is the automatic push-button lift.

Programmed Automatic Assemblers

Manufacturing assembly is essentially a relative-positional process. There are now available, as described in Chapter 12, fully automatic machines which can be data-programmed to assemble different articles.

Railway Signalling Systems

All predetermined traffic signalling systems are examples of the command automation of a positional process.

GROUP 8. FEEDBACK AUTOMATION OF POSITIONAL PROCESSES

In general, this is the field of "navigation according to absolute references," and the following are examples—

Radio Navigational System

This measures the absolute position of an aircraft or ship relative to the ground by reference to a triple radio interference pattern, and deviation from a set course can be corrected.

Star Guidance Systems

These do the equivalent of taking bearings with a sextant to compute absolute position in space, and from the positional reference obtained a corrective course can be set.

Buried-wire Guidance Systems

A vehicle can be made to follow a wire buried in the ground, sensing its position and "homing" on to it under feedback control (*see* Chapter 15).

Los Angeles Road-traffic Control System

This system (*see* Chapter 14) measures the rate of flow of road traffic and adjusts the traffic lights to encourage maximum flow. It is thus a corrective feedback system.

GROUP 9. SORTING AUTOMATION OF POSITIONAL PROCESSES

Here we look for a random-input positional process which requires sorting out. There are many of these in industry and distribution. Some examples are—

Mail Sorting

Sorting of mail is a classic random-input process. The aim is to recognize the writing on the envelopes and parcels and to classify them by destination. A telephone exchange is another example. There the incoming signal has to be routed to the requested outgoing wires (*see* Chapter 14).

Piece-part Orienting

Automatic feeders of piece parts have to convert the random orientation at the input into ordered arrangement at the output (*see* Chapter 12).

Railway Marshalling Yards

Incoming goods trains have to be reassembled at marshalling yards into outgoing trains of wagons that have a common destination. This case is almost identical with that of mail sorting.

DETAILED EXAMPLES OF THE NINE SYSTEMS

The considerations in this chapter lead to the conclusion that the three modes of automation and the three basic forms of material process yield nine characteristic systems. The above descriptions have outlined the general picture, and practical details will be filled in by Chapters 5 to 16 inclusive. Cross references are shown in the following table.

| | TYPE OF AUTOMATION | | |
	COMMAND	FEEDBACK	SORTING (FEEDFORWARD)
CHEMICAL PROCESSES	Sequentially controlled batch processes (Ch. 5) Materials dispensing (Ch. 6)	Negative feedback controllers (Ch. 7) Computor control (Ch. 8)	Feedforward control (Ch. 8)
SHAPING PROCESSES	Machine-tool control (Ch. 9 and 10) Automatic knitting machine (Ch. 19) Steel industry (Ch. 16)	Machine-tool control (Ch. 9) Steel industry (Ch. 16)	Automatic grading machines (Ch. 11)
POSITIONAL PROCESSES	Conveyors (Ch. 15) Automatic stores (Ch. 13) Automatic assembly (Ch. 12)	Los Angeles road-traffic control (Ch. 14) Robot tug (Ch. 15)	Mail sorting (Ch. 14) Piece-part orienting (Ch. 12)

CHAPTER 5

BATCH AUTOMATION OF CHEMICAL AND ALLIED PROCESSES

THE great majority of the processes of the chemical and food industry are of the batch variety (as briefly described in Chapter 4), in which the whole of a relatively stationary material is treated successively according to one pattern after another. This predominance of batch processes is due to their inherent flexibility. It is easy to make changes in them, and they can always be stopped at some stage to check that product quality is satisfactory. Most *commence* as batch processes because their capital cost is lower when they are on a small scale, standard chemical engineering plant being used, and later it seems reasonable to keep to the same procedures when scaling for larger throughputs. Also, the most advanced and complicated processes, say in the pharmaceutical industry, are on a batch scale in order to allow for modifications and developments.

It is quite wrong to suppose that batch working is a rather old-fashioned way of dealing with chemical and allied processes. Batch processes are usually only converted for continuous operation after many years of experience have established all the factors of which knowledge is required for operation and control. One may almost generalize to the effect that only well-established processes should be converted for flow production—evolving processes are better carried out by batch methods.

MAIN ADVANTAGES AND DISADVANTAGES OF BATCH PRODUCTION

The main advantage of batch production is that each stage can be isolated from its predecessors and successors, so the quality of production in the current stage can be thoroughly observed and corrected. With continuous production there may will be considerable overlapping of the various phases of the process pattern, with some interference between adjacent phases, whereas in batch work the whole of the material in a given stage is being treated identically by homogenizing devices such as mixers and fans. In its isolation, the batch can be constantly inspected, and adjusted if necessary, and there is no need to get on with the next operation until the supervisors are quite satisfied with the quality of the product.

The main disadvantages of batching arise from relative under-employment of capital equipment and factory space. Underemployment of plant stems from two causes: (*i*) all stages in a batching system are rarely used simultaneously, and (*ii*) the system is not normally self-cleaning, so requires extra operations. Thus throughput value per pound invested may be relatively low. A further problem is that, unless the process is automated, excessive time may be spent in inspecting and adjusting the product in the various stages, and there may also be loss of productive time owing to dilatoriness in transferring the product from one stage to the next. Also a batch process is very dependent on good supervision.

AUTOMATION TARGETS IN BATCH PRODUCTION

Batch processes are potentially capable of yielding a very-high-quality product, but suffer from a poor plant-utilization factor and critical dependence on the quality of supervision. The aim of automation of batch processes must, therefore, be to improve these characteristics. To this end it is necessary that—

(*a*) as soon as one process stage is completed, material be transferred to the next stage (aim: improved plant-utilization),

(*b*) each stage of the batch process be sufficiently instrumented and automatically controlled to ensure that the final product quality for the process stage is achieved as rapidly as possible (aim: improved plant-utilization and reduction of supervision costs),

(*c*) the system allow simultaneous production in the different stages (aim: high plant-utilization), and

(*d*) the method of programming the system allow use of the plant for the widest likely variety of products and processes; this implies *automatic variable programming* (aim: increased plant-utilization).

AUTOMATIC SEQUENCING

The first requirement for automatic control of batch production is automatic sequencing of successive stages so that there is no time lost between them. A large chemical firm in Britain has collected statistics to show that the gain from elimination of lost time between stages corresponds to an increased plant utilization of between fifteen and twenty per cent.

The core of an automatic sequencing system is the sequencer, which is a kind of switch, and the most common version of this is the "uniselector," as used in telephone exchanges. These switches normally have either twenty-five or fifty positions, and may provide between four and eight sets of electrical contacts in a row at each position of a rotating member. The rotating member is turned one step at a time by a solenoid operating from an incoming electrical impulse.The impulse is usually provided by a signal which means "previous process-stage complete." By arranging the connexions to the switch as shown in Fig. 5.1, and as described in the following notes, it is possible to control the progressive stages of a batch process.

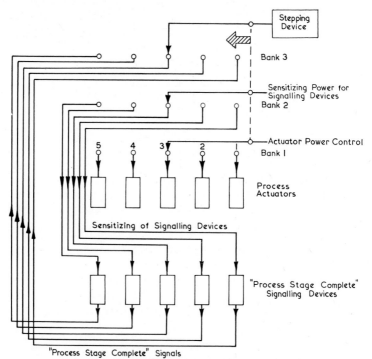

FIG. 5.1.   BATCH-PROCESS SEQUENCING BY UNISELECTOR

Process Instruction Connexions

To one bank of contacts in the sequencing switch are connected wires which go to electrical relays controlling process actuation devices such as fluid valves, pumps, motors, etc. Starting at the first row in the switch, these are connected in the predetermined sequence so that, as the switch rotates, the various operations required are started in the correct order.

"Process Stage Complete" Signals

The *reason* for moving from one step of the switch to the next step must be that the previous stage has been completed. Thus sequencing systems require incoming signal lines to tell that process stages have been completed. The signals are usually provided by closure of electrical contacts on the plant when such measures as liquid level, temperature, pressure, etc., reach set values.

One bank of contacts in the sequencer is reserved to sensitize the device that signals "process stage complete" from the process stage being worked out. Thus if Row 3 of Bank 1 has sent out a signal to start a vat heater, Row 3 of Bank 2 might be arranged to sensitize a thermostat that would signal "process complete." (See Fig. 5.1.)

Sequencer Stepping

After a process stage has been initiated, and the device for signalling "process stage complete" has been sensitized (i.e. provided with electrical power to signal back), a time will come at which the device signals "process stage *is* complete." This signal is taken through a third bank of contacts on the stepping switch to the stepping device (*see* Fig. 5.1), which is usually a pulsing relay connected to the sequencing-switch solenoid. This moves the sequencing switch to the next position, and the next process is initiated.

Other Techniques

The above description covers the essence of the technique involved in sequencing, though there are many alternative techniques. These include solid-state (transistor) sequence-switching systems, and series relays each one of which corresponds to one row of a uniselector.

AUTOMATIC PROCESS-STAGE QUALITY CONTROL

A sequencing system coming on to a new process-stage position will usually close an electrical relay, and this has to be sufficient to control everything required in the process stage. Primarily, such a relay can start a self-contained electrical control circuit. The following actions are typical.

Opening (or Closing) a Chemical Valve

A pilot valve (electropneumatic, electrohydraulic, or all-electric) supplies power to an actuator on the spindle or lever of the chemical valve. The actuator opens or closes the valve.

Starting (or Stopping) an Electric Motor

An electrical relay operates the motor contactor. Hydraulic pumps for moving liquids into vessels, or for transferring them from vessel to vessel, can be automated by starting their motors in this way. A stirrer to homogenize a batch may similarly be driven by an electric motor. In some cases hydraulic or pneumatic may be preferred to electric motors. Then the original signal has to work through electro-mechanical pilot valves operating in air or hydraulic pipelines.

Introduction of Negative-feedback Controllers*

The above two operations, involving motors or valves, are only sufficient to deal with the normal mechanical handling problems of the process, and they will not of themselves control product quality. Quality problems are mainly dealt with by bringing in negative-feedback control.

The specification for a process-stage might, for example, be: "Bring the product to the boil." In this case (as shown in Fig. 5.2) the sequencing instruction signal switches on a temperature controller and at the same time opens, say, a steam valve; but the steam pipe also has a second valve operated from the temperature-feedback controller. The "process complete" signal is given out when the temperature reached is equal to the controller's target temperature.

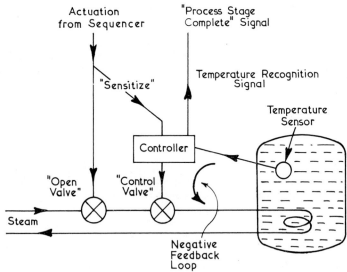

FIG. 5.2.   "BRING THE PRODUCT TO THE BOIL," METHOD A

* For description of negative-feedback controllers see beginning of Chapter 7.

Activation of Sensors with Target-point Switches

The process stage recipe, "Bring the product to the boil," could also have been communicated as shown in Fig. 5.3, by using the sequencing instruction signal to activate a temperature sensor with a limit switch and simultaneously open a steam valve. There would be no control over the approach to the critical temperature, though such control could be desirable.

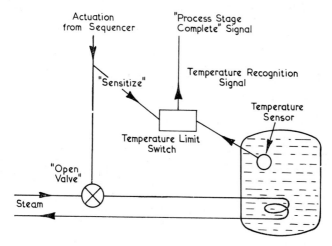

FIG. 5.3.   "BRING THE PRODUCT TO THE BOIL," METHOD B

Activation of Timers

After bringing to the boil, the next stage-instruction might be "Boil for ten minutes." With the completion of the incoming signal from the previous "bring-to-the boil" stage, the next signal would start an electrical timer set at ten minutes; the feedback temperature-controller (described above) would remain in operation. At the end of ten minutes the timer would signal the sequencer to move on to the next instruction.

Attraction of Operator Attention

In many processes it is vital that the operator use his judgement at some critical stage, but there is no reason for him to hang around waiting for his vital few minutes of work. Thus it is important to call on the operator at the correct moment. This can be arranged by means of a sequence stage with an associated sensor. The sensor detects the critical stage (or its approach) and signals back to the sequencer, which then moves on one step and sets an alarm going. The operator then comes and does his job, and the process is restarted manually, by pushing a button. This operation can become complicated if the operator has to choose between succeeding procedures.

COMPLICATIONS IN PRACTICE

The above six facilities cover a great deal of the general operating requirements of automated batch processing. We shall now go on to consider more detailed aspects of the operational design of a batch control system. Below is a practical example.

Worked Example

The preceding general description may give the impression that the working out of the general specification for automating a batch process is quite simple, but in practice one runs into a number of complications. The main complication is due to the fact that what a process chemist would describe as "one stage of the batch" may in fact involve a dozen sequential operations of which he simply has not been aware, because the process operators do so many extra things which are part of their know-how and skill. Thus the full automation of what appears to be quite a simple batch process may well involve a couple of hundred sequential stages in its automated form. I shall try to bring these facts out in the worked example tabulated on page 60.

From this table we note a considerable difference between the process chemist's analysis (left-hand side) and that of the automation engineer (right-hand side). In any important automated process it is highly desirable to monitor the operation of all actuation instructions. This is usually done by placing microswitches on the process actuator body to give "actuation correct" signals and cancel a three-second alarm which should be sensitized each time an actuation is requested. This means usually that chemical valves have to be dealt with in sequence, though it is possible to arrange that several chemical valves are operated simultaneously yet will raise the alarm on individual failure. Roughly speaking, it is cheaper to give each actuator a separate sequence stage if the total operations in the process do not exceed a hundred, and above this figure it may be better to arrange valve groupings with special group-monitoring circuits.

The result in general is that the automation engineer's work-study tables usually show from two to four times as many sequential stages as the process chemist's.

STUDYING VERY COMPLICATED PROCESSES

In very complicated systems, involving over a hundred sequential stages, I have found study by written procedure-tables too cumbersome. I have therefore devised a system of cards (about 3 in. × 4 in. as in small card-indexes) to give flexibility in the design phase, and only revert to a typed list when the design is finished and ready for the contractor.

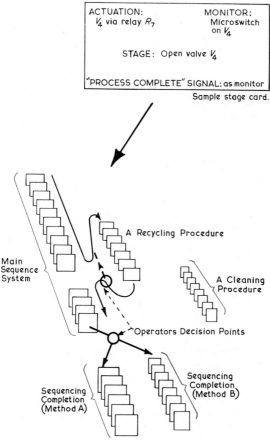

FIG. 5.4.   CARD INDEX METHOD OF DEVELOPING A SEQUENCE CONTROL SYSTEM

Each of the cards represents one stage of the process (*see* Fig. 5.4) and the centre of the card carries the general description of the stage. At the top of the card is written the precise actuation required, together with any details of intermediate devices such as relays or magneto-pneumatic pilot valves, and at the bottom is written the nature of the "process stage complete" signal. By arranging the cards in columns one can see readily how the "process complete" signal from an upper card initiates the sequence change for the actuation on the stage card below, and one can play with the cards until the design is satisfactory.

Any complex sequencing system requires the break-down of the system into subsystems: these are represented by groups of cards. A typical subsystem is an automatic cleaning procedure that is only occasionally required, for example when the use of the plant is changed, or at week-ends, and has to be kept clear of the main sequencing procedures although it may use many of the same actuators. Another typical subsystem embraces recycling procedures in batch filtration, when it is required to carry out a filtration cycle in the middle of a batch process and examine the quality of the filtrate: if the product is not clean enough it may have to be recycled round the same circuit

BATCH PROCESS AUTOMATION: COMMENCEMENT OF TYPICAL ANALYSIS TABLE.

Process Chemist's Description		Automation Engineer's Analysis	
Stage No.	Description.	Stage Actuation	Process Complete Signal.
1.	Start vessel-stirrer by operating starter A and apply steam at 30 lb/sq. in. through valves V_1 and V_1.	1. Press "Start" Button.	"Start Button"
		2. Start Stirrer (through relay)	Stirrer Contactor monitor contact
		3. Actuate V_1	microswitch on V_1
		4. Actuate V_2	microswitch on V_2
2.	Heat for two hours after reaching a temperature of 135 °C.	5. Sensitize temperature-sensor set to 135 °C	limit switch on temperature sensor.
		6. Start two-hour time clock	limit switch at two hours
3.	At end of above period turn off steam by closing valves V_1 and V_2 and apply coolant through valves V_3 and V_4	7. Close V_1	microswitch on V_1
		8. Close V_2	microswitch on V_2
		9 Open V_3	microswitch on V_3
		10 Open V_4	microswitch on V_4
4.	When temperature has fallen to 40 °C turn off coolant, stop stirrer, and eject contents through V_5 by closing vent V_6 and applying compressed air through V_7	11. Sensitize temperature-sensor at 40 °C	limit switch on temperature sensor
		12. Stop stirrer	fallout of contactor
		13. Open V_5	microswitch V_5
		14. Close V_6	microswitch V_6
		15. Open V_7	microswitch V_7

until it is satisfactory. My experience is that it is best to keep such recycling sequencing procedures quite separate from the main sequential process, and to divert from one to the other at a certain stage in the main process.

All that is required in these cases is for the "process stage complete" signal at some stage of the main sequential system to trigger the first stage of a recycling procedure. This stage has its own sequencing switch or unit, and at the end of a cycle the last "process complete" signal raises an alarm. The operator, after examining the product, presses either the "recycle" or the "continue main procedure" button, and in the latter case the main sequential system takes over.

A UNITIZED SEQUENCE CONTROL SYSTEM

One standard proprietary form of hardware for sequence control of batch processes is that produced by Gresham Automation Ltd. All principal functions are incorporated in separate "black boxes" which are combined into various systems. The units are as suitable for small as for complicated systems, and can be used to establish several subsystems and points of operator's choice and intervention. the standard units in this system are—

Sequencing Unit. This unit, as its name implies, is the control mechanism by which one operation is switched on after another in the sequence predetermined by a *variable program unit* (*see* later). It consists of a uniselector capable of controlling processes with up to 25 stages of sequential operation. The move from stage to stage is carried out by closing contacts upon receipt of an automatic signal indicating "process stage complete." A large number of contacts for each stage is brought out to separate terminal blocks so that external circuits can be controlled, either directly for light current or through relays for heavy current. This unit has a self-contained power pack which operates from single-phase, 50 c/s a.c. mains. Several of these units may be employed for extensive systems.

Timing Unit. The standard timing unit consists of pairs of electric clocks. A required time for the process stage can be set on their dials. Signals coming from the appropriate stage of the sequencing unit start a clock going, and at the end of the preset time a relay contact in the clock closes and signals the sequencing unit to move on to the next stage. Standard timing clocks can be preset to better than one per cent accuracy over their operating ranges.

Relay Unit. The relay unit is a link between the sequencing unit and the external power circuits to be controlled. Each unit can accommodate up to twelve relays with push-buttons for manual operation. Each push-button has an associated legend-plate to identify its

c*

control function. Relays in this unit can have extra contacts for actuator monitoring in association with the alarm unit.

Alarm Unit. The purpose of this unit is to attract the attention of a supervisor

(*a*) when the process has been stopped at a certain stage, as laid down in the program, to permit inspection of the product; or, in the case of mixing, to permit the addition of a very small quantity of ingredient such as flavouring or colouring, where the cost of an an electromechanical dispenser is not justified; or

(*b*) when there has been no operation in response to an instruction, owing to some failure.

The alarm unit has bells and lights, and is sensitized by extra contacts on the process actuator relay.

Variable-program Unit. The complete program of operations is preset on this unit. It is essentially a plug board with a number of

FIG. 5.5.   SEQUENCE CONTROL SYSTEM FOR NINE STEEPING PRESSES SUPPLIED TO THE U.S.S.R.

(*Courtesy: Gresham Automation Ltd.*)

FIG. 5.6.   SHOP FLOOR CONTROL AND INTERVENTION UNITS FOR USE WITH SYSTEM IN FIG. 5.5.

(Courtesy: Gresham Automation Ltd.)

wander plugs on flexible leads, and its function is to allow any variation of sequence. Standard templates can be punched, corresponding to each program of operation. These templates are located on dowels in front of the plug board, and ensure that only the correct plugs can be inserted in the right holes to define the program. This unit has been designed for flexibility, and the program can be completely changed within approximately one minute.

Operation Indicating Unit. An operation indicating unit consists of a display of sixteen back-illuminated panels of plastics, which can be signwritten to correspond with the various process stages. The lamps behind the panel are normally wired to the appropriate terminal block on the sequencing unit, and lit in turn to indicate the operations and the stage reached. The legend is a single piece of plastics fitting into slides. If the variable-program unit is used, the whole legend panel can be removed and replaced by another that corresponds to the revised program.

From the above units it is possible to build up almost any possible sequence-control system. But such a system is only the central control feature, and will require peripheral powered atuators and sensors.

An example of a complex batch-sequence-control system is shown in Fig. 5.5. It was designed for the simultaneous control of nine steeping presses for rayon manufacture in the U.S.S.R. Each of nine identical sequencing and timing units controls each of the nine parallel processes, and in addition there are means for controlling the phasing of the nine processes so that they start and complete their process cycles in staggered arrangement to give a reasonably smooth total output to the subsequent processes. This is achieved by a special queueing unit. Also, as shown in Fig. 5.6, each of the nine systems has a shop-floor control unit, enabling the process operators to signal the central system when each of the processes is ready to operate, and to intervene manually in case of emergency.

CHAPTER 6

DISPENSING CONTROL

An important feature of sequential operation of batch processes is the ability to weigh, meter and dispense ingredients. The vital elements of automatic weighing are—

(*i*) Basic weighing techniques.
(*ii*) Data programming.
(*iii*) General layout.
(*iv*) Integration of weighing and dispensing with other facilities, such as overall program sequencing.

BASIC WEIGHING TECHNIQUE

There are many methods of weighing, involving mechanics, pneumatics, hydraulics and electronics, but for the practical purposes of automatic dispensing we shall limit our selection of methods to—

Mechanical Techniques. These are the well-established techniques of the majority of the older weighing companies. Lever or spring-balance systems indicate weight on a dial. It is noteworthy that even the automated versions of such techniques generally leave the dial in place as a visual check on what is happening.

Electronic Load-cell Techniques. A set of fine electrical-resistance wires ("strain gauges") is bonded to a block of steel. The weight distorts the steel block, so stretching the wires by a small amount. This stretching alters their electrical resistance, and the change is detected in appropriate "black boxes." The reading is usually displayed on the same sort of dial as is employed for mechanical weighers. The general form of circuit used in load-cell systems is shown in Fig. 6.1. It consists of four strain-gauges in a Wheatstone bridge. Two of the gauges are arranged at right angles to the other two, and they are not appreciably changed by the load cell's distortion under weight; they compensate for temperature and aging variations in the other two, active, strain gauges. The output of the strain-gauge bridge is compared with the output of an external bridge. The differential current is amplified to drive a motor which moves a contact along one arm of the external bridge until the differential current is zero. The setting of the potentiometer, or the position of the driving motor, is a measure of the final weight reached, and can be shown on a dial or other display device.

Generally speaking, mechanical techniques have been used where greater accuracy is required, but the development of electronic load-cells is now reaching the point where accuracies of 0·05 per cent or better appear to be possible. Furthermore, load cells are very suitable for installations where very heavy weights are involved; and where conditions are dusty and dirty, since there are no mechanisms to be interfered with. Up to the present, weighers for process work have been dominantly mechanical, but in America the leading companies are beginning to take electronic-load-cell weighing more seriously, and we may expect to see a considerable acceleration in the use of this technique. Whilst mechanical weighers must have fairly well exhausted their possibilities, there are many interesting lines for the further development of electronic load-cells. Promising prospects include the non-bonded load-cell, for which unusual zero-load stability is claimed, various systems of pre-aging, individual calibration, and the employment of negative feedback.

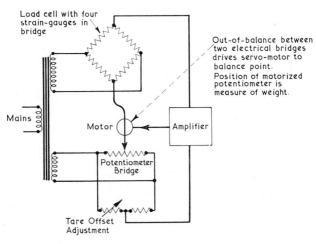

FIG. 6.1.   LOAD-CELL CIRCUIT

At this time, in 1962, it would be going too far to suggest that load cells will entirely replace mechanical devices for process weighing. The ultimate decision will always turn on value for money, but it is now clear that any proposal for an automated weighing system should involve the careful consideration of the merits of both techniques.

DATA PROGRAMMING OF WEIGHERS

There are many possible bases for the data programming of weighers. These include plug boards, punched tape, magnetic tape, punched cards, plug-in analogue resistor or helical potentiometer units, etc.

However, during recent visits to the leading makers of such equipment in Europe and America, I found that they had almost all decided in favour of the punched-card method because it is cheap, easily understood, and provides much more flexibility in sequential or parallel dispensing of weighed components.

Whilst I agree in general with this decision, I would sound a word of warning: *it all depends upon what you mean by a punched card.* If weight dispensing is to be combined with a sequential control system having several hundred steps (quite a common requirement), then the ordinary business-machine punched-card would come to its end long before all the steps of the process had been dealt with. For very complicated weighing and process sequencing it will probably be necessary to devise a very long and unfamiliar punched-card, which is really a "punched card-tape" of the sort used to control knitting machines. An alternative technique would be to use punched or magnetic *tapes* for controlling the sequencing functions, but have separate temporary memories for weight figures. This would allow parallel weighing to proceed whilst providing unlimited sequential-control information. With these provisos in mind, one may accept as satisfactory that the punched card appears to be the presently favoured technique for data programming of weighers.

There are three popular methods of application of punched-card programming to mechanical or electronic-load-cell weighers: (i) the preset-target system for mechanical weighers; (ii) the potentiometer-balance system for mechanical weighers; (iii) the potentiometer-balance system for load-cell weighers.

Preset-target System

This system, which is equally applicable to all weighers with dial-and-pointer display, is illustrated schematically in Fig. 6.2. In the form developed by the Oerlikon Company, known in Britain under the trade name "Sinex", a motor-driven photo-electric cell is attached

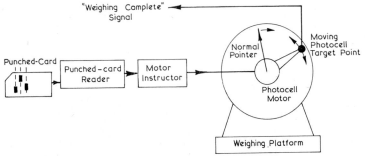

FIG. 6.2.   PRESET DIAL TARGETS SYSTEM USING PHOTOCELL

to the centre of a dial-and-pointer system. The punched-card programming system moves the photocell round the dial until it stops at the required weight reading. This is done before the weigher is operated. The photocell position establishes the "target signal." After weighing has begun, the pointer turns round the dial until it is detected by the photocell, which then gives out a "weighing process complete" signal and stops the operation.

The advantage of this system is that it can convert existing dial-type weighers into punched-card, remotely programmed, robots, but at the same time let the operator revert to local manual weighing if the control system fails.

Potentiometer-balance System for Mechanical Weighers

In this system (*see* Fig. 6.3) the punched-card reader selects a system of resistances, usually arranged in decimal array, to form a

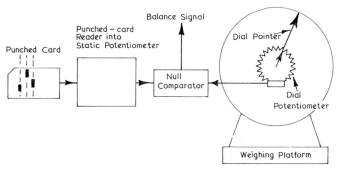

FIG. 6.3.   DIAL POTENTIOMETER BALANCE SYSTEM
(*Also see Fig.* 6.4)

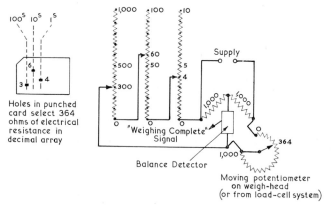

FIG. 6.4.   PUNCHED-CARD WEIGHT SELECTION

potentiometer which is a proportional analogue of the required weight (*see* Fig. 6.4). The pointer on the weigher dial carries a wiper that runs over a circular potentiometer. At a certain position on the dial the resistance of the variable potentiometer is equivalent to the resistance of the potentiometer set up by the punched-card reader. Balance between the two potentiometers is detected in an electrical comparator, and a "weighing process complete" signal is given out. This can be employed to stop further dispensing of material into the weigher.

Potentiometer-balance System for Electronic Load-cell Weighers

This system is very similar to the one previously described for mechanical weighers. It consists (*see* Fig. 6.5) of a static potentio-

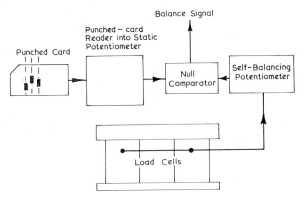

FIG. 6.5.   PUNCHED-CARD SYSTEM FOR LOAD-CELL WEIGHING

meter set up by means of a punched-card system. This is compared electrically (*see* Fig. 6.4) with the potentiometer belonging to the load-cell detection system. When balance is reached in a null comparator this gives out a "weighing process complete" signal to stop further dispensing of material into the weigher.

General Layout of Weighing Systems

Batch-process weighing systems normally involve the dispensing of materials from storage hoppers. Such hoppers may have one of three principal relationships with their weighers (*see* Fig. 6.6.) as follows—

Individual Hopper Weighers. "Individual" systems are those in which each hopper has an individual weigher associated with it and normally located underneath for gravity feed.

Mobile Weighers. If very many ingredients are involved, an "individual" system is very expensive in weighers. To economize on weighing equipment it may be necessary to take a mobile weighing-car to each hopper.

Transfer Weighing. In this system, which is an alternative to the use of mobile weighers, the output from many hoppers is conveyed either pneumatically or mechanically to the weighing station.

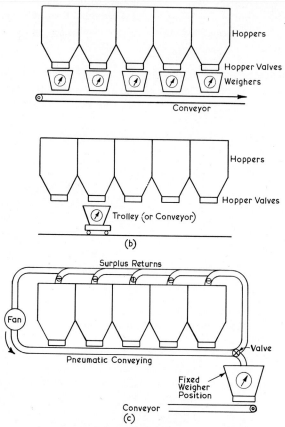

FIG. 6.6. THREE HOPPER-WEIGHING SYSTEMS
(a) Individual-hopper ("parallel") weighing; (b) Mobile weighing; (c) Transfer weighing

The choice between these three methods in a given situation will turn on such considerations as the speed requirement (the individual system is the quickest, since it can dispense several components simultaneously), the nature of the materials (pneumatic transfer weighing is very attractive for flour, which can readily be blown in pipes over considerable distances), capital costs (mobile weighing is usually the cheapest), etc. It is impossible to forecast all the practical circumstances that might lead to a decision. Here we shall consider only the repercussions of the choice upon the data-handling problem. In all cases we shall assume that variable-recipe facilities are required, since fixed-recipe systems are merely a particular simplification of the problem.

PARALLEL AND SEQUENTIAL DISPENSING

If the system consists of individual hopper weighers, then it is desirable to take advantage of the considerable multiple-weighing capacity by dispensing materials to the weighers simultaneously ("parallel" or "matrix" weighing). In either mobile or transfer weighing, only one weigher deals with several weighing operations, so the dispensing must be in sequence. What are the repercussions of parallel and sequential weighing on punched-card programming "black-boxes?"

Multi-component Sequential Weighing

Assume that the punched card requires three decimal columns for each ingredient weight, to give a full-scale program accuracy of one part in a thousand. (This would probably go with the sort of three-digit decimal tapped-resistance system depicted in Fig. 6.4, balancing against a rotary dial-potentiometer, in the weighing head.)

The punched card has to be used three rows at a time for each ingredient, and a sequencing switch (of the sort described in the previous chapter) is all that is needed to "interrogate" the punched card in successive sets of three rows. This is shown schematically in Fig. 6.7. The sequencer itself will be moved on to the next three-

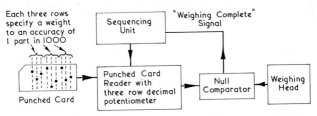

FIG. 6.7. SCHEMATIC DIAGRAM OF SEQUENTIAL INGREDIENT-DISPENSING

row interrogating position on receipt of the "weighing process complete" signal.

These are the bare bones of the system. In most cases quite a degree of process-actuation instruction will also be required.

1. The punched card will require a column for "weigher identification" selection. This (in the case of mobile weighing) will simul-

taneously start the mobile weigher moving and activate a limit switch at the correct destination. This may involve some logical comparison of the original position of the weigher with its required destination, in order to decide not only whether the weigher should move but in which initial direction. Assuming that this is sorted out by an appropriate logical "black-box," the mobile weigher will move until it has operated the program-sensitized limit-switch. The latter then sends a "weigher in correct position" signal back to the sequencer.

2. The sequencer is moved on one step by the last incoming signal (described above), and simultaneously it (*a*) operates the ingredient-input device, (*b*) probably starts a time-limit clock to check that the weighing does not take too long (owing to some fault like powder hold-up, and (*c*) sets the three-digit weighing formula, as described earlier.

From the above it is clear that each sequence stage involves at least *four* rows of the punched card, three rows for the weighing digits and one row for process actuation.

3. When weighing is complete the balance signal will be sent out from the weighing null comparator to the sequencer, which will move to its next position.

4. The process will repeat 1, 2 and 3 above until all the ingredients are dispensed.

The above analysis shows that the combination of the punched-card reader and the sequencing switch has to deal with three essential groups of functions—

1. Data and actuation related to the ingredient identity and correct position of the weigher. (*Where* the operation is wanted.)

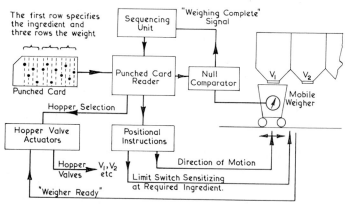

FIG. 6.8.   BASIC SCHEME OF INGREDIENT DISPENSING WITH MOBILE WEIGHER

2. Data related to the ingredient and hopper-dispensed weight. (*What* is wanted.)

3. Actuation of the hopper valves. (Weighing *operation*.)

In practical installations the complications mount progressively as arrangements are made for operation monitoring, for emptying the mobile weigher after each operation, and so on. The simplified schematic drawing of a typical system in Fig. 6.8 would, if it included all these, expand until it covered a sheet of double-elephant paper.

The partial description given above does show how the punched card is being rapidly used up in groups of at least four rows at a time. Such a system calls for a very considerable punched-card interrogator with a great number of contacts, and the sequencing unit also requires to be of very considerable capacity. The principles remain basic to all systems, although the technique gets cumbersome for extensive ones.

Multi-component Parallel Weighing

Consider the control problem when individual weighers for many components are arranged for simultaneous weighing. The simplified control scheme is shown in Fig. 6.9. All that is required is a single punched card on which all the component weights are specified by three decimal rows, but the complication is that the card reader must have a static array of decimal resistances for *each* of the three rows of the card, since each weigher has to have a target for correct weight. Similarly, a correspondingly large number of null balance comparators is needed to indicate that the individual weighings are complete. Finally a logical unit is wanted; all the "weighing complete" signals are received in the AND circuits of this unit, providing a further signal to the system when the last weigher has completed its mission. Then either all weighers can be discharged on to some common conveyor, or a new program can be commenced.

DISPENSING OF LIQUIDS

The general principles of dispensing systems apply equally well to both solid and liquid materials, but whereas in the former case it is more convenient to *weigh* the materials, in the latter case it is usual to *meter* them by volume. If the specific gravity is known, volume is as good a criterion as weight.

The normal device for metering liquids is a positive-displacement pump, either reciprocating or rotary. When the liquid displacement per pump cycle is known, total volumetric delivery is found simply by counting cycles.

For batch processes the normal control system is to set up a number corresponding to the required delivery on an electronic or relay counter, and then count down the outcoming pulses from the pump until zero marks completion. Such counters may be set up by push buttons, rotary switches or punched cards.

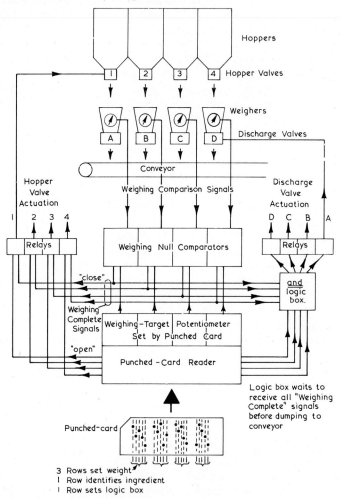

FIG. 6.9.   PARALLEL DISPENSING BY PUNCHED CARD

Continuous Liquid Proportioning

So far we have considered dispensing in batch processes, but there is an equally important requirement for the continuous proportioning of solids and liquids.

Typical of these is the liquid proportioning system developed by Constructors John Brown Ltd. This system is known as the "Auto-blender." Each installation consists of (*a*) a control panel on which the proportioning requirements may be set up, and (*b*) peripheral equipment consisting of pumps and positive-displacement flowmeters. The system can handle any number of liquids, and special programming facilities are provided for each of these components.

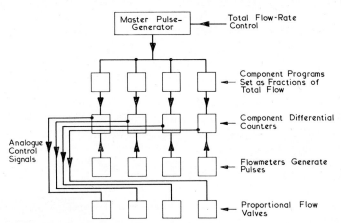

FIG. 6.10.   PROPORTIONAL CONTROL OF CONTINUOUS LIQUID BLENDING

The system (*see* Fig. 6.10) uses a master oscillator to generate electronic pulses at a rate which may be varied at will. The pulse train is fed to all the component programmers. The rate of pulsation virtually sets the *total* supply required, and the programming of each contributory component is governed by selecting a fraction of this rate. Thus once the porportioning factors have been set, the total flow can be varied without affecting the component fractions.

Each positive-displacement flowmeter in the individual component-flow lines generates pulses which are taken to the individual component-control units. The difference between the number of pulses from the component programmer and the flowmeters is accumulated in a differential counter—for correct operation this difference should be zero. Any actual difference is converted into an analogue signal and fed to the individual component-proportioning valves. The valves operate to bring the differential count figures down to zero. An accuracy of 0·25 per cent is claimed for the system.

CONTINUOUS PROPORTIONING OF SOLIDS

The proportioning of solids in continuous chemical processes is usually by continuous-belt weighers. The instrumentation includes means both for determining the weight on the belt and the speed of the belt. The measured weight has to be combined with the measured speed in some appropriate mechanical or electronic integrator to give the weight flow rate. Such systems are currently accurate to about 0·5 per cent, and there is considerable need for improved accuracy for many applications.

DISPENSING INSTALLATIONS

Foundry at Automobile Factory

The Ford installation at Dagenham, by Sinex Ltd., is one of the most modern in existence for the formula-weighing of foundry-sand constituents. It comprises four identical units. Each unit weighs two grades of sand, three bonding ingredients, and three liquids, all of which are fed into a mixer. The whole operation is automatically controlled by a punched card.

Each unit can produce a batch of approximately one ton every three minutes, and the formula can be completely changed in a matter of seconds by replacing the punched card. Two weighing scales are used to obtain the required accuracy for both the heavier doses of sand and the relatively smaller amounts of bonding material. The liquids are accurately metered into pressure vessels from which they are blown into the mixers.

The scales are mounted on mobile carriers. They are of the mechanical type, the target weight being set on the weigher dial by remote control from the punched card. A coding system is used for setting up the weights on the punched cards, so the formula can be kept secret. An override permits the formula to be set up manually on a switch board.

The control system can handle twenty ingredients per weighing machine, i.e. forty ingredients from the two weighers on the one punched card.

Blending by Weight

One of the most highly developed commercial systems for dispensing materials into mixers and blending them is the Richardson "Select-O-Weigh" illustrated in Figs. 6.11 and 6.12. The desired weights of ingredients, and the order in which they are to be fed into the final mixer, is punched in an I.B.M. card and fed into the central

FIG. 6.11. "SELECT-O-WEIGH" SYSTEM
(*Courtesy: Richardson Scale Co.*)

control system through a specially developed punched-card reader. The system is designed to operate on the "transfer system"—many ingredients in hoppers are conveyed or piped to a central weigher

FIG. 6.12. DETAIL OF PUNCHED-CARD READER ON "SELECT-O-WEIGH" SYSTEM
(*Courtesy: Richardson Scale Co.*)

which, after weighing, dumps them in the mixer. The conveyors involve vibrating feeders, screw conveyors and belt feeders. The scale system itself is also provided with vibrators to ensure smooth, quick and accurate operation. The entire system is dust-tight, with flexible connexions between storage bins and the vibrating feeders. Flexible connexions are also provided between the vibrating feeders and the feeder turret above the scale.

An inventory counter and totalizer takes the results of all weighings in digital form (from a gear digitizer on the weighing head) and keeps the score on all ingredients for total inventory control.

In the control system shown in Figs. 6.11 and 6.12 the two punched-card readers are for controlling pre-mixes and final mixes respectively. A coded interlock gives the alarm if the identity on the two cards is not the same. The system provides for the proportioning of 24 main ingredients plus sixteen pre-blended additives, and facilities are also available for controlling liquid additions metered by counting methods.

Biscuit Factory

An interesting control and dispensing system has been supplied by Elliott-Automation Ltd. to Robinson's Ltd. of Rochdale for installation in Carr's biscuit factory at Carlisle. This consists of a punched-card system for totally automatic blending of seven grades of flour, with additions of such ingredients as sugar, syrups, fats and so on.

Each recipe is coded on a punched card which is stored below the program panel. The recipe cards for the day are collected and placed on the program panel for the various baking ovens. Through each hole in the cards a plug is inserted to register the various ingredients required. The request to the automatic programmer for a mix is made from a panel in the oven area by means of a "request" push-button. This activates the programming device, and ingredients begin to be dispensed into a container above a mixer. The automatic programmer is continuously scanning for requests from the oven area, but a human supervisor decides priorities.

The programmer will omit any request coming from an oven whose containers already contain ingredients or have their discharge valves open. This will apply in particular to shared containers. To compensate for the omissions, sharing ovens have more than one chance of selection. The scanning order has also been arranged so that the sharing ovens are not adjacent; this gives them a further chance.

The programmer will reject a recipe requiring an ingredient that is not available. A rejected request is indicated by flashing the "request" lamp. This indicates the offending oven to the supervisor, and he can replace either the recipe in the store or the deficient ingredient. When an ingredient is replaced, the request is automatically made available again to the scanner.

In a digital form, the weight from the receipt stores is compared with the translated output from a disk encoder, on the main shaft of the weigh-meter. An output to stop the feed into the weigh-hopper is given by the comparator when the actual weight is equal to the weight required. The average overshoot and amount of ingredient in suspension are compensated for at each weighing.

Mixes can also be weighed by push-button operation of the plant from a mimic diagram. When the indicator shows the correct amount of flour, the supervisor directs the feed of ingredient away from the weigh-hopper and back to the storage hopper. The feeder valve is closed, and when the lines are clear a new flour can be selected.

The flour hoppers may be refilled from lorries, railway waggons or sacks. This operation is independent of any weighing cycle and may be performed at any time. When a lorry arrives the driver connects the appropriate pipes. He then signals to the supervisor by push-button. The supervisor endorses the lorry driver's action, and the appropriate starters automatically extract the flour from the lorries. When flour ceases to flow, as indicated by the pressure difference in the blow-lines, the lorry driver checks his load, stops the air supply, and disconnects his pipes. The flour is first transported into test bins, where it is graded, and then distributed to the main storage bins. Outlets are provided for unwanted flour, dusting and bagging.

A teleprinter of standard pattern gives a complete record of the ovens selected and recipes supplied. The recipe is printed with letters before each weight, to denote the grade and type of each ingredient used. The weights printed are cumulative for each ingredient, and this not only simplifies the equipment required for print-out, but provides an immediate check on stock of each ingredient.

CHAPTER 7

CURRENT PRACTICE IN CONTINUOUS
CHEMICAL PROCESS CONTROL

FOR the last twenty years or so, control technique in the chemical industry has been relatively static. This is not to say that progress has not been made, but it has been in the direction of increased reliability rather than innovation.

At the same time there has been a great deal of research and development, of a revolutionary nature, leading toward control by computer. This is only now reaching the practical stage, in 1962. It is so far-reaching that I shall devote the next chapter entirely to it, and restrict the present chapter to a consideration of established process-control technique.

THE GENERAL POSITION

The current position of the art in continuous chemical process control is characterized by three main features: (i) the use of unit negative-feedback controllers with which are associated automatic sensors and automatic control valves; (ii) highly centralized control rooms; and (iii) data reduction systems. Only the last of the three factors is anything like a recent development. The wide-spread application of the first two has created a most dramatic impression, with particular reference to the reduction of manual labour. Many modern chemical plants already represent almost the ultimate in labour-saving possibilities relative to the value of the capital equipment involved, and further automation is essentially directed towards improved quality control and increased plant utilization. As far as the man in the street is concerned, a modern chemical plant appears to be an example of almost complete automation, and future improvements will be detectable mainly by process chemists and financial experts.

CONTINUOUS CHEMICAL CONTROL

In Chapter 4 a continuous chemical process was described as one in which the materials had to be moved past a static process pattern; so automating a continuous chemical process involves (a) a continuous materials-handling system, and (b) a control system for maintaining a constant process pattern for such variables as materials input, temperature and pressure, chemical state, etc.

In principle all this should be the easiest matter possible, first because the materials-handling problem with chemicals is very easy (they are usually in liquid form and a simple pumping system is adequate), and secondly a constant process pattern merely involves making sure that no conditions change at any point of the plant. If the chemical reactions involved are essentially simple, stable, and well behaved, almost total automation is achievable. This particularly applies to several sectors of the oil industry, where the end-point quality specification is not critical. However, when the chemical reactions tend to be unstable, a constant process pattern will not induce a constant quality of end product, and severe difficulties arise. Thus, very broadly, current techniques are almost ideal for stable processes but they are not adequate for the quality control of unstable processes, and this has led to the search for computer control, which I shall describe in the next chapter.

THE UNIT NEGATIVE-FEEDBACK CONTROLLER

In order to keep a process pattern constant (*see* Fig. 4.10), the local conditions must be kept constant at each important point along the length of the chemical plant, and suitable controls have to be provided for this purpose. An ideal or target condition (the local "command program") is specified for each control point, and negative-feedback controllers installed to hold the conditions there to the ideal. Since many such control points are required, each controller is referred to as a "local-loop controller," the local-loop embracing the circulation system shown in Fig. 7.1.

A local-loop negative-feedback controller compares the sensor signal with the target signal and from them creates an error signal. If the subsequent corrective signal is directly proportional to the error signal, the device is known as a *proportional controller*. Such a simple controller tends to make a process oscillate about the target point if (as is normal) the process has any thermal or chemical inertia. This is because the corrective action will not stop in time to prevent the process from overreaching the target point.

It is highly desirable for feedback controllers to contain some anticipatory features. These are usually of two kinds. Firstly a *derivative* signal, proportional to the rate of change of error signal, can be added to the proportional signal to give a quick reaction to any sudden change of error signal. Secondly the error signal may be *integrated* with time, so that corrective action may be greater the longer the error persists.

Most modern controllers contain all three of the error signal "terms," proportional, derivative and integrating, and have control knobs to set the relative amount of each corrective feature. For this reason they are known as *three-term controllers*.

It is of interest, remembering the discussion in Chapter 3 on simulation of process know-how, that the mathematical simulations involved in three-term controllers are a prime example of the effectiveness of such techniques. Indeed, the attempt to run processes with computers is to some degree an extension of three-term control on a much larger scale.

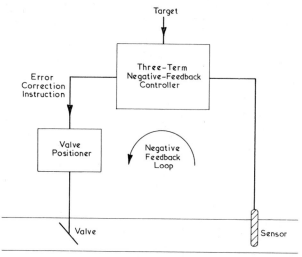

FIG. 7.1.   LOCAL-LOOP CONTROL

Note, however, that the sensors used with three-term controllers are almost always *physical*, controlling physical quantities such as temperature, pressure, and material flow rate, and they do not normally act by measuring and controlling chemical factors directly. The possibilities of controlling directly from chemical quality sensors will be considered in the next chapter.

THE CENTRALIZED CONTROL ROOM

A complex chemical plant may have hundreds of local-loop controllers installed to maintain a constant process pattern, and with these there may be associated a great number of instruments for the better information of the process supervisors. Since chemical plants are often very tall and exposed to the open air, it is a major problem of communications to co-ordinate any required changes on a plant. The natural development has therefore been to centralize the control apparatus in one room, as shown in Fig. 7.2, and this involves the following factors—

1. If there are many loop-controllers of the type just described, then they must be of the "remote set point" type. With this kind of controller the local target points or command program can be set from a distance. This allows all target setting to be centralized, perhaps on a single control desk.

2. All chemical valves and other actuation devices must be of a remote-setting type.

3. All instrumentation must be of remote-reading type.

FIG. 7.2.   MAIN CONTROL AT B.P.'S RUHR REFINERY, DINSLAKEN, GERMANY
Courtesy: British Petroleum Co. Ltd.)

It is usual to place all centralized instruments on a process display diagram to facilitate quick understanding by the human controller. He will also require good telephone communication with the various parts of the plant where there may still be a few process operators.

Presentation of data in a centralized control room may lead to very considerable labour-saving, but in spite of the very dramatic superficial impression, such installations do not necessarily provide the best control possible. It is still a matter for human judgement to make process adjustments from guidance provided by the profuse instrumentation. The centralized control room is not really an instance of complete automation as defined in this book (i.e. complete transfer to control by data), and will undoubtedly be supplanted by more compact and automatic installations of the sort considered in the next chapter.

MULTI-POINT SCANNING SYSTEMS

Where it is desired to establish some central control over a complex process extending over a considerable area, it is necessary to transmit many messages to and from the process. The transmission channels may be expensive, and there may be danger of loss of data owing to confusion of signals by extraneous electrical "noise." In these cases it is desirable to use some form of coded transmission of data (*see* Fig. 7.3) which is less sensitive to such "noise," and the usual method

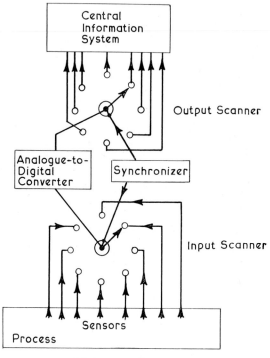

FIG. 7.3.   MULTI-POINT SCANNING

is to convert amplitude (analogue) signals into a digital code for transmission. But analogue-to-digital conversion is expensive, and it is economic to use one set of conversion apparatus for all the signals, taking them in turn. Then only one transmission link is required between process and control system, though it does involve a second data-distributing device at the receiving end to direct the digitized signals to their correct final destination. Altogether, the following apparatus is involved—

Various sensors picking up process data, probably in analogue (varying-amplitude) form.

A sequencing data-scanning unit, which takes the data signals one at a time. The scanner is probably in the process area.

An analogue-to-digital converter.

A transmission link from the process to the control area.

A second sequencing scanning-switch for redistributing digitized signals to the correct destinations in the control system.

A synchronizing device to make sure that the two sequencing switches keep correctly in step.

The above arrangement is possible on the assumption that the control system can use digital signals directly. If it is essentially an analogue control system, then either: (a) the signals may not be converted to digital form in the first place (this will turn on the distances involved, and the likely interference from sequencing and transmission noise), or (b) a digital-to-analogue converter may be inserted just before the second (output) scanning unit.

DATA-LOGGING AND DATA-REDUCTION SYSTEMS

The conventional central control room is rather a cumbersome system. A great number of individual instruments and recorders must be observed if one is to know what is happening in the plant. Over the last few years an effort has been made to simplify the problem by means of "data-logging" systems. The purpose of a data-logging system is to collect all the measurements transmitted from the process and convert them into digital form so that they may be automatically printed by typewriter on a log sheet. All the important figures obtaining at one particular time are shown along one row. The system may also produce a punched-tape version of the figures, and this may be processed in a computer to correlate variables for research purposes.

A data logger is a simple means for centralizing all measurements. Where it is used, graphical recorders may be restricted to those measurements whose trend is best observed in a graphical presentation.

FIG. 7.4. DATA LOGGER AT I.C.I.

(*Courtesy: A.E.I. & I.C.I.*)

In a system devised by A. E. I. Ltd. (*see* Fig. 7.4), the data logger includes a luminous digital indicator on which any selected variable can be displayed at demand. With this system the automatic logging can be carried out continuously or after predetermined intervals of time.

When feeding a data-logging system from a complex set of incoming signals, it may be necessary to adapt non-linear signals to make them proportional to the measured variable. This adaptation (or "compensation") may be done in an appropriate "function generator" —another electronic "black box."

Such systems are intended to simplify the presentation of data to a human controller, and it is desirable that the printed figures be appropriately scaled up or down to represent quantities in directly recognizable units of temperature, pressure, flow rate, etc. This scaling of readings will normally only require the interposition of appropriate electrical calibrating potentiometers, but in a few cases it may be necessary to combine one or two readings to make them more intelligible. Thus a given signal line may be carrying incoming information on flow *rate* in a pipeline, but this information can also be converted into cumulative delivery over a given time by automatic integration of flow rate with time in an appropriate "black box."

The practical operation of data-logging systems often starts with a great number of commissioning problems. For example, there is no point in printing figures to the third decimal place when the accuracy of the original sensor may only be accurate to one decimal place, and steps must be taken to ensure that such misleading inaccuracies are eliminated.

In general, data-logging systems are not considered to be very satisfactory. They tend to produce too many figures. They cannot be easily digested by the control staff, and the tendency is therefore to create data-*reduction* systems, which only print those measurements which show that a process quantity is incorrect in terms of the target. A complementary development is the provision of short-period electronic "memories." If readings are going in an undesirable direction, such memories can be called upon to provide the recent history over the last hour or so.

PRESENT STATE OF THE ART

At present, the art of continuous chemical process control is largely dominated by three characteristics—

1. Negative-feedback-control units, each capable of stabilizing one process variable.

2. The central instrumentation room.

3. A trend towards data-logging and data-reduction apparatus, to reduce the excessive amount of displayed information in central instrumentation rooms.

In the next chapter you will see how these features are becoming out of date for complex chemical plants, and how the new trend is towards automatic control by computers.

CHAPTER 8

NEW DEVELOPMENTS IN CONTINUOUS
CHEMICAL PROCESS CONTROL

THE main line of attack on the problem of the improved control of
continuous chemical processes is by means of electronic computers.
Of all practical developments in automation this is the one that is
commanding the greatest technical effort. This is not entirely because
problems in the chemical industry are the most demanding, but rather
because their solution would clear the way to the computer control
of many other forms of complex process. The solution by computers
of chemical control problems implies the solution of the general
problem of simulating a human being's complex process know-how.
Once this has been achieved, the way is open to the universal application of thinking robots on a scale difficult to envisage—but equally
dangerous to underestimate. At the 1960 conference of the Internatioal
Federation of Automatic Control, held in Moscow, the great majority
of the three hundred or so papers was devoted to one or another
aspect of the computer control of complex processes, and the detailed
mathematical and electronic ramifications of these studies are both
bewildering and fascinating.

THE PRINCIPAL OBJECTIVES

The underlying assumption is that, at the present time, continuous
chemical processes are not being controlled as well as they might be.
The objectives of increased automation here have very little to do
with increased labour savings, since so few operators are required
in an advanced chemical plant with centralized control (*see* last
chapter). The principal objectives are three. They are to (i) make
exactly the quality and balance of products of a production program;
(ii) manufacture this correct and balanced product with a minimum
consumption of raw materials and energy; and (iii) make the maximum
use of capital investment in process plant, i.e. maximize the plant's
throughput at the correct quality and balance of products.

A considerable part of chemical industry, notably in the petroleum
sector, is particularly concerned with the economics of its product
balance in processes where various products are made simultaneously.
It may be most important to make exactly the balance of products
currently demanded by the market, for otherwise too large a capital
investment may be tied up in tankage and warehouses. Indeed, one

of the main advantages of highly integrated automatic systems is their potentially rapid adaptability to changing market conditions.

EVOLUTIONARY NATURE OF COMPUTER CONTROL

With existing forms of centralized control, where two or three human operators may sit at the centre of an instrumental network, it might be imagined that the residual judgement and experience required from these human controllers are relatively simply, and easily automated out of the picture. This would be a very considerable misunderstanding of the situation. The amount of process know-how that can be carried in the head of a single individual is immense. It is almost impossible to overestimate the difficulties of replacing all this by means of some computing robot.

Not only has a human operator a great deal of experience of the normal running of a chemical plant, but in addition he develops a sixth sense for abnormalities and the approach of dangerous conditions. He is often able to take anticipatory corrective action well before such abnormalities attain serious proportions. As well as having these capabilities he understands how a chemical plant is continuously changing its state of "tune" and responsiveness between overhauls, and he is able to take progressive corrective action against such conditions as the slow furring-up of boilers and heat exchangers, the progressive deterioration of filtration systems, and many other similar insidious plant deteriorations. To put it shortly, after twenty or so years of experience a plant operator knows the whole system inside out, and no computer will be as effective as a human operator unless it has assimilated an equivalent amount of process know-how. This means that there is no question of simply applying a computer to run a continuous chemical plant in the expectation of some immediate improvement. On the contrary, the first problem is to ensure that the plant is run at least as well as by the human operator. Even this would be an achievement of the highest technical order, and tremendous additional problems are involved if a computer is to operate a process better than a human being.

The philosophical expectation for computer control of chemical plant is as shown in Fig. 8.1, where the quality of control by a human operator is indicated by a relatively horizontal line in time, while the level of control by a computer is indicated by an inclined line which commences at a much lower level than existing human operation.

There is a close analogy between the evolution of computers and teaching animals to do tricks. Every trick has to be acquired by much study and experimentation on a slowly progressive basis. The problem is not so much to find suitable computers for the purpose, but rather to teach computers to do men's present tricks. In all this the electronics experts are at the mercy of the process chemists and operators, who alone have an inkling of the details of the tricks that they require to be performed.

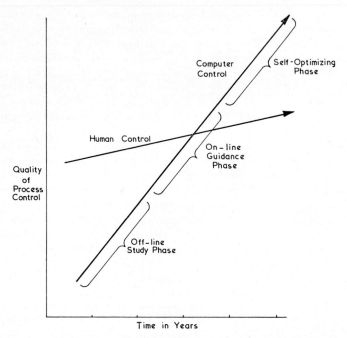

FIG. 8.1.   COMPUTER PROCESS CONTROL AS AN EVOLUTIONARY PROCESS

Thus computers have to be introduced to chemical process control by degrees, and apparently in three well-marked stages—

Off-line Computer Studies. In these the principal aim is to inject process know-how into a computer by constructing a mathematical model of the know-how as a basic reference for a possible control system.

On-line Monitoring or Guidance Systems. Here the computer is directly coupled to a chemical process to receive instrumental signals. As a result of robot deliberations it produces an instruction sheet for a human controller. This is sometimes called "guidance computing." One of its purposes is to retain the full weight of operator experience whilst allowing the computer to try out its wings.

On-line Computer Control. The computer controls the process directly.

Off-line Computer Studies

It is generally agreed by the experts that the only feasible method for computer control of a chemical process is first to establish a mathematical model of the process and then to place this model inside an analogue or digital computer. (*Note:* I consider that there is an exception to this rule, described later in this chapter under *The Logical Juke-box Computer.*)

Now what is meant by a "mathematical model" of a chemical process? The most important mathematical concept involved is the so-called "transfer function" of the process. This may sound complicated, but it is simply the ratio between the mathematical formula for the input to a process and the mathematical formula for the output from the process.

Examples of Transfer Functions

A. If an input is varied and always causes twice as big a change in the output, then the transfer function is "two."

B. If an input is proportional to $\sin \omega t$ and causes an output variation proportional to $\cos \omega t$, the transfer function is proportional to $\cos \omega t / \sin \omega t$, or cotan ωt.

The importance of the transfer function is that it gives the mathematical relationship between *causes* and *effects*, between input variations and output variations, and this is the essence of process-control know-how. Transfer functions simply tell you that if you make *this* variation at the input you will get *that* variation at the output.

In practice the mathematics have to take into account all factors which can affect the output of a process, not only variations in the input but also subsequent intercombinations during the process itself. One could not attempt in the scope of this chapter to give any extended examples of practical process mathematics, but as an example of what can be done one can adduce the mathematical models that have now been worked out for such processes as distillation columns. Whilst these mathematical studies of chemical processes are still in their infancy, they appear to be at once the main hope and the main obstacle for process control by computer.

Mathematical studies have to be worked on progressively, and usually commence with an attempt to write the equations (or transfer functions) for the chemical process in terms of what knowledge may be available. But classical chemical kinetic theory will rarely do more than establish a first guess at the problem. The next stage is to acquire more detailed mathematical information from the process itself, and this can be pursued in one of two ways. The first way is to examine all the past records of the plant and attempt to construct cause-and-effect patterns in mathematical form. This second way is to experiment on the chemical plant by introducing deliberate changes in control factors, and to see what the effect is. By means of all these techniques the earlier mathematical skeleton begins to grow flesh, although it may still only be a ghost of what really happens in the process plant.

This is where the off-line computer commences its operations. The provisional mathematical model of the process can now be put into an analogue or digital computer, and experimental variations can be introduced into the model at the same time as corresponding experiments are being made on the process itself. Then the hope is that by modifying the model in the computer, either empirically or logically, it may gradually be made to follow the same behaviour pattern as is displayed by the process plant.

At the time of writing, in 1962, I am not aware of any very successful outcome of this technique in Britain, but the Standard Oil Company (Indiana, U.S.A.) claim that they now have a mathematical model of some of their oil-refinery processes embedded in an I.B.M. 704 computer, and that this really works.

On-line Computer Monitoring

Providing that a computer has assimilated a reasonably adequate mathematical model of a chemical process, it may pass to the next stage. This is to begin collecting information directly from the process in the hope that it may be able to begin to produce some of the correct control answers, or at least suggestions to guide human controllers. In essence, the computer observes the direction in which the measurements are going and refers to its own mathematical model to see what the other variables should be doing to correct the situation.

Later in this chapter I shall touch upon four alternative views as to how all this should be done. In the meantime, the important feature to note is that a monitoring or guidance computer is, as it were, *practising* its control function under *real* conditions, but is not short-circuiting operator experience and final human decisions. The human operator has full control of the situation. If the computer keeps making successful control suggestions to him, of course, the operator will acquire greater and greater confidence in his robot friend, and in due course may be prepared to let it take the whole job on.

Full Computer Control

No one has yet reached the position of trusting a computer with the sole control of a complex and difficult chemical plant, though the Indiana installation may go solo before long. This may therefore be an appropriate point at which to comment on some of the principal proposals. They appear to be—

1. *The Logical Juke-box System*, which has no full mathematical model of the process in its computer, but which does go a long way towards the incorporation of a maximum of empirical operational experience.

2. *The Feedback System, Based on Quality Measurement*, uses a mathematical model in its computer.

3. *The Feedforward System, Based on Observed Input Variables*, has a mathematical model of the process in its computer.

4. *The Feedforward System, with Self-optimization*, is based on 3 above, but has additional self-optimization features for a small degree of quality correction.

The Logical Juke-box Computer

As its name implies, the "juke-box" system of control is based on alternative selection of pre-arranged programs, just as in a juke box one is able to call for the playing of a particular gramophone record by pressing a particular button. The juke-box concept embraces a very wide range of detailed systems, and the underlying assumptions are as follows—

1. The process can be specified by a series of relatively stable conditions which are related to a few measured factors in the process.

2. The process is one where reliability is so important that it should be possible to revert in some degree to local control if the central control breaks down.

3. The laws of the process are not fully known, and it is desirable to incorporate the maximum amount of empirical know-how in the control system.

A rudimentary approach to juke-box control can be made by reference to Fig. 8.2. There the various factors of the continuous process are taken to be under some degree of control by local-loop controllers of the type discussed in the previous chapter. If it is desired to secure some degree of integration of the system, the first task is to establish empirically a number of compatible target-settings of the local controllers for a given measured state of the process, and to incorporate these targets in a set of alternative programs associated locally with the various feedback controllers. Such a matrix program may well consist of potentiometers with alternative tappings to establish different set-points for the local controllers. In addition, a program-selecting switch at each local controller is required. All compatible programs on the different controllers are to be remotely selected by the same number on these switches.

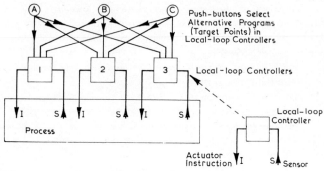

FIG. 8.2.   JUKE-BOX CONTROL

By way of illustration, consider a simple process in which it has been empirically determined that for "half-volume throughput" the following conditions are required—

Temperature......90°C
Pressure..........50lb/sq.in.
pH..............6

We assume that three controllers are involved, one each for temperature, pressure and pH, and that on a certain selecting-switch setting, say No. 4, the target points on potentiometer tappings in local-loop controllers correspond to the preferred values tabulated above. On central selection of the No. 4 program the local controllers will attempt to steer the three conditions to the required targets. If some other set of process conditions is required, then the selection of (say) No. 7 or No. 2 program will simultaneously change the three set-points of the controllers to the new targets.

Such a system is essentially equivalent to centralizing control of a multi-local-loop system: an operator has to press the program-selection buttons. The next development is to put overriding automatic computer control at the centre to make program decisions and initiate correct programs. This sort of controller may take many forms. One form, which is very similar to the system used in the Los Angeles traffic-light control system (Chapter 14), is described below.

Assume that the state of process know-how is such that a skilled operator knows when to make the change, and that the problem is to incorporate the logic of his decisions in an automatic device (Fig. 8.3). Assume also that the process is simple, involving only three local-loop controllers; that the choice of program-change depends on correct interpretation of readings from two instruments which are separate from the three sensors associated with the three process controllers; and that a unique combination of any two readings from the two independent sensors is adequate to establish the choice of program.

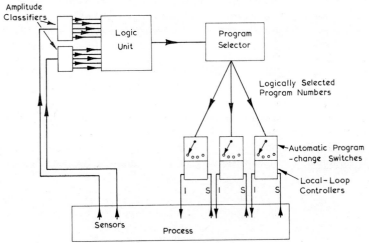

FIG. 8.3.   AUTOMATIC LOGICAL JUKE-BOX CONTROL SYSTEM

The outputs from the two independent sensors are taken to two amplitude-classifiers, which split each output amplitude into discrete steps, say five each. The ten total classifications are then taken to a logical unit of the sort described in Chapter 3, and combined in the manner indicated by empirical know-how.

The unique decision from the logical unit falls on the appropriate number of the program selector, which in turn calls up the corresponding programs in the three local controllers.

Whilst the logical juke-box system is probably limited to the control of those continuous processes that are inherently rather stable, it can be considerably elaborated to cater for such refinements as: (i) arranging sensory classifying system to detect not only signal amplitudes but also *directions of change*, to modify the associated logic appropriately; (ii) using the logical decisions not only to switch a particular matrix of local controllers' set-points in, but also to initiate timed procedures for transferring between two stable states, starting up, suspense, and shutting down. Such auxilliary functions imply the addition of sequencing procedures of the type discussed in Chapter 5.

Perhaps the strongest argument for the use of this type of system is that, with it, a beginning can be made where the initial process knowledge is rudimentary and empirical. At first the system simply copies what the operator does. With experience, the rules for operation evolve into the correct logical form, and ultimately a study of the control data may show the way to mathematical simplifications which allow virtually full computer control. The system therefore offers considerable scope for the future, and at any time is giving of its best in the light of existing process know-how. It is *not* basically self-optimizing in the same sense as the advanced forms of computer control that are described below.

FEEDBACK SYSTEMS BASED ON QUALITY MEASUREMENT

Some years ago most experts considered that the ideal method of controlling a continuous chemical process was to install an on-line quality analyser at the *output* of a process and then have a computer (somehow!) take all necessary steps to ensure that this quality was maintained. This idea is shown in Fig. 8.4 and is simply the negative-

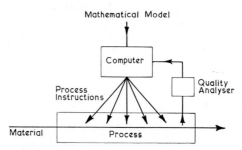

FIG. 8.4.   COMPUTER CONTROL ON QUALITY FEEDBACK INFORMATION

feedback concept taken to its logical conclusion. The fallacy in the argument is to assume that negative-feedback control, which is capable of stabilizing simple physical factors such as temperature and pressure, can in principle be extended to the complex process-pattern targets involved in chemistry. I consider that there may be some fundamental misconception in this matter, a confusion of feedback corrective control with *teleological* control.

Teleological control is apparently natural in living matter. One teleological programming device is in a *seed*. If you plant a certain seed you know that it will produce a certain plant. Somehow the seed contains all the control information to ensure that a most complicated but accurately forecast result ensues. Nobody is certain, or even suggests, that seeds embody a feedback corrective system, but rather that, *in nature, all the answers are "known" in advance*. There does exist in computing a system known as *feedforward* control, which comes near to the teleological concept of process control, and I shall deal with this in the next section.

Nevertheless, many process experts are still struggling with the concept illustrated in Fig. 8.4, attempting to make computers work directly from feedback of a final-product-quality measurement. So far these efforts have met with little success. In my personal view, if they do stumble on success they will find that they have unknowingly converted their systems into feedforward systems. This is not to say that *some degree* of feedback corrective control cannot be used, but rather that it has to be subsidiary to feedforward control. The practical results with feedback quality-control systems are not encouraging to date, and there may be a fundamental inadequacy in the approach.

FEEDFORWARD SYSTEMS

The feedforward system of computer control for continuous chemical processes is operated on the following plan (*see* Fig. 8.5.)

1. Establish a mathematical model of the chemical process and put it into a computer. The model is the potential command program.

2. Automatically measure the *input* variables of the process. Refer these to the mathematical model so that it corrects the process program accordingly.

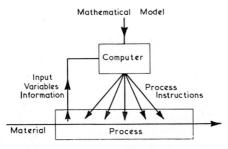

FIG. 8.5.   COMPUTER CONTROL (FEEDFORWARD) BASED ON INPUT VARIABLE ANALYSIS

You will recognize that this approach corresponds to "sorting automation" plus "command automation," as described in Chapters 3 and 4, and in my view this system could be the closest to the natural control of organic growth according to a predestined pattern.

The essential problem is to establish the correct mathematical model of the process. This is a *command* approach to the problem of control, and all the important answers must be predetermined. The only freedom permitted is in variation of the inputs, which are analysed and used to correct the program. Later in this chapter I shall describe the de Havilland "Anatrol" computing system, which is based on this approach.

FEEDFORWARD SYSTEMS WITH SELF-OPTIMIZING FEATURES

Feedforward implies that, with certain inputs to a process, the process must be controlled according to a predetermined program in a computer which issues commands to impose a corresponding pattern on the process. In spite of this action the quality of the product may not be adequate.

A final product-quality analyser could be used to measure deviations from ideal, and the information could be used *in a limited way* for feedback control of those causal factors known to affect quality. This scheme is shown in Fig. 8.6. Comparison with the descriptions

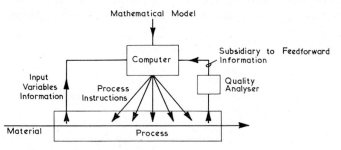

FIG. 8.6.   COMPUTER CONTROL USING BOTH FEEDBACK INFORMATION FROM QUALITY ANALYSER AND FEEDFORWARD INFORMATION FROM INPUT VARIABLE ANALYSIS

given in Chapters 3 and 4 shows that this system represents *maximum automation*. It combines "sorting," "command" and "feedback" automation in a single system. This may represent the ultimate in chemical process control; it is difficult to see how one can go further.

SYSTEM AT AN OIL REFINERY

The computer guidance system at the Standard Oil Company refinery at Whiting, Indiana, is shown schematically in Fig. 8.7. An I.B.M. 704 digital computer scans 196 instrumental readings every four minutes, and every twenty minutes it types orders for control of the refinery. The orders are based on reference to 75,000 stored instructions. The computer itself is a mile away from the refinery, and spends only part of its time on this task. At present the operation is restricted to a crude-oil distillation plant, but plans are in hand for extension to the control of a catalytic cracker, an ultra-forming unit and an alkylation plant.

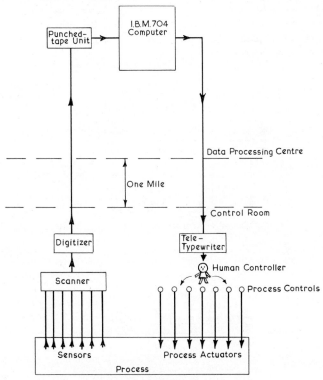

FIG. 8.7.   SIMPLIFIED SCHEMATIC DIAGRAM OF COMPUTER GUIDANCE SYSTEM
AT REFINERY OF STANDARD OIL CO., INDIANA

The Standard Oil engineers say that they have succeeded in creating a working mathematical model of the crude oil distillation process, that this is contained in the computer, and that the achievement is unique in the process-control world. A team of chemical and control engineers from both Standard Oil and the I.B.M. have, since July 1958, studied a 60,000-barrels-a-day crude-oil still. They have extracted about a hundred different readings, processed them on an I.B.M. 650 computer to extract laws of correlation, and supplemented this work with experimentation on the plant.

The team soon concluded that considerably finer control was possible than had been exercised by manual methods. Preparations were then made to give computer guidance to the larger 140,000-barrels-a-day unit. The studies showed that, out of a hundred independent variables, only nineteen required hour-to-hour adjustment, and computer guidance was thus limited to these. In addition there were altogether 160 constrained variables, of which it was considered important to control 54. It was thought desirable also to take into account economic factors based on such variables as current raw-material costs.

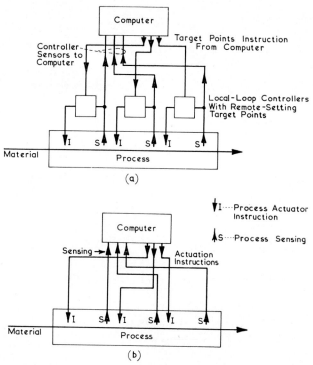

FIG. 8.8.   (a) LOCAL-LOOP CONTROLLERS SET BY COMPUTER; (b) INTEGRATED LOOP CONTROL

The basis of control is twofold. In the first place the computer has to ascertain the current operating conditions. Secondly it has to optimize the control functions. For the former duty the machine relies mainly on the scanning of the 196 instrumental points, but this may be supplemented by the results of laboratory quality analyses. Such results are notified separately to the computer through punched cards.

Optimization is by relating process measurements to current

control settings, and using linear programming on economic equations to determine improved settings. Account must be taken of what will be the effect of changing any prime variable upon the dependent variables, including the overall profitability of the plant. All this requires a great deal of computing, including a search for the optimum values by carrying out systematic experiments originated by the computer.

DIGITAL COMPUTER FOR PROCESS CONTROL

The Ferranti company in England have developed a solid-state digital computer, working in binary arithmetic, specially for process control. The computer was designed for extreme reliability, and incorporates many interesting features. Ferranti's have operated such a computer to control a simulated model of a power-station boiler, and Imperial Chemical Industries have installed one to operate a chemical process at Fleetwood in Lancashire.

The case of this computer illustrates one very important question. Is it better to control a system through many local-loop controllers, or to integrate all incoming and outgoing signals directly into the central process-control computer?

The two points of view are illustrated in Fig. 8.8. The important issue is that, if control is integrated, the computer must be 100 per cent reliable; if the computer fails, there is no way of operating the process piecemeal. Hitherto, no one has had the courage to integrate all control in this way, but the I.C.I. installation does so.

To meet this requirement the Ferranti "Argus" computer is based on all-solid-state devices, and the makers claim that the system requires no preventive maintenance. A very interesting feature is the programming system. This is normally the weak link in a computer's chain of reliability because it usually includes electrical contacts for card or punched-tape readers. Programming is contactless in the Ferranti system, two sets of printed-circuit grids being magnetically coupled for programming by insertion of ferrite pegs. Also the computer uses magnetic-core memories. Thus there are no moving parts at all, and nothing to burn out.

In the I.C.I. installation the computer will at first be used to take over all the functions normally performed by the many local-loop controllers, as shown in Fig. 8.8b. In other words it will contain instructions for all the set points of the process pattern and will originate correction signals if the incoming signals differ from the targets. The actual chemical process to be controlled is rather docile, so a simple form of integrated local-loop control may be adequate for operation. The computer has capacity for some mathematical models, either for feedforward or optimization, and it will be interesting to see if this installation evolves into something more sophisticated.

ANALOGUE COMPUTER FOR PROCESS CONTROL

The de Havilland "Anatrol" system is an analogue computer (*see* Fig. 8.9) specially devised for economical process control. At the

FIG. 8.9.   "ANATROL"
(Courtesy: De Havilland Aircraft Co. Ltd.)

time of writing, it has not been used to control a practical installation, but it is of some ingenuity and technical interest.

The objectives set in producing this computer were—

1. *Low cost*. This is achieved by using a few analogue mathematical units in a sequence of twenty-five steps. Four basic units do the work which would normally be done by seventy-five such units. A time of one second is allowed on each of the steps so that the system cycles every twenty-five seconds.

2. *Compatibility with existing instrumentation*. Almost all signals coming into a process are of the analogue amplitude variety. Outgoing signals to local process controllers and actuation devices

are mainly wanted in the same form. Therefore the "Anatrol" system has been designed to use analogue language throughout.

3. *Reliability.* The "Anatrol" system is based on the idea of controlling the set points of separate local-loop controllers in the way shown diagrammatically in Fig. 8.8a. This means that, should the computer fail, some degree of control of the process is possible by direct manual setting of the local controllers.

The "Anatrol" system is wholeheartedly based on a feedforward control philosophy. The policy is to set up a mathematical model of the process in the analogue computer, to modify this model according to sample input variables, and thus to derive correcting signals for the local controllers.

As may be recalled from Chapter 3, the basis of the analogue computer is the operational amplifier. This, in association with various potentiometers, resistors and capacitors, can be used to perform a variety of mathematical operations. The sequencing system on the "Anatrol" computer always uses the same three operational amplifiers and one multiplier, but at the various steps of the sequencer switch it selects the appropriate component to change the mathematical operation required on that particular step. This "time sharing" principle is common to digital computers, and effects considerable economies in apparatus, but normally can be done effectively *only* with digital computers. Chemical process control problems are mostly very-low-speed problems, since usually nothing much happens in less than a few minutes, so the same time-sharing principle can be used in applying analogue computers to them. Means are provided for checking the circuitry every twenty-five seconds. The time sharing makes a substantial contribution to reliability because fewer components are used altogether.

This computer relies upon the establishment in it of an accurate mathematical model of the ideal steady state of the process. The model must be valid for a range of variable input factors, and the computer must derive from it the corresponding, ideal, dependent-variable values. Measurements of actual dependent-variable values are compared with these ideals, and corrective action is taken through remote changes of set point in local-loop negative-feedback controllers. The mathematical model has to take time into account in feeding forward corrective signals based on input variables, since process inertia requires some consideration of phasing. Analogue technique is naturally suitable for this.

It is of interest that the makers of "Anatrol" gave main consideration to the steady state of a process. This is in accordance with the fundamental philosophy developed earlier in this book:

that continuous processes require a constant process pattern for a moving material, and one should only need to control the badly-behaved segments. If this is so, the proper feedforward phasing of corrective action based on measured changes is likely to go a considerable way to securing that control, and is itself likely to cause minimum shock or disturbance to the process.

The makers suggest that the best control system may use an analogue computer for feedforward control based on a mathematical model, but that the final degree of optimizing control might be arranged according to the scheme shown in Fig. 8.10. This system has three additional features—

1. The use of data-acquisition equipment. This records information of the change of input variables and output consequences.

2. The availability of an off-line digital computer for working out correlations from the above.

3. The use of an experimental optimizer which causes regular changes to the process through the central computer.

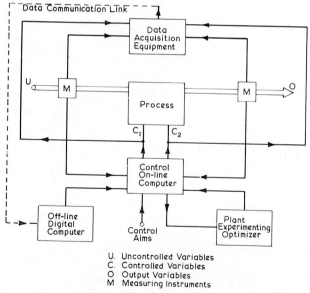

U. Uncontrolled Variables
C. Controlled Variables
O. Output Variables
M. Measuring Instruments

FIG. 8.10.   DE HAVILLAND "ANATROL" PROCESS CONTROL COMPUTER WITH OPTIMIZING AUXILIARIES

(*Courtesy: De Havilland Ltd.*)

The experimental optimizer carries out a program of changes in the input variables of the system, whilst attempting to optimize one or two particular output variables (*see* next section). When the optimizer is contributing more than 10 per cent to the control of the system (i.e. when it is forcing the mathematical model more than 10 per cent away from the position the latter would choose), the alarm system switches on the data-acquirer. The acquirer begins to log all the control figures related to this partial failure of the system. The figures can be digested at leisure in the off-line digital computer, and the control staff can decide on the modifications required in the mathematical model.

Here again we see the evolutionary philosophy at work. A computer is put in to commence some sort of process control, but steps are also taken to improve the operation of the system progressively by experimental optimization and mathematical readjustment.

THE SITUATION IN SUM

Whereas in 1955 the idea of controlling chemical processes with computers was just an idea, it is now clear that much practical progress is being made in the development of hardware for such applications, and already one or two processes are at least under computer guidance. Perhaps the most striking development is in the realization that feedforward and command control have at least as important a part to play as negative-feedback control. Great practical improvements are in evidence in computers like the Ferranti "Argus," which are all solid-state and therefore inherently very reliable. Overriding is the philosophy that computer control is evolutionary, to be developed by each process firm. This means that process chemists may need greatly to improve their mathematical understanding of their processes.

CHAPTER 9

DATA-CONTROLLED MACHINE TOOLS

THE data control of machine tools is not new. For at least thirty years automatic machine tools have been available for copying from a model of the piece-part to be made. For example, the Keller copying machine was devised for the manufacture of large steel dies for the crank presses of the motor-vehicle industry. This works directly from a wooden or plaster model of a motor-car wing, door or similar part, and reproduces the three-dimensional profile in a block of steel. The product requires a good deal of hand-finishing before it becomes a tool suitable for use. Such model-copying machines, both for three-dimensional contour work and for turning, are still with us. In some instances they are capable of very considerable accuracy, through the means of hydraulic servo-positioning devices.

The newer developments in data-controlled auto-positioning machine tools stem from a need to manufacture three-dimensional piece-parts to mathematical-design-law accuracy without the labour of making an accurate physical model first. Such a need arose when it became necessary to produce accurate wind-tunnel models of aircraft sections, and the first machines were three-dimensional millers.

The modern method is to produce a data program in such a medium as punched card, punched tape, magnetic tape, or even plug boards. The program is automatically carried out for all the operations required on such machines as jig-borers, millers, lathes, flame cutters, etc.

POSITIONING AND CONTOURING SYSTEMS

There are two basic forms of automated metal-machining—

1. *Positioning Systems.* If each operation is distinct from the next, the system may be regarded as a discrete sequential one. Typical of this category are jig-borers and drillers, in which a drilling or boring is completed before the tool is moved into a different position for the next operation. The accuracy required for this type of system lies in *location* of work points; *between* work points the tool may move relative to the workpiece in any reasonable fashion, since it is not cutting metal.

2. *Contouring Systems.* In continuous metal-cutting the tool has

to be accurately controlled all the time. Perhaps the most advanced example of this type of system is the three-dimensional milling machine.

THE FOUR PRINCIPAL COMBINATIONS OF
DATA-CONTROLLED MACHINING

In the earlier part of this book I defined two forms of automation as (*a*) program control and (*b*) feedback control, the former characterized by the issue of commands from some sort of program device, and the latter by the issue of corrective instructions related to measured deviations from an ideal.

It will be clear that all machine-tool-control systems must essentially be of the programmed kind, but for very accurate work it may be desirable also to superimpose a feedback control to correct deviation from the program.

This leads to the notion that there are four principal modes of machine-tool automation, resulting from the permutations of positioning and contouring systems with either simple-command or command-with-feedback control, as follows—

1. Positioning system with command automation.
2. Positioning system with command-feedback automation.
3. Contouring system with command automation.
4. Contouring system with command-feedback automation.

In considering the above combinations it is important to note that measurement of the actual machine-tool position is what is fed back in these cases. This should not be confused with the servo-positioning technique, which may be used in command control. Thus some degree of feedback may be used in an auto-positioning system which rotates the leadscrew of a milling table, but this may not be checking the true position of the table relative to the workpiece, and any backlash in the system would be undetected. A true command-feedback system will have some form of independent measurement of the accuracy of the overall system, perhaps by independent measurement of the actual result of machining on the workpiece, or if this is not possible then at least by independent measurement of the motion of the workpiece relative to the tool. In the latter case, reference is to measuring bars or scales, usually mounted on the bed of the machine.

POSITIONAL CONTROL SYSTEMS

Almost all positional control systems are concerned with moving a tool-holder through rectangular-co-ordinate displacements to a final accurate position for the commencement of a machining operation such as drilling, boring, or punching. The tool holder is normally moved by the rotation of an accurate leadscrew. The following are the principal data-actuating methods.

Digitizing-disk Systems

These systems usually have an accuracy of a half to two thousandths of an inch. They compare information coming back from a digitizing disk on the leadscrew with a digital number set up in the data programmer. The difference between the two sets of numbers (i.e. the error) controls the leadscrew servo-motor. The error signal may be left in digital form to drive a digital stepping motor, or alternatively it may be converted into analogue form and amplified to drive the normal type of servo-motor.

Synchro Systems

A synchro is an analogue version of a digitizing disk. It represents an angular position (of the leadscrew) by a corresponding analogue voltage. Such systems can give an accuracy of about 0·001 in. with a 0·1-in. pitch leadscrew. Program data are converted into a form suitable for instructing the system by means of tapped voltage-transformers.

Developed in a linear form by Ferrand Control Inc., this system (known as the "Inductosyn") is the one adopted by E.M.I. Electronics Ltd. (*see* Fig. 9.1). Each measuring element of the linear "Inductosyn"

Fig. 9.1.   An "Inductosyn" Measuring Element, Scale and Slider
Shown in Photograph

(Courtesy: E. M. I. Electronics)

is in 10-in. units with a single hairpin winding, and a corresponding short slider detects coincidences of windings. The linear "Inductosyn" can be attached to the machine-tool bed to act as an independent measuring framework, so a true command-feedback system can be based on its use. It is capable of an accuracy of 0·0001-in. Since the system "homes" to coincidence between many turns of the fixed and slider windings, winding inconsistencies are averaged out and a high degree of positional accuracy is assured.

Differential-transformer Systems

A primary winding is let into the two grooves of a two-start thread cut in a long insulating bar. A similar secondary winding is located in a short two-start-thread bar which slides over the primary winding bar. The windings have a 0·1-in. pitch, and the voltage induced in the sliding secondary winding alternates sinusoidally, a maximum and a zero occurring for every 0·1 in. of relative movement.

Points at which zero current is detected mark off the positional intervals. Finer gradations may be obtained by *rotating* the secondary winding so that a zero is found somewhere between the 0·1-in. positions. The rotation is transmitted to a fine leadscrew for positioning the tool. As with the "Inductosyn," coincidence of many primary and secondary turns compensates for the minor differences between turns and gives accuracy.

Measuring-bar Systems

Typical of the measuring-bar technique is the B.T.H. system, which depends on brass inserts accurately let into a steel bar at 1-in. intervals. The bar is fixed to the machine bed. A sliding magnetic sensing head can be made to "home" accurately on to a zero signal obtained when there is symmetry about the brass inserts. Fine adjustments are provided on either side of the brass inserts to distort the magnetic field for calibration. The claimed accuracy of calibration is fifteen millionths of an inch. Such a system requires the addition of an inch of intermediate fine control, usually provided by a an automatic micrometer screw.

Optical-grating Systems

This type of system is used by Ferranti. It is based on two transparent optical gratings, each with a series of fine parallel lines marked on it. When the lines on one grating are at a slight angle to those on the other, movement of one grating relative to the other, at right angles to the lines, is seen as a much magnified movement of the line intersections. The latter can be photo-electrically sensed. The system is accurate to 0·0001 in. using 5000 lines per inch on the gratings.

Alternatively a coarser system can be used, with optical magnification. Such a system has been developed by Mullard Equipment Ltd. for the Coventry Gauge and Tool Co. jig-boring system.

These systems depend on counting, and lend themselves to digital programming.

Electrical Capacitance Systems

The leadscrew of a machine may be surrounded by a non-contacting sliding nut. The slider registers high and low values of electrical capacitance as it moves over the screw, and can be rotated for finer gradations. Averaging accuracy is obtained when several turns are used on the slider.

This technique may be used either in a command system, employing the leadscrew of a machine, or in a command-feedback system, with the measuring screw fixed to the machine bed and with a separate leadscrew to position the table or tool.

An electrical capacitance system has been developed by the Oerlikon Co. in Switzerland.

Potentiometer Systems

A bank of potentiometers with wipers coupled to the leadscrew may be used for analogue positioning. Such a system has been developed by Ekco Electronics Ltd. It may be considered as another analogue version of the digitizing disk. Program data must first be converted to analogue form. The system homes on to a null difference signal from the leadscrew potentiometers and program potentiometers. This is not a true command-feedback system since it defines leadscrew motion, not table or tool position.

CONTOUR CONTROL SYSTEMS

Contour control adds two extra problems to those of plain positional control.

In the first place there is the problem of dealing with the continuous path of the tool. This path is often a three-dimensional one, and as contour machines normally work on rectangular co-ordinates, six dimensional parameters may have to be specified, three for the current position and three for the position towards which the tool should be going.

The second problem arises because the cutting speeds for contouring are prescribed, and the velocity of motion is a basic factor to be dealt with.

Part of the first problem is how to deal with curves between defined points. In three-dimensional milling there is usually no indication on the drawing of what path the cutter should take. For example, a hemisphere will be represented in a very simple drawing giving only one dimension, the radius of the hemisphere. How does one translate this into an instruction for a milling machine using rectangular co-ordinates? The problem is further complicated by the need to allow for the thickness of the cutting tool, and the cutting path will by no means be a simple hemispherical one.

PROGRAMMING OF CONTOURING SYSTEMS

Whereas positioning systems can be adequately defined by punched-card programs, contouring systems require some sort of tape system to deal with the much larger amount of control information involved.

In America the Aircraft Industries Association has defined four types of tape control as follows—

Class I. Tape Template. Given physical dimension on the tape is equal or proportional to a dimension on the part. The tape is equivalent to a rolled-up template. This kind of control can describe either one or two dimensions. Examples: a rivetter and a drill press.

Class II. Cycle programmer. Tape is substituted for electrical or mechanical cycling devices, either simple or extremely complex. This class may control machinery, index the tools, actuate clamps, etc. Examples: lathes and stretch presses.

Class III. Point-to-Point Locators. The spindle is guided by tape to a numerically defined point, usually described in only two axes, and the tape then cycles the operation. The path from one defined point to another is not controlled. Examples: turret drill boring mill, and hole spacers.

Class IV. Continuous-Path Control. The path of the working tool is continuously controlled in at least two of the three axes, and may be controlled in three, five or more dimensions. Contours and complex curves can be produced. Examples: profilers, skin mills, and spar mills.

Essentially only the last of the above groups is involved in contouring machines, and requires the preparatory operations of programming, computing and interpolation between points.

Drawing Information

The preferred kind of drawing is of the usual plan-and-elevation type, in which the plan view carries the greater part of the contouring information. Drawings need not be accurately to scale, but must show all the points and dimensions required to define the part. In particular, these must define all changes in direction.

The drawing must include the end-points of straight lines intersected by circular curves, together with the radii and centres of radii of such curves. If non-circular curves are used it is necessary to specify both their end-points and the mathematical equations that define their shape. All non-functional curves have to be kept as simple as possible, preferably as segments of circles or ellipses.

On the drawing the workpiece has to be dimensioned in X, Y, Z co-ordinates, using a decimal system. The origin of the axes must be at a datum point well outside the workpiece and corresponding to the datum used on the machine. Partly this is to allow adequate dimensional references for cutter thicknesses, and for radii of operation that lie outside the part being machined but yet come within the common co-ordinate system.

Tabulation

Drawing information has next to be tabulated on change-of-direction points of X, Y, Z dimensions, radii, tool dimensions and feed rate. I shall deal with a practical example in some detail in the later description of the Ferranti system.

PRACTICAL NUMERICAL CONTROL SYSTEMS

In general, automation of machine tools is aimed at short-run or even one-off production. The main objectives are to save setting-up time and costs, and to ensure great accuracy without dependence upon highly paid craftsmen. There are great numbers of practical applications in the field, some of which will now be described.

Punching Automation

The punching of holes in metal sheet calls for a great deal of work where the cost of multiple dies cannot be justified. The type of machine developed for this work is the turret press, which holds a variety of punches and dies in a head that can be indexed round. The Wiedemann Machine Co. have specialized in the production of machines of this type, and a recent development of theirs incorporates the General Electric Mark III automatic positional control system (Fig. 9.2).

The Weidemann turret punching press has a capacity of a hundred tons, and can pierce a metal plate up to 60 in. $\times$ 100 in. $\times$ $\frac{3}{8}$in. Table speed for positioning is 600 in. per minute. The turret holds thirty-six sets of punches and can rotate at 90 per second. Hydraulic cylinders move the table under the control of proportional servo-valves, and a piston type of hydraulic motor turns the turret.

The General Electric control equipment is in a console and is operated by 1-in. punched tape. As one hole is being punched, the tape reader advances and puts the next set of operating information into a rapid-access memory so that there may be no hold-up from slowness of tape-reader translation. Tape is simply prepared from a chart listing the *X* and *Y* co-ordinates of the hole positions and the tool number to be used.

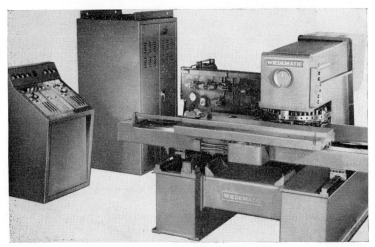

FIG. 9.2.   WIEDEMATIC MODEL A.15 TURRET PUNCH PRESS WITH GENERAL ELECTRIC NUMERICAL POSITIONING
(Courtesy: Wiedemann and Dowding & Doll)

General Electric have also produced an automatic programmer which will make the tape from an undimensioned line drawing. The draughtsman has to make an accurate drawing, defining hole centres. An electronic scaler is manually centred over the centre marks and transmits positional data to the tape encoder.

The general accuracy of the system using a dimensioned table for input data is —0·005 in. Accuracy using the automatic programmer depends on the precision of the draughtsmanship and take-off.

This machine is installed at General Electric and is estimated to have saved about £17,000 during its first year of operation, about £7,000 of which was saving of direct labour. These savings were left after allowing for £3,500 annual depreciation.

Boring Machines

A typical modern data-controlled borer is the Kearns machine fitted with a B.T.H. control system (Fig. 9.3). This system can be programmed from punched cards (Fig. 9.4). The machine uses the measuring bar described earlier in this chapter. The accuracy of

FIG. 9.3.   KEARNS DATA-CONTROLLED BORER FITTED WITH B.T.H.
CONTROL SYSTEM
(Courtesy: A.E.I. Ltd.)

positioning about the brass inserts is to 0·00002 in., but allowance
has to made for the micrometer fine-adjustment screw, which has
a guaranteed accuracy of 0·000025 in. Under normal conditions it is
claimed that overall accuracies of better than 0.0005 in. are achievable.

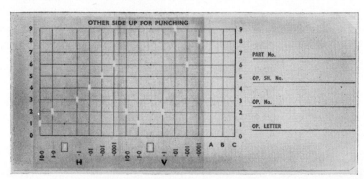

FIG. 9.4.   PUNCHED-CARD PROGRAMMING OF B.T.H. CONTROL SYSTEM
(Courtesy: A.E.I. Ltd.)

A Tracer Control System

No account of data-controlled machine tools would be complete
without reference to the modern descendants of the earliest type of
automatically programmed machine, the copying machine. These

are nowadays known as tracer-controlled machines, and they use an accurate piece-part or a model as the data-programming device.

Tracer control can be applied to machine tools of single-, two-, or three-dimensional operation, and is thus applicable to lathes, millers, borers and almost any conceivable machine requiring contouring control.

The modern machine is electronically controlled and has four main units. In the B.T.H. system these function as follows—

The Tracing Head is the moving stylus which touches the master model. The motion of the stylus sets up control voltages which are applied to the electronic control circuits. The stylus varies an air gap in a magnetic circuit to give an electrical output related to displacement.

The Electronic Control Circuits determine the feed speeds and directions required to cause the stylus to slide tangentially along the model. They supply appropriate field currents to a Ward Leonard generator set.

The Ward Leonard Generator Set has one generator for each leadscrew feed motor.

D.C. Feed Motors for the larger machine-tools are normally of $\frac{1}{2}$ h.p. or above and operate the tool-slide leadscrews. For small machine-tools the Ward Leonard sets may be dispensed with, and the d.c. feed motors may be operated directly off the electronic control unit.

A schematic diagram of the above functions is shown in Fig. 9.5 for a lathe and in Fig. 9.6 for two-dimensional control of a vertical milling machine.

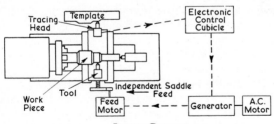

FIG. 9.5.   LATHE CONTROL

Single-dimensional Control for Lathes. In this case only the motion of the cross slide is under automatic control, whilst a constant feed is applied to the lengthwise movement of the saddle. The B.T.H. system will maintain a controlled feed of up to 60 in. per minute with a change in stylus deflexion of only 0·001 in. This high sensitivity permits the accurate machining of rapidly changing

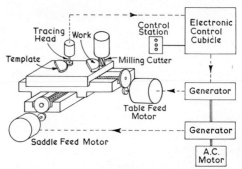

FIG. 9.6.   TWO-DIMENSIONAL CONTROL OF VERTICAL MILLING MACHINE

contours, including non-circular ones; in the latter case, the motion under automatic control is reciprocatory as the workpiece revolves.

Two-dimensional Control for Millers. With this system, as shown in Fig. 9.6, the one sensing head operates two separate feed-motors controlling the cross slides. The tracing head is sensitive to deflexions parallel to both feed motions, and puts out a signal from which both the amplitude and direction of stylus deflexion can be obtained. From this signal the electronic circuits determine the feed speeds and directions that the stylus must have to move tangentially along the model under a constant working deflexion. The deflexion can be allowed for by making the stylus tip larger in radius than the cutter by the amount of the deflexion. Feed speeds of 2 in. per minute can be used, with copying errors not exceeding 0·001 in. The error is about 0·004 in. at feed speeds of 10 in. per minute.

Three-dimensional Control. Large three-dimensional forms, like the punches and dies used for pressing steel, can be automatically machined. In this case it is necessary to control all three slide co-ordinates from a single tracer head. In most cases it is satisfactory to make a series of parallel cuts across the workpiece. In the B.T.H. "3D System" the tracing head is sensitive to deflexions in all three directions, and the electronic system automatically selects the required combination of signals. It is noteworthy that the system will always follow the surface of the model irrespective of the steepness of contours involved, even including re-entrant cavities if the cutting tool is of a suitable type.

The Ferranti Computer Control System

The Ferranti system of true-path numerical control of machine tools, particularly milling machines, is one of the most effective yet developed in either Britain or the U.S.A.

Behind this system is a very interesting philosophy. On the one hand it was assumed that the techniques for the physical operation of machine tools by automatic devices had already reached a high state of development, and that scope for further improvement was limited. On the other hand it was considered that the scope for data processing was almost unlimited in the future, and that the best system would be one which took cognizance of this. Perhaps this outlook included an assumption that the engineering products of the future would have an increasedly mathematical design basis, with the great prize of time saving in the drawing office. Certainly this philosophy appears to have been consistently pursued by Ferranti's, and particularly in the field of automated shipbuilding, as you will see in the next chapter.

The Ferranti system is, therefore, to be seen as not only a matter of hardware, but perhaps mainly as the embodiment of a philosophy of product design. The system is based on a central computing service in which improvements in data-handling technique are continually being made. This central service supplies magnetic tapes to the users of data-controlled equipment that consists essentially of servo-mechanical actuators which, although unlikely to be much improved in performance in the future, may well become cheaper and simpler as developments proceed over the years.

This development could be of considerable interest to British jobbing industry. In principle, it enables jobbers to install not-too-expensive data-controlled machine-tools, and yet eliminates the major capital cost of the associated computer techniques.

The Ferranti system possesses the following four main features—

1. The *teleprinter* equipment used to encode the drawing and planning data on a punched tape.

2. The *computer*, which converts the raw data on the punched tape into control information for the machine-tool servo-mechanisms, and records this on magnetic tape.

3. The *control unit*, which receives the magnetic tape and plays it to control digital devices and give commands to the machine-tool servo-mechanisms.

4. The *machine tool*, equipped with measuring systems and servo-motors controlling the actual machining operations.

THE DESIGN AND DRAWING STAGE

All drawings should be made in terms of rectangular co-ordinates from a datum point outside the workpiece. A typical drawing is given in Fig. 9.7. This shows the five principal features that must be determined in the marking of the cutter path, the establishment of where the cutter shall start from, etc.

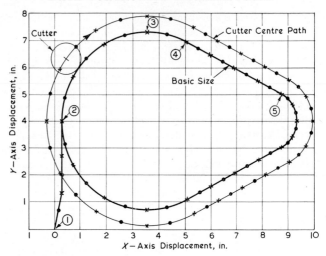

Fig. 9.7.   Drawing of Cam in Preparation for Data Extraction

Program Planning

This consists of tabulating data from the drawing in a form suitable for the preparation of the punched tape. The table for the cam shown in Fig. 9.7 is given in Fig. 9.8. It consists essentially of the abstraction from the co-ordinate drawing of the change-of-direction direction points that define the curves in the machining sequence. Two points are required to define a line: the X, Y co-ordinates of the start and end of the line. Three points are required to define a circular arc: the X, Y co-ordinates of the start and end of the arc and the centre of the arc. For more complicated contours a smooth curve is interpolated between points. Different sorts of curves, such as circles, conic sections, etc., are called up by the planner by marking a code word against the X, Y dimensions given, and the computer will do the rest. The computer will also automatically allow for the effect of cutter diameter.

The information required on the planning sheet is—

Machine setting point. If the cutter's starting point is different from the drawing datum point, this starting point must be specified; the computer will do the rest.

Cutter diameter. This is usually called up by means of a standard code.

Feed rate. The rate of material movement must be settled beforehand and entered on the sheet against the various operations.

Compensation sense. Instruction codes are standardized to give

INITIAL SIGNAL	DATUM CO-ORD OF X	DATUM CO-ORD OF Y	DATUM CO-ORD OF Z	CUTTER DIA	END OF LINE		PLANNED:- N. FISHER	TYPED:-	DRG Nº:-	OPERATION:-
+STA≡				DIA≡ 01 0000-	x x		DATE:-	DATE:-	TITLE:-	MILL PROFILE
							FIRM:-		FILE Nº	

Nº of co-ord line point	Instructions	Cutter feed rate	Type of curve / Plane curve	Co-ordinates of change points	End of line	Co-ordinates of pole of curve	Miscellaneous curve constants	Cont'd End of rate line
1	TCR-TNY≡ θ 100000-	RAT=160000-		COX-02 6000- COY-01 0000-	x x	POX- POY- POZ-		◇
at 1				COX-03 6000- COY-02 0000- COZ-02 0000-	x x	POX- POY- POZ-		
2				NOR≡	NOR≡ x x	POX- POY- POZ-		NOR≡ x x
3	COD=032500-	RAT=060000-	CIR≡ YAZ≡	COX-05 0240- COY-01 0780-	NOR≡ x x	POX-03 6000- POY-04 0000- POZ-		NOR≡ x x
4			CIR≡ YAZ≡	COX-08 8430- COY-02 9890-	x x	POX-08 3500- POY-04 0000- POZ-		
5	COD=011250-		CIR≡ YAZ≡	COX-05 0240- COY-05 9210-	x x	POX-08 6000- POY-04 0000- POZ-		
6	COD=032500-			COX-06 6000- COY-01 0000-	NOR≡ x x	POX-03 6000- POY-03 0000- POZ-		NOR≡ x x
7				COX-04 2500- COY-01 0000-	x x	POX- POY- POZ-		
at 7	TCC-TNY≡ θ 100000-	RAT=150000-			x x	POX- POY- POZ-		STO≡ x x
Datum				COX- COY- COZ-		POX- POY- POZ-		
12				COX- COY- COZ-		POX- POY- POZ-		
13				COX- COY- COZ-		POX- POY- POZ-		

FIG. 9.8.

FERRANTI PLANNING SHEET FOR DATA CONTROLLED MACHINE TOOL

CODE	COMPUTER INSTRUCTION		
XAY≡	Select XY plane curve clockwise	GRD≡	Approximate radius of circle
YAX≡	,, XY ,, ,, anticlockwise	COD≡	
YAZ≡	,, YZ ,, ,, clockwise	TNX≡	
ZAY≡	,, YZ ,, ,, anticlockwise	TNY≡	Tangent normal (for tool diameter compensation)
ZAX≡	,, ZX ,, ,, clockwise	TNZ≡	
XAZ≡	,, ZX ,, ,, anticlockwise	INT≡	Commerce interpolation
CIR≡	Set up circle	END≡	End interpolation
MIS≡	Miscellaneous curve (general second degree, or specifically, ellipse, hyperbola, or parabola)	TCL≡	Tool compensation (tool centre to left of profile)
		TCR≡	Tool compensation (tool centre to right of profile)
DAX–		TCC≡	Tool centre cut
DAY–	Co-ordinates of datum (machine tool setting point)	DIA≡	Tool diameter
DAZ–		RAT≡	Feed rate
		NOR≡	Switch off rate control
COX–	X	STA≡	Start computer magnetic tape deck
COY–	Set in Y co-ordinate of final point section	STO≡	Stop
COZ–	Z	∴ ∴	Clear all stores
		0.0	End of instruction
POX–	X	◇	End of tape
POY–	Set in Y co-ordinate of pole or curve	θ	Minus
POZ–	Z		

The – , = and ≡ signs are purely of significance for automatic digital checking unambiguous definition to the relationship of the cutter to the part dimensions (i.e. as to direction of travel and on which side of the drawing line the cutter is to operate).

Co-ordinates of change points. As mentioned earlier, these must be extracted from the drawing and entered in appropriate columns.

Type of curve. The coded instruction for curve types is entered in the same line as the corresponding change points defining the start and end of the curve.

Plane of curve. This specifies the plane in which the curve is to be generated.

Co-ordinates of pole of curve. The co-ordinates of centres of circles or poles of conics are entered as required.

ENCODING

The planning sheet for the Ferranti system is encoded by copy-typing the planning sheet line on a teleprinter. This produces a correctly coded paper tape, and simultaneously a red copy of the planning sheet for comparison with the original. The tape may then be fed into a reader on the teleprinter, which produces a duplicate tape and a black copy of the planning sheet. The three versions of the planning sheet may be compared so that any encoding errors can be quickly spotted.

THE COMPUTER

The calculation necessary to obtain the magnetic-tape program is done by a special computer. This is essentially a digital differential analyser that can define the cutter-compensated forms of straight lines and of any second-degree curve at any angle to the axes. It can also make cutter-compensated parabolic interpolation between specified points, so that curves on either side of change points run smoothly into one another. Controlled by the input punched tape, the computer rapidly calculates the cutter track and records this on the output magnetic tape.

ALTERNATIVE COMPUTER ARRANGEMENTS

The Ferranti system can use four alternative computer arrangements (*see* Fig. 9.9), as follows—

Special-purpose computer. This is ideally suited to the running of a computer service, but is so expensive that it can only be justified if fairly fully occupied. The output of the machine is about eight times as fast as the ultimate machining speed. A machine-tool load factor of 50 per cent would imply that about sixteen data-controlled machine tools should be in operation to balance load against such a computer.

General-purpose computer plus differential analyser. If an organization already has a general-purpose computer, this can also be used in combination with an additional unit, a digital differential analyser, to fulfil the required functions. It will be slower than the special-purpose computer, but may be fast enough, and economic, if the general-purpose computer has other load.

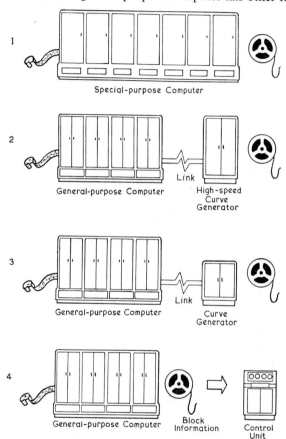

FIG. 9.9.   ALTERNATIVE ARRANGEMENTS OF COMPUTERS AND MAGNETIC
              TAPE PREPARATION FOR FERRANTI MACHINE TOOL CONTROL
              SYSTEM

(Courtesy: Ferranti Ltd.)

General-purpose computer and curve generator. This is rather similar to the previous arrangement but uses a slower curve-generator, and may give a low-cost solution where a modest output involving a few machine-tools is involved.

General-purpose computer and control units with integral curve generators. The curve-generating ability is incorporated in the control unit associated with each individual machine tool. This can be an economic solution for an organization which only has one or two data-controlled machine tools.

The views of the Ferranti company on general policy are that, whilst a large works may well find it economic to install a group of numerically controlled tools and a computer, the vast majority of machining units in Britain are highly specialized in small works, any one of which can hardly afford the cost of its own computer facilities. Also, it is just these small firms that carry out the most complicated machining operations. These call for a high computer activity if they are to use data-controlled tools. Clearly this situation can admirably be dealt with by a central computer service, and Ferranti's have established such a service in Edinburgh. It is at present supplying tapes for machine tools throughout Britain, and a new service is available in London to cope with complex multi-dimensional work.

The current practice is for the customer to send Ferranti's his roll of encoded punched tape, which has been prepared by his planning staff, together with the planning sheet. These are processed on the Ferranti special-purpose computer and are dispatched back to the customer on the same day. Perhaps development of the telephone system will one day allow such data to be transmitted as speedily and reliably as if the computer were installed in the customer's own works.

THE CONTROL UNIT

In order to keep capital costs down, the control units associated with each machine tool are designed to be as simple as possible. Each unit contains a magnetic-tape reading-head which can read four magnetic-tape tracks simultaneously. The general function of the unit, in conjunction with the machine-tool servo-mechanisms and measuring system, is to move the machine-tool slide in accordance with the commands from the magnetic tape. The associated electronics are essentially of a digital counting and logical nature.

Control System Without a Separate Computer

The E.M.I. control system is fundamentally different from Ferranti's. It employs analogue positioning devices, and the control console directly associated with the machine tool has self-contained facilities for curve interpolation, so a separate computer is not required. The basic system operates from a punched-paper-tape reader, and has both an information store and an electrical curve-interpolation unit all fitted in the control console. The machine-tool-slide-operating units are either electrical or hydraulic servo-motors.

Two further items can be added on a unit basis, a cutter-radius-compensation unit, and a unit for setting the cutter datum at various positions. The purpose of having separate units is to establish a lower basic cost for the machine-tool control, and to allow more complicated systems to be built up according to the customer's particular requirements. The systems thus appears to be particularly suitable for the smaller operator, who does not wish to be involved in the cost of a separate computer within his own establishment.

Programming. The original drawing information is first put into the usual X, Y co-ordinate table for change-of-direction points. All curves, whether circular or otherwise, are defined by three points, and the interpolator on the machine tool produces a parabolic curve through these points. Even circular arcs are approximated in this fashion, and a design formula is available for specifying how close the three defining points must be to limit the error from the truly circular to a predetermined amount. When these data have been tabulated they are put into punched tape through a standard teletypewriter. This produces two items: a five-row punched tape, and a normally typed sheet for checking that the encoding is correct.

Machine Operation. The punched tape is fed directly into the machine-tool console. This contains all the equipment for curve

FIG. 9.10   E.M.I. EMICON 3D CONTINUOUS CONTOUR CONTROL FITTED TO
A DROOP AND REIN F580 VERTICAL MILLING MACHINE
(*Courtesy: E.M.I. Electronics Ltd.*)

interpolation. The three points required to specify the curve are registered in advance in a relay memory.

Machine-tool Positioning. The basic technique for positioning the machine-tool slide is by reference to a linear "Inductosyn" as shown in Fig. 9.1, and as explained earlier in this chapter. The system is thus one of command-plus-feedback control. The positional reference is absolute, and the analogue voltage representing the difference between the punched-tape commands and the position detected by the "Inductosyn" is used to produce servo-amplified currents to drive the electric or hydraulic servo-motors. The accuracy claimed for this system is $\pm$ 0·0002 in., with a repeatability of $\pm$ 0·00005 in. Fig. 9.10 illustrates this system fitted to a Droop and Rein vertical milling machine, complete with the associated controlling console.

CHAPTER 10

AUTOMATION IN SHIPBUILDING

ANY belief that automation applies only to mass production should be finally dispelled by the development of data-controlled processes in shipbuilding. At the same time it may be fair comment that no industry is so overdue for the overhaul of its methods and their replacement by new techniques. Nevertheless, the new developments are revolutionary, and it may well be that the largest jumps in automation will be made by those industries which have resisted change the longest.

COMPUTER-CONTROLLED CUTTING MACHINE

In 1957 two British companies, British Oxygen Ltd. and Ferranti Ltd., announced a joint project for a computer-controlled cutting machine (Fig. 10.1). Designed for cutting steel plate in the engineering

Fig. 10.1.   BRITISH OXYGEN COMPANY LTD. AND FERRANTI LTD., DATA CONTROLLED FLAME CUTTING MACHINE FOR SHIPS' PLATES
(Courtesy of the mentioned companies)

industry in general, the machine has specially important application in shipyards. The system is a true data-controlled shaping process.

This computer-controlled machine leads the way to revolutionary change in the technique of cutting large and complicated shapes in steel plate. No costly templates are needed, and there are possibilities of considerable saving in planning and drawing. The machine is capable of simultaneously cutting left-hand and right-hand "mirror-image" steel plates from information recorded on a magnetic tape produced by a computer. Owing to the considerably greater cutting accuracy, the necessity for extensive manual fairing during assembly is considerably reduced. Whilst the shipbuilding field is perhaps the most obvious one for its use, the system can also be applied to other important sectors of the engineering industry, including structural engineering, locomotive building, and the construction of industrial boilers and heat exchangers.

Data Input. The dimensional details of a ship's plates are extracted from the steelwork drawings used in conjunction with a table of "offsets" (this term will be explained later). Whilst exact plate drawings are not required, it is convenient to make freehand sketches to check that all details are being taken care of.

The next step is to write these dimensional data in computer language on a planning sheet, which includes details of cutting speeds required and kerf width. From this planning sheet a punched paper tape is prepared by simple copy-typing, for input to the computer. This tape is sent to the computer centre for the preparation of a magnetic tape to be used on the gas cutting-machine.

The Computer System. The computer may be housed at the shipyard of the engineering works concerned, or it may be at a common computer centre serving a number of users. The computer is a Ferranti "Pegasus" plus a digital differential analyser. As the information on the paper tape is processed in the computer, the digital differential analyser prepares a magnetic tape for controlling the continuous path of the oxy-acetylene cutting heads. The use of this computer greatly reduces the amount of programming required. Thus it is only necessary to specify the beginning and end of straight lines and circular arcs, no intermediate points being required. The computer itself can store standard programs for insertion into the magnetic tape of repetitive features such as notches, scallops and manholes, and they can be called up by inserting a simple reference code in the original planning sheet.

The Gas-cutting Machine. Once the magnetic tape has been prepared in the way described above, this completes the work of the computer, and the tape is then ready to be inserted into the reader of the console controlling the gas cutting-machine. The machine itself can simultaneously cut two mirror-image plates, of size up to 12 ft. by 40 ft., and up to a thickness of 3 in. Power-driven roller-tables with retractable stops may be used to locate the plates relative to the datum position of the cutting heads, and to bring the plates from the loading area to the cutting area and out again to the discharge area after gas-profiling. Hydraulic servo-mechanisms with feedback devices and anti-backlash features are fitted to the longtitudinal and transverse drives.

Flame Cutting. In addition to controlling the movement of the cutting heads, it is also necessary to control the other functions associated with oxy-acetylene cutting. These are—

Gas control. A new balanced-pressure regulating system has been evolved to ensure that a neutral flame is obtained irrespective of pipeline pressure variations. The ignition of the preheating flame is automatic.

Nozzle height. A special height-sensor ensures that the distance is always maintained between the nozzle tip and the plate.

Flame monitoring. The flame is monitored to ensure the continuity of the preheating flame and of the cutting process. In the event of failure the machine is instantly shut-down automatically, and a restarting sequence can be initiated as soon as the fault has been cleared.

All the above functions are controlled automatically by the auxiliary-functions console on receipt of an impulse from the main magnetic tape. "Fail safe" principles are built into the system throughout.

INTEGRATION OF SHIP DESIGN AND AUTOMATED PRODUCTION

The foregoing description demonstrates that the numerical control of ship-plate cutting is being practically achieved, and it would appear fairly certain that the employment of such methods will penetrate many shipyards in due course. A second possibility now on the horizon concerns the substantial integration of the design of the ship's hull by computer techniques, followed by automatic plate-cutting of the sort already described. This possibility is made stronger by the fact that much of the existing design work is of a numerical type. Providing that certain outstanding problems are overcome, the possibility could become actuality within a few years. If this were to be achieved it would represent perhaps the greatest single break-through by a data-controlled process, and we may imagine that it would cause something of a revolutionary change.

In the following description of these implications I am particularly indebted to the work of Mr T. Hysing, as reported in his paper "On the Use of Numerical Methods in the Design and Manufacture of Ships," which was read in 1960 to the Moscow meeting of the International Federation of Automatic Control.

General Considerations

The existing technique for hull design commences with the general basis of requirements laid down in the customer's specification, and these requirements are then interpreted into drawings of the principal cross-sections of the ship. Cross-sectional contours are reconciled with longtitudinal contours by continuous, experimental, three-dimensional readjustment, until adequate fairing is reached and the external shape is free from any changes likely to cause unnecessary turbulence or waves. Clearly such a procedure calls for considerable experience and know-how.

When this work has proceeded to a satisfactory state, tenth-scale drawings of the cross-sections are made. These contain all the information required for further design, although the information may not be in a very convenient form for all purposes. For example, these drawings refer to three-dimensionally contoured plates, whereas the actual plates must be cut from flat metal.

After this stage, decisions must be made on the dividing up of the hull skin into plates, the plates must be detailed, and manufacturing drawings must be prepared giving the developed shape—that is, the flat shape that can be worked into the required double curvature of the plates.

A study of the existing procedures reveals that many numerical methods are already in use and, furthermore, that many existing graphical procedures could not only be replaced by numerical techniques but that the work would thereby be simplified. The prospects for the use of numerical methods therefore depend, to some extent, upon how far empirical know-how regarding shape can be codified into numerical procedures, and to some extent on the possibility of evolving mathematical formulae representing a three-dimensional streamlined form. The prize to be won is the ability to go directly from such numerical procedures to the production of magnetic or punched tapes embodying the flame-cutter instructions.

The New Method

A considerable amount of study has been put into these possibilities, both in Norway and Britain, and has revealed that many of the existing drawing techniques are based upon numerical procedures that could be followed in computers, and this applies both to hull lines and to details.

Accordingly Hysing suggests a design procedure which commences with the established practice of making a hull drawing. From the drawings of sections a set of *coarse* "offsets" is taken. Offsets are simply the dimensional specifications of the main sections referred to a datum line, and thus correspond in some measure to the change-of-direction points used in data tables for numerically controlled machine-tools. They are not, of course, change-of-direction points on a ship's hull, but simply those points for which a cross-sectional drawing has been made.

The next step is to place this information in a computer to derive a set of *fine* offset points. Presumably at this stage computer checks could be made for smoothness of any conceivable geodesic line on the hull surface.

These operations virtually establish within the computer the specification for the hull shape, albeit from somewhat empirical beginnings.

The next move is to derive the boundary lines and locations of the plates. At present this is done from a model of the hull. Whether in due course this model can be dispensed with remains to be seen, but at least there would seem to be no reason why this model could not be made on a three-dimensional milling machine using numerical control derived from the computer's fine-offset information. Such a procedure might also be a prudent check on the correctness of the basic numerical information in the computer, and could also enable one to perform tank tests to find the resistance to motion through water.

The plate arrangements having been decided in this way, they may be put into the computer, combined with the offset information, and the actual shape of each plate computed. Virtually, this computation is a mathematical unfolding of the hull's three-dimensional shape into flat plates. At the same time the contoured curves of the final plates can be derived for curve-rolling instructions.

Present development is towards a method that does not need the making of a model hull, and that allows the whole calculation to be done by digital computer. This appears to involve the mathematical determination of hull geodesics (great-circle curves) which will lead to hull plates with sides very close to straight lines.

In passing, it may be noted that the development of such methods for hull formation is leading to equivalent methods for hull framing, partly to make the most of computer technique and of capital tied up in numerically controlled flame-cutting equipment, and partly because it links the best and most logical technique in any case.

The above possibilities involve two very recalcitrant mathematical problems. The first relates to the trial-and-error work at present done on a drawing toward "smoothing" a ship's lines. Even to commence on a mathematical, and hence possible computer, solution for this problem implies a mathematical specification of ship's lines, and this stage is not yet reached. But even if it were reached, there appears to be no numerical solution to the general problem of three-dimensional interpolation. The second unsolved problem relates to the optimum grouping of a number of ship's plates to be cut out of a minimum quantity of standard plates. Work is proceeding toward a solution of these problems.

So far one has not heard of a numerically controlled machine for automatic rolling of the plates after their automatic flame-cutting, but no doubt this will come in due course. A further factor, so far not taken into consideration, is the repercussion of these automatic methods on the ship's design itself. Presumably, if these methods come into use and promise to make substantial financial savings, shipowners may be prepared to take a ship which is designed entirely on mathematical curves, even if this gives rise to unorthodox shape. It seems barely conceivable that the best shape of hull is not mathematically law-abiding.

CHAPTER 11

AUTOMATIC INSPECTION MACHINES

MANUFACTURING equipment has been brought to a high pitch of perfection over the last hundred years or so, *but*, the most perfect machines available cannot guarantee the quality of the product. In the final resort it must be inspected and compared with its original specification. The inevitable deviation, however small, is a measure of the imperfection of control, and this imperfection is inherent in the productive equipment.

It is interesting to look back upon the history of the striving for product perfection, and perhaps to single out the quite extraordinary contribution made by the Ford organization in general (and perhaps by Henry Ford in particular) to the evolutionary process. This is an especially interesting point to look into because we are now at the threshold of a new sort of effort to improve production processes.

Before the Ford era we had a machine-and-tool age in which we made things as well as we could to drawings, and all the imperfections appeared at the assembly stage. Then it was the job of a fitter to adjust the parts until they made an adequate assembly. Henry Ford was perhaps the first to realize that a new technique was essential if precision parts were to be mass-produced and assembled without the hard labour of fitting. He set about this task with the foreknowledge that somewhere the science of statistics was involved, and that if precision assemblies had to go together to a mating fit of 0·001 in., then it was highly desirable to make the individual parts to about one order of magnitude better than this, so that even parts with high and low tolerances on the pair were likely to fit to the required limits. Henry Ford thus saw the problem of mass production as one that involved holding the production processes of industry to a far higher degree of accuracy than before, in order to ease assembly problems. He set out to achieve this by calling for gauge blocks, the master key to physical measurement, to be made to even higher standards of accuracy than previously, and he also realized that the mass production of the gauge blocks themselves was fundamental to the operation. Thus, by mass-producing gauge blocks, he was able to supply the machine-tool industry with the standards required, so that eventually he was able to purchase a range of manufacturing equipment capable of making parts, day in and day out, to far higher standards than had been thought feasible. It then became possible to assemble motor-car connecting-rods on to their crankshafts knowing that the assembly was as good as anything that had hitherto been done by the laborious fittings of bearings.

This opened the way to the establishment of mass-production plants in which the flow of production was uninterrupted by time-wasting manual fitting, and established the basis of the modern mass-production era. It may not be generally realized how considerably that Herculean labour of Ford's has contributed to productivity, and how its effect is now felt in all processes depending upon the accuracy of machine tools.

But the possibility of improving accuracy by means of better machine tools is limited, and it is probably a truism that it simply does not pay to try to achieve production accuracies greater than 0·0002 in. because at this point one is at the mercy of even slight wear and tear in the producing machine. Even the most advanced ideas on negative-feedback control of machine tools would not begin to imply that higher accuracies could be dealt with under continuous production conditions.

Yet an accuracy of 0·0002 in. is no longer good enough for many mass-produced precision products, especially for the fine-limit parts of modern motor-car engines, such as piston pins, hydraulic tappets, etc., so a new technique has to be found for producing mating assemblies to an *accuracy of fit better than is possible with the production equipment.*

That italicized statement may sound a paradox, but it is a paradox with a statistical solution. The solution is to inspect and classify the products from a machine *automatically*, and to mate these products with other parts that have also been automatically inspected and classified.

In other words, the answer is automatic sorting for selective assembly, and it is mainly this that has led to the development of a remarkable series of automatic inspection machines now used in America and beginning to be used in Europe.

FIVE VARIETIES OF AUTOMATIC INSPECTION

There are five principal varieties of inspection equipment now available in various parts of the world—

1. *"In-process" inspection devices*, which can be applied to existing production equipment and which are slowly coming to be provided in modular form so that customers can begin to apply automatic inspection techniques to their own machines.

2. *The automatic inspection machine* proper, which will usually take randomly oriented parts and orient them for feeding to the machine. It then senses the particular property to be inspected

(dimension, weight, hardness, etc.) classifies the result into "accepted" and "rejected" classes, and sorts the product into two groups.

3. *The grading machine* is an automatic inspection machine, generally like 2 above, but the acceptable class is subclassified into grades appropriate for selective assembly. In principle there is very little difference between the automatic inspection machine and the grading machine, except for the number of classes involved, and, by implication, the finer discrimination and accuracy of the measuring device.

4. *Process control systems*, which are based on the measuring information provided by any of the above three systems.

5. *Digital inspection machines*, which correspond to reversed-operation digitally-controlled machine tools.

In-process Inspection

The whole advantage of "in-process" inspection, compared with "post-process" inspection (groups 2 and 3 above), is that data are produced at a time when they can indicate that the process is going off-beam. Therefore "in-process" inspection should also be made the basis of process control by some sort of rapid system. The sort of control facilities which "in-process" inspection offers are—

An alarm system to warn of out-of-limit trends from undue cutter or machine wear.

Operating a change-over system so that the producing machine goes on to fine-finish tool-feed from coarse-finish tool-feed.

Stopping and retracting the tool when the correct dimension has been reached.

Information, capable of statistical digestion, to indicate systematic and random variations in the system (small and cheap computers are now coming on the market to deal with this sort of information). In general, what is needed is quality control information where it can be used before scrap is made.

At the time of writing, there is great controversy in the U.S.A. over the relative merits of in-process and post-process inspection. These depend on the particular case, and many people take the view that one should install all the automatic inspection equipment that seems economic after adequate work-study on the alternatives.

Automatic Inspection and Grading Machines

SENSING ELEMENTS

Most automatic inspection machines for dimensional measurement are concerned with checking parts for very small variations from target figures. A typical dimensional sensor is therefore probably only required to cover a total dimensional range of some 0·010 in. but within this range it may be called to measure dimensions to an accuracy of 0·00001 in.

Available machines make use of five principal forms of dimensional sensor: (*a*) air gauge, (*b*) air-electric gauge, (*c*) air-electronic gauge, (*d*) electrical capacity gauge, and (*e*) differential transformer.

Whilst the pure air-gauge and the air-electric gauge are quite useful for highly accurate visual indication on manometer tubes or dial instruments, the form of presentation and output is not very suitable for further data processing. This really calls for a continuously variable electrical analogue signal, proportional to dimensional change, and I shall therefore limit the following discussion to the last three sensors above: they appear to have the greater scope for automatic grading and complex automation.

Capacitive sensor. This is the type of sensor which has been adopted by the Radio Corporation of America for its wide range of automatic inspection machines, some of which will be described later in this chapter. Changed spacing of two metal plates changes their capacity. As we know from our radio sets, an electrical capacitor is the device used for tuning the frequency of the set to different wave-lengths. The dimensional capacitor works in the same way, by varying the frequency of an electronic oscillator. Thus a dimensional change causes a change in the frequency of an alternating current passing across the plates. This alteration in frequency is detected, and is the output signal from the system. Such a system would not normally give an output directly proportional to the change in spacing of the capacitor plates, but proportionality can be substantially achieved by putting in correcting circuits.

This sensor has the advantage of being extremely robust. It is not affected by the magnetic field that may accompany some steel piece-parts under inspection, and it can discriminate down to 0·000005 in. or so. The usual technique of using the sensor to inspect a workpiece is to fit the former with suitable metal probes.

Differential-transformer sensor. The differential transformer is a dimension-sensor of extreme accuracy. It depends on the fact that the electromagnetic coupling between two coils is influenced by the presence of a common magnetic core. If this core is moved whilst an alternating current is passed in one coil, extremely sensitive coupling can be obtained with the second coil, so sensitive that a dimensional change of 0·000002 in. may be detected. It is noteworthy that the Sheffield Corporation (Dayton, Ohio, U.S.A.), perhaps the largest firm in the world specializing in automatic dimensional-inspection machines, has now adopted this type of sensor. That company claims that these sensors work at high speed and give repeatable dimensional indications of the order of millionths of an inch.

Air-electronic sensor. The air-gauge principle has the basic advantage that dimensions can be measured without actually touching the workpiece, since the operation depends upon the change of pressure-drop between a jet and the workpiece. Thus the system is particularly applicable to "in-process" inspection, and also to bore measurement —here one may resort to all the well-developed tricks with air-gauges spaced round a periphery. By taking the pressure variations to a diaphragm and then measuring its movement (with either capacitive or differential-transformer sensors as described above), one can convert the air-gauge into an electronic system providing electrical signals proportional to dimensional change.

PRACTICAL EXAMPLES

In my experience, by far the most advanced examples of automatic inspection and grading machines have been designed to suit the American automotive industry. I have in mind particularly the machines emanating from such well-known firms as the Sheffield Corporation, Radio Corporation of America and the Pratt and Whitney Co. Below are descriptions of some of these machines.

It should be noted that one of the problems in automatic inspection is how to deliver the piece-parts from random bulk orientation to the ordered orientation required for reception by the machine. This problem has been solved by the development of special orienters and feed hoppers. As these are common to many other machines, including automatic assembly machines, we shall consider them separately in the next chapter on automatic assembly.

PISTON-PIN GRADER

This type of machine, made by Radio Corporation of America, is suitable for the automatic inspection and grading of gudgeon pins or similar small cylindrical parts.

The pins are fed from an automatic parts-feeder-and-orienter to the first station of the inspection machine, where they are checked for length to tolerances of 0·0001 in. and segregated into over- and under-size sets. At a second station the parts are rotated in a V-block having a 60° included angle, and are inspected for out-of-roundness within tolerances of 0·0002 in; rejects are automatically segregated. This latter is a true roundness test, and is unaffected by the size of the part. Outside diameter and taper are checked at a third station, where the pins are classified into four acceptable categories in increments of 0·0001 in. as well as for over- or under-size. Parts having a taper of more than 0.0001 in. are also rejected. The machine speed is about 3000 parts an hour.

The machine senses capacitively. Counters automatically total the number of pins in each classification, and lights and dials on the back panel also give a continuous visual presentation of the entire operation. This is valuable in connexion with any servicing the machine may require.

VALVE GRADER

This machine, also made by the Radio Corporation of America, is intended for very comprehensive automatic inspection and grading of automobile engine valves at speeds of over 3000 pieces per hour. Valves are dropped from an 8 cu. ft. bulk hopper and orienting system into a guide track on the machine, and are fed individually to the first inspection station. Here they are automatically positioned in a fixture and rotated 360°, and during this operation they are automatically checked for stem and seat concentricity and for stem straightness. Those out of tolerance are rejected and segregated into predetermined catagories. Valves which, because of dimensional inaccuracies, fail to rotate fully, are diverted to the "no spin" chute.

The valves which pass this first inspection are gravity-fed to the second station, where they are checked for head thickness and length. Those out of tolerance are rejected and segregated into specific groups. Those meeting specification slide down a track on to a conveyor or a "tote" box.

Any valve approximating the size desired can be used to set the concentricity limits on the system, and any valve of known size, falling within the limits of the classification groups, is adequate for setting up the other stations.

RANGE OF DIMENSIONAL INSPECTION MACHINES

It would be quite impossible, within the scope of a single chapter to give more details of individual automatic inspection and grading machines, but the following is a list compiled as a result of a visit to the United States in 1960.

Machines exist for the measurement of—

Automobile engine valves	Helical springs	Seals
Ball bearings	Horn diaphragms	Spacers
Ball retainers	Hydraulic tappets	Sparking plugs
Bolts and screws	Magnets	Studs
Business-machine parts	Piston rings	Transmission parts
Cams	Pistons	Trunnion bearings, crosses, and cups
Connecting rods	Plain bearings	Typewriter parts
Electric motor parts	Pump vanes	Universal joints
Gears	Push rods	Valve guides
Glass tubes	Rivets	Watch parts
Gudgeon and other pins	Rocker-arm-parts	Wire gauges
	Roller bearings	

and so on. Most of the above machines are running in the range of 2,000 to 6,000 parts an hour, the higher figure for small parts such as balls for ball bearings, and the lower speeds for larger parts such as pistons and connecting-rods. In many case the machines have several inspection stations, and in most cases automatically grade the acceptable products into a range for ultimate selective assembly with corresponding graded parts.

SPECIAL-PROCESS INSPECTION MACHINES

Probably about nine-tenths of the automatic inspection and grading machines in use are of the dimensional type just described, but there is a growing class of special inspection machines which are unique to a given process. To illustrate these I shall give two examples, both of which are products of the Radio Corporation of America.

Paper Inspection Equipment

The R.C.A. optical paper-inspection system consists of electronic equipment that detects and classifies visual defects in the surface of large rolls of paper. The sensing head monitors the surface quality of the paper continuously as it passes over a roller at up to 1,000 ft./min.

Changes in the light reflected from the surface of the paper are measured and transmitted to the classifying circuitry. These circuits apply the preset inspection standard to the defect signals, in order to establish their severity. In this manner creases, calandar cuts, holes, dirt spots, and gloss imperfections are detected and may be classified in either of two or three catagories "Accepts and Rejects" or "Firsts, Seconds and Rejects," depending upon the customer's requirements. Digital read-out controls are provided on the rack. These permit the paper-machine operator to predetermine the visual severity a defect must have to be classified in each catagory. The controls allow the predetermining of separate classification levels for surface imperfections, as opposed to defects like holes and spots.

The sensing head (Fig. 11.1) is located close to a chrome-plated roller over which the paper is passed. Two banks of incandescent lamps, associated with the sensing head, provide uniform illumination of the paper surface. The light reflected from the paper surface passes through a lens system to sensitive photo-conductive cells, and in this manner the visual quality of the paper is converted into electrical data signals. A separate sensing head is provided for each $\frac{3}{4}$ in. width of the paper. The head thus observes a small area of the paper and gives signals corresponding to the various types of flaw.

A separate rack contains the signal-collection-and-classification circuitry which processes the information collected from the surface of the paper as it travels at high speed past the inspection apertures.

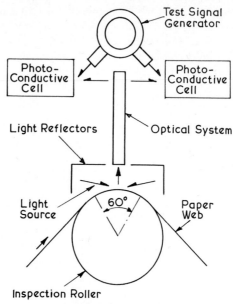

FIG. 11.1.   OPERATING PRINCIPLES

"Dark" and "light" signals from the various defects which exceed the normal formation patterns are handled by separate channels. This permits more effective control over the inspection criteria, since some defects (such as dark spots and holes) produce a negative or "dark" signal and may not be as objectionable as the more subtle wrinkles, creases and gloss imperfections that produce a positive or "light" signal. Controls for both dark and light channels are easily adjusted for criticality.

Illustrated in Fig. 11.2 is the wave-form typical of this system. The diagram shows the three "light" and three "dark" classification levels for registration of defects, together with a middle band for the acceptable normal product.

The performance of the machine is as follows—

Dark spots.—The minimum size of flaw which will be detected is a spot of area equivalent to a $\frac{1}{16}$in diameter circle, and with a length-to-width ratio of two or less. The diffuse visual reflectance of the spot must be less than half that of the surrounding paper. Dark, coloured, or transparent paper cannot be inspected by the system.

Smudges.—Sensitivity to creases running in the direction of paper-travel can be calibrated against samples.

Holes.—Holes of the same order of size as the dark spots mentioned above are distinguished by a reflectance exceeding that from the underlying chrome-plated roller.

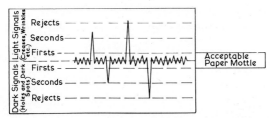

FIG. 11.2. CLASSIFICATION OF FLAW TYPES

Beverage Inspection Machine

Still another R.C.A. automatic inspection machine looks out for foreign bodies in bottles holding transparent beverages. The machine is completely self-contained, and fits into any $3\frac{1}{4}$ in. conveyor system of the kind used in bottling plants.

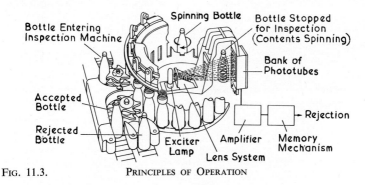

FIG. 11.3. PRINCIPLES OF OPERATION

The essential elements of the optical and electronic system are shown in Fig. 11.3. The lamp-and-lens system projects a strong, narrow beam of light through the bottle and its contents on to a bank of photocells. These are followed by an amplifier, so that a small change in light can actuate a selector. The latter automatically sets aside those bottles containing particles.

To betray its presence, a particle must move through a light beam. This movement is made certain by spinning the bottle at high speed and then braking it to standstill just before the inspection period begins. Because of their momentum, the liquid contents continue to swirl, and foreign particles intercept the light beam. Since the bottle itself does not move during inspection, fluting, lettering and imperfection in the glass do not change the transmitted light pattern, and therefore do not actuate the rejection mechanism.

As well as rejecting bottles containing foreign particles, the inspection machine will also reject under-filled bottles in most conditions, as well as bottles containing oil, grease or caustic matter if the latter is sufficient to cause bubbling during inspection. Furthermore, freshly-filled bottles with leaking crowns or cracks are rejected, since they bubble excessively.

To protect is own operation, the machine has a check circuit which superimposes a synthetic signal on the system after each bottle is inspected, to verify that operation has been correct.

AUTOMATIC INSPECTION AND SELECTIVE ASSEMBLY

In the introduction to this chapter I referred to the coming tendency to secure fine-limit fits in mass production processes by means of automatic inspection and grading followed by selective assembly. For products of substantial size, such an operation requires the co-ordinated working of several different machines. For example, two machines for grading the mating parts may feed one automatic selective-assembly machine. Such systems are coming into more frequent use in automotive factories.

If the product is small, the whole operation can be dealt with in a single machine "unit." An example is the machine for automatic inspection and selective assembly of tapered roller bearings, made by the Sheffield Corporation (Dayton, U.S.A.).

The completely integrated inspection-assembly machine is shown in Fig. 11.4. It automatically assembles tapered roller bearings at the rate of 1,000 per hour, while under the observation of only one operator. Each complete bearing assembly consists of an inner race, eighteen rollers and a cage.

At the beginning of the cycle, finished rollers are loaded according to size classification into six separate hoppers, and are fed from this point by gravity, as required. Cages and inner races are also fed to the machine from separate hoppers, by gravity. To start the operation a button is pressed and an inner race moves into position at station 1. Two dimensional sensors then gauge the standoff flange thickness and any out-of-tolerance parts are rejected. The acceptable races next move to station 2, and while this is going on a special ratchet loader arrangement feeds eighteen correctly selected rollers to a transfer jig. This selection of rollers is controlled by four sensing heads, embracing six classifications. Feedback of previous race dimensions from station 1 actuates the discharge of the correct-size rollers from their storage hopper. The rollers are fed one at a time to the transfer jig until it is full, and at the same time a cage is fed into position underneath the race at station 2.

The rollers next move into position over the cage, where they are dropped into place, and an air cylinder then forces the inner race down into the loaded cage until it snaps into position at the lower level. The assembly then moves forward to station 3, where it is rotated past a "finger" to detect any missing rollers. At station 4 a special die presses a slight bulge in the side walls of the cage to lock the assembly together. If this die does not travel a predetermined distance and operate a limit switch, the entire assembly is rejected.

FIG. 11.4.   COMBINED AUTOMATIC INSPECTION AND ASSEMBLY MACHINE FOR
BEARINGS
(Courtesy: Sheffield Corporation)

Station 5 turns the assembly over for final inspection at station 6. Here a permanent outer-race master is rotated and forced over the assembly under high pressure. The torque characteristics of the race are then determined by measuring the rise in current in the driving motor. At the same time a contact point touches the bottom face of the inner race. With its accompanying electronics, this picks up any noise that would indicate a misfit. Standout dimension is also measured by a dimensional sensor. All assemblies are segregated at the discharge point into "okay," "standout reject," "torque reject," and "noise reject," and the acceptable assemblies are automatically conveyed to washing and greasing operations.

FEEDBACK FROM INSPECTION MACHINES

In this chapter we are not concerned with machine tools which have built-in inspection devices and closed-loop control of tool position. But there is a half-way house method of feeding control data back from an automatic inspection machine. This is to display reject information to preceding machine-tool operators so that they can take quick avoiding action.

An example is a system developed by the Sheffield Corporation. This system is called a "multi-feedback device," and it is designed to measure precisely and at high speed the parts being produced by a series of machines. It consists of gauge tooling, with provisions for receiving and measuring precision parts from each of a series of machines. Individual parts are conveyed through a series of part-handling devices. A "memory" system positions parts in gauging stations one at a time as they flow from different machines. Controls go into action as each part is being inspected. Electrical sensor signals received from the part are transmitted to the particular machine which produced the part, and make lights flash on a panel mounted conveniently for the operator. These signals indicate when to stop and adjust the machine tool if it has produced a predetermined number of rejects.

In cases where all parts passing through the gauging control unit are not quite the same, two sensing stations are incorporated in the device. In cases where basic dimensions may be the same but overall sizes may be different, a primary sensing station inspects the basic dimensions and a series of secondary stations inspects the variable dimensions of the part. Here the memory system performs the additional job of determining which secondary station will inspect the part after it leaves the primary station.

The memory system may also be used for a third dimensional-quality-control function—that of directing acceptable parts into individual chutes corresponding to the types of part being produced. Multi-feedback machines of this type, controlling as many as twenty machine tools simultaneously, are in use.

IN-PROCESS INSPECTION MODULES

There is a pronounced move in the U.S.A. towards developing standard modules, or inspection "black boxes," for incorporation in processes by machine users or machine builders. A group of typical modules, manufactured by R.C.A., has the following functions:

The master gauge-control accepts signals from the type of capacitive sensor described earlier in this chapter, and converts it into a signal which deflects the pointer of the associated meter. Full-scale sensor displacement gives a 20-volt output signal, which can be used directly or may be fed onwards for further manipulation.

The sum comparator resolves the sum of the measurements of two master gauge-controls into a single answer. Typical uses are in checking trunnion crosses and valves. In the former case each arm is measured individually, and the sum of the readings indicates total length. When valves are being checked, the distance from the groove to the seat and from the groove to the tip are measured individually and added in the unit to give the total length.

The difference computer computes the difference in the outputs from two master gauge-control units, and is particularly useful for determining tapers. It also contains its own thyratron limit-switch (see below), so that if a dimensional difference exceeds permissible limits the thyratron will operate a classifying gate in the subsequent mechanical handling system.

The thyratron units are essentially electronic limit switches or single-point classifiers, and are used with the master gauge-control unit to establish grading levels. Thus, if it is required to grade a product into seven incremental dimensional grades, seven thyratron units would be wired into the output of a single master gauge-control unit and set at incremental triggering points for operating the gates in the mechanical classifier.

FINISHED-PRODUCT TESTERS

The total cost of inspection in a factory can form a considerable fraction of the total cost of production. The purpose of inspection is to give the customer a reliable product, and one which will perform according to its specification. But there is no guarantee that factory inspection of individual parts will ensure the reliable *functioning* of the finished assembly. Sometimes, too, a part is inspected for qualities which are irrelevant to the function of the assembly it will go into, and sometimes there is no inspection for the really important factors.

The realization that this is indeed the situation, and that the costs of normal inspection procedures are truly formidable, is now leading engineers to thorough inspection of the *finished* product for its *function*—what the customer is paying for—and to use the information from such testing to determine the required extent of earlier piece-part and subassembly inspection in the factory.

To some degree this is generally done by studying complaints from the field statistically, and dealing with these complaints in the factory by intensifying inspection procedures related to the worst cases. Such a procedure is by no means always satisfactory. It may displease the customer who is used as a statistical sample in a functional inspection system, and then lead to loss of goodwill and orders; it is often too late—especially when the product is subject to evolutionary design changes (as in the motor-car industry, with new models introduced each year); and the customers'-complaint picture may not be accurate because it tends to be based on opinion rather than measurement— service-complaint committees, sitting in on statistical service-complaint lists, rarely know just how seriously to take a given complaint group.

In order to meet this situation there is a move by some progressive companies to install *automatic finished-product testers*. These put the finished product through its functional paces and give measured inspection figures having a high degree of statistical accuracy. By this means there is hope that the potential customers'-complaint picture can be calculated so that avoiding action may be taken.

It is not possible to deal with the techniques involved in particular instances, since these will vary enormously according to whether one is making a ball-point pen or a motor-car, but the principles are common. They are—

1. The finished-product tester should be devised to measure the main functions of the finished product. These measured figures should preferably be automatically printed out, so a complex tester will probably be based on some scanning system of multiple sensors, common digitization, and print-out.

2. The system should be designed with considerable flexibility, so that new tests can be rapidly introduced at the first sign of suspicious behaviour related to a particular function. To extract these factors is the real job of the quality-control chief, and good contacts with the design and service departments soon give clues to where the next trouble is coming from.

3. All data should be processed by statistical methods to find the random and systematic variations from specification, and also to determine the "average product." This is no mean task, and very few designers are sure of the real average characteristics of the product they design.

An Example—Programmed Transformer Testing

A highly automated, electric-transformer-testing system has been developed and installed by Westinghouse Electric at their Sharon factory in Philadelphia, U.S.A. The aim of the project was the automatic testing and recording of all the commercial tests required for pole-mounted distribution transformers. The tests are automatically programmed from punched cards, one card for each transformer, and test results are automatically recorded on the same card.

THE PRODUCT-HANDLING PROBLEM

There is a main, 52 ft. slat conveyor which takes the transformers through the test set-up, and this provides stations for thirteen transformers: there are two stations for connexion, nine testing stations, and two stations for disconnexion. Above is a corresponding conveyor which carries the connexion leads between the transformers and the test equipment. Moving connectors on this overhead conveyor mate with stationary contacts at the test facilities, and thus connect the transformers to the testing devices, the whole being indexed on a 4 ft. progressive movement.

DATA-HANDLING

Data are sent from a centre to the test stations in time and form to establish the test program. Since there are nine different test stations, nine I.B.M. cards are working simultaneously to give the program instructions. A special card-reader was devised to receive the programming cards. This consists of a miniature indexing conveyor corresponding to the main system. The cards traverse this system in synchronization with the full-scale system. Also associated with the card-reader is a logic system which takes the readings from the punched cards and converts them into switching impulses to set the test stations. The various incoming results from the sensed tests are stored temporarily, and then the results are punched into the cards at the tenth station. All results are reported as *Pass, Fail,* or *No-test.* The system has very comprehensive checking and alarm features.

OPERATION

The system is operated by two men, one at the card-reader and one at the discharge end. The former is also responsible for making the incoming electrical connexions to transformers. It has been found that the system gives much quicker turn-round of information for use by the productive departments, reduces test costs and, incidentally, provides safer conditions for the testing staff.

NUMERICALLY CONTROLLED INSPECTION MACHINES

The automatic inspection and grading machines described earlier in this chapter are very valuable tools for quantity production where the rapid checking of a few key dimensions is adequate to ensure the maintenance of quality. However, these methods are of little value for very complex articles produced in small quantities by manual methods; the inspection time may well exceed production time. It is for such cases that the numerically controlled, automatic inspection machine has been devised. This is virtually a numerically controlled machine-tool, with the tool replaced by a probing stylus whose position is controlled by a punched-tape system. Such systems allow rapid automatic inspection of complex three-dimensional shapes like those of turbine blades, pump impellers, etc. Typical of such systems is the Pratt and Whitney "Data-limit" system.

The "Data-limit" System

This is a six-co-ordinate inspection system for gauging points in three-dimensional space, and operates from punched-tape instructions. Differences between a master tape and the actual dimensions are printed out automatically. It is claimed that the repeat accuracy of the system is to within 0·000025 in. The basic measuring system is a stainless steel bar having $\frac{1}{2}$ in. raised sectors at $\frac{1}{2}$ in. intervals, with null magnetic sensing to give accurate 1 in. space register. This system is combined with a small slide driven by a micrometer screw to give intermediate readings. Under automatic operation the coarse and fine systems are moved by servo-mechanisms, and the programming tape system issues separate instructions to the coarse and fine systems.

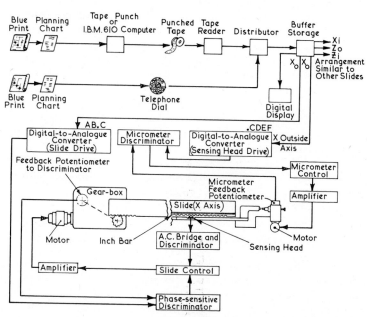

FIG. 11.5.   BLOCK DIAGRAM OF EQUIPMENT USED TO POSITION ONE SLIDE
(*Courtesy: Pratt and Whitney Inc.*)

There are altogether three functions: (1) positioning the sensor heads, (2) taking the readings, and (3) recording the readings. When operation is under tape control, the programmed information for sensor positioning and for sequences of inspection is carried entirely on the tape. For tape preparation a planning sheet and I.B.M.610 computer are used. The computer can be human rather than electronic, but for complex jobs the machine is found to be an economy. In such complicated work, six machine-movements may be required for each gauging position, and whereas the workpiece may be simply described by polar co-ordinates, the machine itself works on rectangular co-ordinates. Thus it is necessary to find the perpendicular angle for the sensing heads at each point of inspection, and these complicated calculations are much better done by speedy computers. The difference between the programmed position of the gauge head and its actual contact point is caused to produce a proportional analogue signal which is converted into digital for printing out. A schematic diagram of the "Data-limit" system is shown in Fig. 11.5.

The "Universal Probograph"

Equipment, somewhat simpler than the above, for semi-automatic numerical inspection is the "Universal Probograph" made by Warner and Swasey. This operates by comparing nominal dimensions, recorded on an eight-channel punched tape, with actual dimensions checked by means of a probe, the deviation being recorded on a strip chart. In order to check a contoured part, the operator places it in the machine, inserts the tape into a punched-tape reader, and presses the "start" button. Three rectangular co-ordinate slides then move the probe until it touches the part, and this contact is recorded on the strip chart as a dot. The position of the dot relative to vertical lines running along the chart indicates deviation. There are two nominal position lines on the chart, one for progressively increasing dimensions and one for progressively dimishing dimensions. This pair of comparison lines can be used for thickness measurements, with pairs of dots which fall within the lines indicating under-thickness, and pairs which fall outside the lines indicating over-thickness. Contour errors are indicated by a wavy pattern in the successive dots.

NUCLEONIC GAUGING

The use of nucleonic gauges for automatic inspection is rapidly increasing. Such gauges are particularly suited to the measurement of material thickness. The principle on which these gauges depend is that if nuclear radiation falls on a material, part of the radiation is scattered and part is absorbed. This effect can thus be used in two ways: (*a*) for a *transmission* gauge, which measures the amount of radiation passing *through* the material, or (*b*) for a *backscatter* gauge, which measures the radiation *reflected from* the material (Fig. 11.6).

In the case of transmission gauging, the measured transmission is related to the weight per unit area of the material. For constant-density materials a transmission meter can thus be calibrated as a thickness gauge. If it is desired to measure the thickness of coatings on a base material, it is usual to use two gauges, the first "looking" at the uncoated material and acting as a standard, and the second "looking" at the coated materials; the difference between the two signal outputs measures the weight per unit area of the coating.

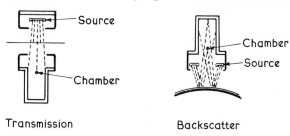

Transmission   Backscatter

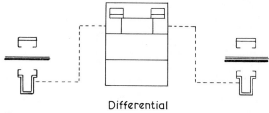

Differential

Fig. 11.6.   Nucleonic Gauging Technique

(*Courtesy: Baldwin Instrument Co. Ltd.*)

The back-scatter method is normally used where the material is accessible from one side only, for example for controlling an automatic cutter on a coal-mining machine, to ensure that the cutter keeps a fixed distance away from the rock when removing coal from the rock face.

Nucleonic gauging has several advantages in thickness measurement. It is reasonably accurate—in the order of 1 per cent—and no contact with the moving material is required, so errors are not introduced by gauge-bounce, and there is no danger of marking delicate surfaces such as those of paper or foil.

Principal applications are in metal rolling, paper and board making, plastics and rubber sheet manufacture, and coating of such materials as waxed paper, adhesive tape, etc.

One of the problems in thickness measurement is that the sheet to be scanned is often very wide. This difficulty can be dealt with either by oscillating the nucleonic gauge and its detector across the width of the sheet mechanically, or by using a number of fixed scanning heads. One machine has been developed specially to take a sample strip off the width of a sheet and process the strip rapidly along its length to acquire very accurate information. This is post-process information, but, in the many processes that have stable production equipment, it may give quite satisfactory results.

QUALITY-CONTROL RECORDING

It is rather surprising, when one has considered the great variety of automatic inspection devices mentioned in this chapter, that more serious and wide-spread attempts are not made to centralize this information automatically in quality-control rooms.

One small system available is the Pratt and Whitney quality analyser. With this system the output from a number of automatic inspection devices can be monitored and converted into digital form, and this is combined with counting to give such information as: (1) number of accepted and rejected parts per hour, (2) average size of a given number of parts, (3) range of size for a given number of parts, (4) number of corrective signals sent per hour to machines producing parts, (5) record of operator's number, time, date, temperature etc., and (6) automatic analysis of dimensional relationships.

There would appear to be a considerable field for such processing of inspection data, including treatment by standard quality-control mathematical methods, to give quick guidance as to machine conditions and very accurate machine-control feedback signals based on systematic variations.

MARRIAGE OF MECHANICS AND ELECTRONICS

There is little doubt that the general field of automatic inspection is one of the most important for the future of automation, since by such methods alone can one maintain quality under the high pressure for production.

The general application of these techniques is far more developed in the U.S.A. than in any other country of the world, and if we are practically involved in such techniques then it is important to keep a constant close scrutiny on American developments.

All the devices described in this chapter are truly forms of "data-controlled process" (see the original definition of automation in Chapter I), and as such represent a particularly intimate marriage between mechanical engineering and electronic technique.

F

CHAPTER 12

AUTOMATIC ASSEMBLY

THE main production processes of manufacturing industry are already highly mechanized. Development is also active in automatic quality-inspection, as discussed in the last chapter. The remaining major productive sector to be automated is that of assembly, and this historical phase had hardly begun yet. The reasons are—

1. Automatic assembly involves very complex mechanical handling, and the economics are often on the side of human labour.

2. Automatic assembly implies that the component parts will go together without difficulty; otherwise the process will come to a grinding halt, to the accompaniment of very expensive noises. In turn this involves either 100 per cent inspection of the components to be fed to an automatic assembler (or their inspection within the machine itself), or alternatively the component parts must be designed so that any conceivable act of mis-manufacture cannot cause assembly trouble. This latter is a very unlikely achievment.

3. Unlike most machine tools, automatic assemblers are custom-built to suit a particular assembly, and since they are expensive the obsolescence risk is very high if product changes are liable to be made.

GENERAL REQUIREMENTS OF AUTOMATIC ASSEMBLY

Whilst partially automated assembly is possible with hand-fed machines, full automation requires acceptance of piece-parts in random orientation, for assembly without jamming or damage to the machine. This implies a general scheme as shown in Fig. 12.1 involving the following seven main functions—

1. *Bulk feed.*—The different groups of parts coming from previous productive processes are tumbled into bulk-feed hoppers.

2.—*Piece-part orientation.*—Bulk-fed parts must be oriented for presentation to the assembly machine in a consistent fashion. This requirement could be eased if the previous process were capable of maintaining orientation of the parts or of feeding them directly into magazines, but this is rarely so.

3. *Interference inspection.*—All parts should be inspected after orientation for that factor (usually dimensional, but it might be hardness) which could either damage the machine or lead to incorrect assembly. Of these two factors the former is paramount, since the latter involves only rejection of the particular assembly. Every important dimension does not have to be inspected here—only "interference dimensions" such as pin oversize, plastics flash, missing holes, burrs, etc. If such interferences are detected, the machine must immediately reject the part and not proceed until that part has been successfully replaced.

4. *Transfer.*—After interference inspection (if carried out) it is next necessary to transfer the component from its oriented alignment to its correct

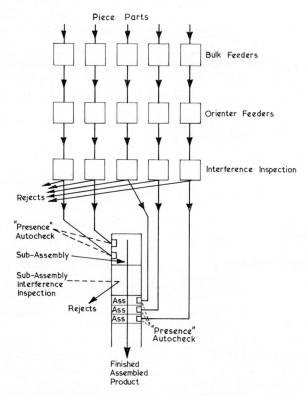

FIG. 12.1.   GENERAL SCHEME OF AUTOMATIC ASSEMBLY

place in the assembly machine proper, and this usually calls for two devices (*a*) an escapement system which meters the component parts one at a time and extracts them from their previous side-by-side or end-to-end alignment, and (*b*) a transferring device, virtually a mechanical hand, which takes the component after its escapement and places it correctly in the appropriate stage of the assembly machine. The escapement device and the transferring device often co-exist in one indistinguishable mechanism.

5. *Presence detection.*—The machine may incorporate sensors to detect the correct presence of all components required to make up an assembly in the sequential assembly zones. With some components it is possible to use this presence detection to evade part or all of the earlier interference inspection. This can be the case when an over-dimension of the part prevents it from entering the assembly station; the lack of a signal from the presence detector can raise an alarm. This is not a very satisfactory system. It implies that every incorrect part will stop the assembly machine, and the preliminary inspection of components is greatly to be preferred.

6. *Assembly proper.*—This will normally involve sequential progressive assembly of the piece-parts. It is a matter of correct mechanical design, together with presence detection as described above.

7. *Subassembly inspection.*—Each phase of subassembly should be automatically checked for those features of incorrect assembly or damage which could endanger later assembly stages, and the subassembly should be automatically rejected if found incorrect. This system also implies some subassembly-presence sensing at all stages of progressive assembly.

ORIENTATION

There appear to be three ways in which bulked components may be oriented for consistent alignment.

Statistical Technique

This involves presentation of randomly oriented parts to a mechanical filter which will only accept those parts that are correctly oriented. These parts pass on, and the remainder are returned to be re-randomized to give a further small proportion of parts which will be correctly oriented at the next presentation.

Polarizing Technique

The most difficult product to orient in a particular direction is a sphere. True, there is normally no need to orient a sphere (for example in a ball-bearing-assembly machine); but if a sphere has a small hole in it, and the sphere must be held with the hole in a particular place, this is very troublesome. The difficulty is that a sphere is not polarized, i.e. it has no distinguishing features. If a body has distinguishing geometrical or weight-distribution features, it is often possible to use these to encourage orientation. For example, if long pins are conveyed towards an angled guide in random orientation they will tend to line up to become parallel with the guide. The more difference there is between two properties of a body at right angles, the easier it is to orient the body with some simple gadget. Consider the following examples—

1. Long pins will line up against angled guides better than short pins of the same diameter. The ratio of length to diameter should never be less than 4:3 for this to be effective.
2. A bolt or screw is easily oriented because the head is different from the shank. It is first roughly oriented by being fed against an angled bar, and then allowed to fall between parallel rails so that the head is kept uppermost.
3. A part which is much heavier at one end than the other can be oriented over knife-edges or spill ledges.

Half the battle in orienting is to see that the parts have polar properties, either of geometry or weight.

Sensing and Correction Technique

If parts cannot be oriented by use of their natural geometric or weight properties, it may be necessary to sense their orientation and make a corrective movement. This particularly occurs on parts like split pins, which are easily put end to end but which may just as easily lie the wrong way round. Fore-and-aft orientation is possible, sensing by photo-electric or similar techniques for 'which way round?' and arranging for a 180° rotation if incorrect.

SOME AVAILABLE DEVICES

Commercially available component-orienting feeders are based on a combination of the statistical and polarizing methods described above. A bulk reservoir presents randomly oriented parts to an orienting filter. A percentage of components gets past this device and is oriented; the rest fall back into the random feeder, where they are stirred so that a certain percentage will succeed at the next attempt. The three most popular systems are: (1) vibrating-bowl feeders for small parts; (2) rotating-disk feeders for small parts; and (3) elevating-belt feeders for larger parts.

Vibrating-bowl Feeders

In vibrating-bowl feeders the bowl is vibrated tangentially by means of an electromagnet and inclined springs. The components to be fed are dumped into the main volume of the bowl, but the tangential vibration carries them to the outside of the base. There they begin the ascent of a spiral ledge to the top of the bowl. The parts are projected upwards and forwards during the upward half of the vibratory cycle, but they fall vertically under gravity during the downward half of the cycle. The system is thus virtually a vibrational rectifier, and the parts progress against the incline.

Such a system only ensures that there will be a continuous feed of parts to the top of the bowl, but it does not ensure that their three geometrical axes will be correctly aligned. A "mechanical filter" is needed at the top of the bowl to reject parts which are incorrectly aligned. For example, the parts may have to pass by on a narrow ledge so that those which have their longest dimension fore-and-aft in the direction of motion will get by, and those which approach the ledge sideways-on will overbalance and fall off the track. Alternatively, an overhead scraping finger may remove from the track all parts standing on their ends. The tricks which can be played for orientation are many and various, and I have one catalogue that lists about seventy different devices.

In general, vibrating-bowl feeders are particularly suitable for rather small parts and for those which are particularly stable when seated on one face.

Rotating-disk Feeders

Rotating-disk feeders are not often seen in this country but they are very popular in the U.S.A. They have recently been introduced into British manufacture and we shall see much more of them. The rotating disk (*see* Fig. 12.2) contains radial slots which dip at an angle of about 30° to the vertical into a bowl. The bowl carries the bulked components to be fed.

FIG. 12.2.   ROTATING-DISK FEEDER
(Courtesy: Aylesbury Automation Ltd.)

This feeder is particularly suitable for parts having geometrical axes of different lengths, since the width of the rotating slots in the disks can be adjusted to accept only one width of component. Parts which have entered the disk are carried round and up, and then discharged on to an outlet track. If the parts are axially symmetrical shapes, no further orientation is required, but if a "heads or tails?" distinguishing operation is required, then some sort of mechanical filter must be inserted into the system, either associated with the upper part of the rotating disk or put into the outlet track so that rejected parts can drop back into the feeding bowl. In general, the orienting tricks used for this purpose are very similar to those employed with vibrating feeders, though parts being fed in rotating-disk feeders usually sit on their smallest side whilst parts in vibrating feeders usually sit on their largest side. In fact this latter difference, and its connexion with the possibilities or mechanical filtration for the desired orientation, provide the main reasons for choosing either a disk feeder or a vibrating feeder for a particular problem.

Elevating-belt Feeders

The elevating-belt feeder (*see* Fig. 12.3) works essentially on the same principle as the rotating-disk feeder, but it is particularly suitable for handling larger parts: for example, up to 8 in. dimensions, or where a much greater initial bulk-storage capacity is required (these two aspects are related).

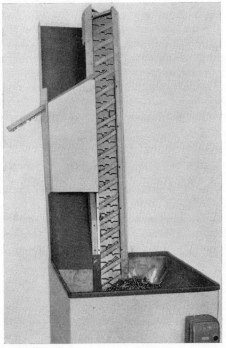

FIG. 12.3.   ELEVATING-BELT FEEDER
(*Courtesy: Aylesbury Automation Ltd.*)

In Fig. 12.3 is shown an elevating-belt feeder designed to deal with large rivets. The bulked components are in the base hopper and on an almost vertical belt. The belt has projecting and inclined ledges which raise parts from the base hopper. Like the rotating-disk feeder, this machine is primarily suitable for parts having one long axis. This is because the width of the ledges on the belt can be adjusted to support a minor dimension. Thus a part such as a simple rod is carried upwards and discharged at an outlet track, but if there is a "heads or tails?" problem then some orienting filter has to be inserted at the commencement of the outlet track so that rejected parts can fall back into the base hopper. In the example shown in Fig. 12.3 this consists of parallel rails, which allow the shank of the rivet to fall through but keep the head uppermost.

Special-part Feeders

As well as the above three principal types of part-feeder, which between them probably cover 80 per cent of applications, there are some four or five other special feeders for parts such as very long bars, finish-ground parts, rings, etc.

One of these special feeders is particularly designed for the handling of such finish-ground parts as hydraulic tappets. They are gently fed on to two rubber bands travelling in opposite directions and connected by inclined stationary surfaces. The parts circulate in this system until those which are encouraged by an angled guide can find their way out through a tube. Those not adequately oriented to go through the outlet hole continue to circulate until their turn comes, as statistically it must.

DESIGNING FOR AUTOMATIC ASSEMBLY

Provided that the problems of automatic part-feeding have been solved, the design of an assembly machine for a specific purpose is basically a matter of good mechanical handling and tooling. Perhaps the real problem is the product itself, and how to design it so that it facilitates automatic assembly. Some of these design considerations are as follows.

Component Accuracy

For automatic assembly, component accuracy should normally be higher than for manual assembly. This is because the problems of part tolerance all focus at the assembly stage. Parts automatically rejected on tolerances would probably be usable in manual assembly: a little selective discrimination would be exercised in choosing the mating parts. Product design should therefore allow the widest possible mating tolerances. If plastics are involved, these may well have to be of the thermoplastic variety to allow some degree of physical distortion. Alternatively, if the parts to be mated are very accurate, then automatic *selective* assembly may be the only answer. (See previous chapter for description of automatic selective assembly of roller-bearing races.)

A particular variation of the automatic selective-assembly machine, which can be economic, employs selective spacers to fill gaps. Two parts can be made to have a good fit given a choice between shims of different thickness. This implies automatic gauging of the two parts for their mating dimensions, automatic classification of the difference dimension, and automatic presentation of the appropriate shim for insertion into the gap.

Accuracy may also be required on surfaces which do not have to be at all accurate for manual assembly. This particularly applies to external surfaces used for part location in an automatic machine. Much consideration must be given to tapers and chamfers, to allow the maximum of self-centralization.

Component Positioning

The original orienting of the piece-part in the feeder, and its subsequent positioning in the assembly machine, may often be made easier by incorporating in the part some special geometrical feature which the machine can "recognize." This may be an additional flat, lug, notch, groove, etc., which will easily register with a sensing finger, spring-loaded ball, etc.

Part Presence

The three normal sensing devices used for presence detection are electrical limit-switches, photocell beams and magnetic proximity-detectors. Of these the photocell is probably the most universally useful. Its detecting ability is substantially unaffected by the nature of the materials in the piece-parts. Either obscuration or surface reflecting properties can be used, and the signals from several photocells can easily be combined in logical units to sense that "all parts are present and correct." Very rarely may it be necessary to add to the geometry of a part to facilitate recognition of its presence.

Fastenings

Wherever possible, parts should be fastened together in the assembly machine by means of devices that require a simple, straight, plunging motion, rather than rotation. This makes for speed and simplicity. Rivets, pins, pressure adhesives, interference fits etc. are better than screws and nuts.

Finishing

Parts which have been through automatic orienters and assemblers tend to come out with surfaces a little the worse for wear. Wherever possible the parts should have an "all-through" finish (*e.g.* with aluminium or plastics) or should be finished *after* automatic assembly.

PRACTICAL EXAMPLES OF ASSEMBLY MACHINES

Assembly machines can be either simple or very complex, and may handle from two up to twenty or thirty component parts. A typical example of a very simple machine for automatic assembly is used for putting spring-washers on to bolts. The machine is fed with washers by a vibrating feeder and with bolts by a rotating-disk feeder. The latter is fed from a primary bulk floor hopper. There appears to be considerable future for the use of such very simple automatic assemblers in putting only two or three parts together, especially where the operation would be rather slow and fiddling with manual labour.

When one comes to more complex automatic assemblers for many components, there are two main lines of development. In the first place there is the rotating-table machine and a typical example of this is shown in Fig. 12.4. The machine is used by Vauxhall Motors Ltd to assemble shock-absorber piston units. 600 units are produced an hour. Twelve progressive assembly stations are arranged round a circular indexing table. The first part to be inserted into the machine is the main piston rod, this by a specially designed rod-feeder. At

Fig. 12.4.   Automatic Assembler at Work
(Courtesy: Vauxhall Motors Ltd.)

later stages other parts are added, some fed from vibrating-bowl feeders and some from pre-magazined stacks (mainly very thin washers, which are very difficult to feed by conventional means because of oil stiction).

All devices that transfer the outputs of feeders to the assembly station are pneumatically operated, and thin parts such as washers are lifted by suction. Eleven out of the twelve stations are concerned with the addition of the further extra part for assembly, but the last station adds a nut which is run on to the thread of the assembly rod.

The main disadvantage with the rotating type of automatic assembler is that it is not infinitely extensible in the number of indexing stations that can be conveniently located round its circumference. A demand is therefore arising for automatic assemblers capable of indefinite extension. Hence the idea of single-operation assembly-station modules that can be coupled together in trains of indefinite length.

Automatic assembly is a progressive concept. After one has established certain satisfactory subassembly operations one may wish to proceed with further integration. So there appears to be much in favour of extensible modular plant, and indeed, it is now coming into vogue in the U.S.A.

DATA-PROGRAMMED AUTOMATIC ASSEMBLY

The economic limitations of existing automatic assemblers would largely be overcome if they could be data-programmed for different operations. They would then acquire the same sort of flexibility that is expected from human operators. A move to this end has been substantially completed in the "Transferobot" automatic assembly machine made by U.S. Industries Inc.

This machine is virtually four data-programmed mechanical hands, capable of a great variety of motions within a swept space corresponding to a hollow cylinder of 36 in. external and 28 in. internal diameter and 6 in. height. Within this space it can grab, push, pull, twist or release whatever it is handling. The only tool-change required is in the claw or fixture on each hand. The machine can work into almost exactly the same assembly jigs as are normally used by human workers. (This same company has now also produced a simplified version of this type of device, which is virtually a single mechanical hand as illustrated in Fig. 12.5.)

Program Setting

The basis of the data-programming is a group of fifteen rows of switches. Each row represents a sequence of movements such as arm swinging, extension, lowering, grabbing, etc. These switches give only the general form of the instruction, not the amount. Quantitative instruction is by means of knobs, in a rather ingenious manner. The operator first sets up the sequence of motion on the switches. Then he puts the machine into operation and uses the knobs to control the amount of motion. The quantities are electronically memorized and can afterwards be used automatically. Thus the machine embodies a degree of "skill copying."

FIG. 12.5.   ROBOT MECHANICAL HAND
(Courtesy: U.S. Industries Inc.)

Feedback Homing

For precise work the tool has a mirror and photo-electric assembly which will home on to one thousandth of an inch. This enables the machine to perform accurately the sort of work which would normally require human activity with magnifying glasses and tweezers. Whilst the machine is essentially a programmed positioning device, it can be arranged that some of the motions are for auto-inspection of fitness of parts for assembly, and indeed, the machine has unusual potential as a multistage automatic inspector, using inspecting sensors instead of assembly jigs.

AUTOMATIC PALLET-LOADING AND UNLOADING

A very special type of automatic assembler is the automatic pallet-loader for automatic stores. As you will see in a later chapter, the main application of automation in that field is on the outlet or "order-picking" aspect, and it is usually more economic to hold the input and more passive of the stores in palletized form. The automatic pallet-loader-and-unloader is therefore to some extent the missing link in automation, missing, that is, between production and bulk storage, and between bulk storage and the automatic order-picking output of the stores. Automated pallet-loading can also be valuable on the extreme outlet side of automatic stores, where a conveyor line of cases must be re-palletized for truck loading.

Stack Handler

The F.M.C. series 389000 machine, made by the Food Machinery & Chemical Corporation, may be considered as an automatic assembler in two sections. The first section is an automatic stacker. It takes single crates and builds them up to heights of 4, 5, 6 or 7 crates. This is done by a relatively straightforward hydraulic lift which raises the first case and permits a second case to be inserted underneath it. This cycle is repeated until the required stack height is reached. The second operation is to transfer the stacks to a loader section which accumulates them on a pallet until a row of three stacks is completed. The machine can proceed to load further rows of three stacks until the total pallet-load is completed and removed on a roller conveyor to fork-lift or other conveyance.

The F.M.C. combined pallet-loader-unloader is a "unitized" machine comprising a case stacker and a case unstacker integrated with specially developed pallet- and case-handling equipment. The machine unstacks a pallet-load of cases and sends them singly on their way. Emptied pallets from the unloader side move automatically into position to receive loads of full cases for stacking and palletization. The system has also been developed to handle barrels and drums.

Automatic Load-assembler for Non-standard Packages

One of the crying needs in automation is for a device that will load trucks automatically without requiring that all crates, cartons or packages be of the same size. This problem is being worked on at the present time.

The machine must either sense vacancies and their dimensions, or it must "remember" past loading operations so that an incoming package can be "considered" in the "memory" for its handling program. It would appear likely that the solution could involve a compromise between both methods.

IS AUTOMATIC ASSEMBLY TRUE AUTOMATION?

In Chapter 1, on the philosophy of automation, I suggested that true automation could be distinguished from mechanization because it possesses the element of progressive data-control. Reading the present chapter you may well wonder where the data-control comes in, either now or in the future. The main scope for data control is probably in protecting a machine from parts of incorrect size. It is in the requirement for vigilance in automatic inspection that data control is mainly involved. Sometimes this will be directly incorporated in the machine, and sometimes it will be a separate process.

And automatic orientation: is this a purely mechanical process or is it one of data control? My own view is that it is basically a data-controlled process, since the mechanical filters required are selective against the unwanted geometry. There is no difference in principle between achieving this result with an electronic eye or by means of the geometrical or gravitational properties of the component itself. Indeed, it is as though the component carried its own identity code and presented it for acceptance or rejection, and this is certainly a most economical and simple form of sorting automation. On the newer developments, incorporated in such machines as the "Transferobot," the data-controlled aspect of automatic assembly is basic.

CHAPTER 13

AUTOMATIC STORAGE

AUTOMATIC storage and warehousing make one of the most rapidly developing sectors of automation. It is strange that storage, such a costly aspect of manufacturing and distributing industry, has in the past been so neglected, and not been brought into line with parallel advances in production. However, the newer concepts of data processing are causing the automatic warehouse concept to develop rapidly, since there is a desirable connexion between the movement of goods and their corresponding paper-work.

Past neglect of warehousing as a candidate for automation appears to have been due to a number of reasons—

1. In a modern manufacturing organization the spotlight is usually on productive technique, and warehousing tends to take second place in the interest of management—except in so far as stores tend to occupy excessive space and represent excessive work-in-progress and capital tied up.

2. A common fault in industries like those concerned with pharmaceuticals and similar packaged products and consumer goods is that warehousing and distribution are not recognized to be the main problems involved. It is not realized that it might be more profitable and important to arrange for rapid discharge of goods from distributing centres than to improve the productive process itself.

3. Warehousing problems tend to be special ones, varying greatly from industry to industry and from building to building, and the stores-equipment suppliers have not in the past been too eager to look for special problems (each further complicated by the particular data-processing system involved) and have preferred to supply standard storage racks, stillages and fork-lift trucks.

4. Costs and savings are difficult to establish. Almost certainly one can rule out any suggestion that a warehouse should be *totally* automated, since it can hardly be profitable to tie up capital in mechanical handlers where a product only rarely moves. Close study is required to determine the exact economics of the partial automation of a stores system.

In approaching warehousing problems with some degree of auto-mation in mind, one must take five factors into account—

(i) The factor of *data*—knowledge of total stocks in the warehouse at any instant, and processing of data on incoming and outgoing goods.

(ii) Getting the product from the producer (or other source of supply) into the warehouse.

(iii) Storage of the goods in a passive state in the warehouse.

(iv) Order-picking, i.e. the issuing of instruction to the warehouse to collect goods together.

(v) Material handling for orders picked and dispatch of goods.

An appropriate data-processing and materials-handling system will be economic in a given set of circumstances if it is properly related to the average size of goods handled, the quantity and variety of goods, the number of incoming production batches per period, the number of outgoing orders dealt with in a period, and the average size of the order with reference to both the number of individual items and the variety spectrum involved. Consideration must also be given to the technique of handling, with particular reference to whether the goods will be handled in their natural state, perhaps involving their natural "packaging," or whether some standard packaging or groupings of packages shall be adopted to facilitate mechanical handling. Thus any approach to automatic storage involves a great deal of work to determine the economic and technical consequences of all these variables.

Hitherto the great majority of warehouses has met the five requirements stated above by means of manual techniques, supplemented by a little mechanization. The clerical work usually consists of reference to stock-record and stock-location cards and listed orders, orders being picked with the aid of hand trolleys.

GENERAL FORM OF AUTOMATIC STORES

Any automatic store has two main parts, a data-processing system and a materials-handling system. The general relationship of these is shown in Fig. 13.1.

Data Processing

The prime requirement of the data-processing system is a "memory" for all current information on the identity, quantity and location of stock. In principle this may be compared to the usual stock-records index, and in practice it will consist of such an existing system, or it may consist of files of punched cards or a magnetic-tape or magnetic-drum memory.

Round this central memory must be arranged three further data-processing functions.

GOODS INPUT

All paper-work on incoming goods has to be processed to determine the change in the stock records, and also to originate specific instructions for the automatic or semi-automatic locating of goods coming into the stores. Such data-processing will involve checking on vacant locations in the stores, and, in view of the magnitude of the problem, it is highly desirable that the memory be of the random-access type, to avoid sequential checking of the whole memory. As we shall see in the description of practical examples of automatic stores, punched cards are the main means for governing the mechanical handling in automatic stores.

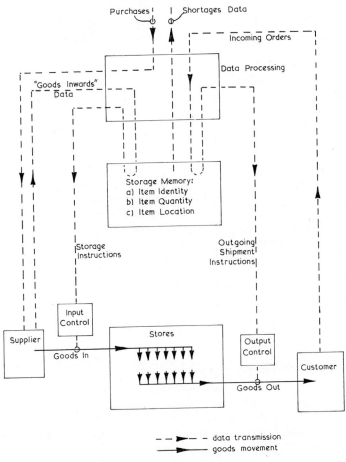

Fig. 13.1.   AUTOMATIC STORES CONTROL

GOODS OUTPUT ("ORDER PICKING")

All incoming orders have to be converted into a form suitable for reference to the data-processing system. The usual technique is to originate punched cards for each item on the order. This information is referred to the stores memory to determine the availability and location of the goods. Goods output instructions are given, and the stores memory is modified to allow for the withdrawals. Goods-outwards instructions to an automatic store are also usually in punched-card form.

PRODUCTION ORDER INFORMATION

The stores memory is periodically scanned for stock movement, depletion and trends, to give information for re-ordering.

Materials Handling

Handling problems in an automatic store are as various as the items handled, so it is hardly possible to generalize more than to say that all movements must be data-controllable by such devices as punched cards or tape, or by push-button programming. There is, however, a special aspect of data handling which can be involved: automatic identification.

Whilst it is possible to devise automatic storage systems which do not require any automatic identification, these will generally be much slower-moving than systems including automatic identification. An automatic identifier can work just as fast as the goods will flow, and there is no need to allow safety margins for goods to clear the system. Automatic product-identification is still in its early stages, but the subject is receiving increasing attention in postal systems, automatic stores and supermarket check-out devices.

There can be automatic identification of goods passing a given point (or their associated conveyor boxes), or of position stations, particularly at junction points.

Some of the techniques developed to deal with these situations are given below.

READING PUNCHED CARDS ON THE MOVE

The dispatcher may place a punched card on goods or their trays. As the goods pass by a recognition station, the cards may be examined by a card reader. The drawback with this system is that the punched card must always be in the right position on the conveyor, and it is difficult to arrange this when the card is attached to the product itself. However, the method may work well enough if the goods are borne by carriers fixed in relationship to the conveyor.

This system can be used either to identify moving goods at a fixed station, or to identify a fixed station from the moving goods.

MAGNETIC MARKING

Another method is to mark cartons or carriers with magnetic ink, usually in binary code, so that magnetic pick-ups can read the identity of the goods as they pass by. This is virtually equivalent to the cheque-marking system. It is usual to mark the carton on its side at a fixed height above the conveyor.

COLOUR MARKING

Coloured pattern codes may be read by several photocells wired to combination logic circuits. Black markings are preferred on buff cartons, but fluorescent inks (illuminated by ultra-violet light) can also be used with appropriately sensitive photocell arrays. Such systems can also be used with lenses. An image of the colour pattern is projected upon a screen with a photocell array in it. Such systems are virtually decoding cameras.

FLUORESCENT INK CODING

The disadvantage of the above systems is that they all require good registration between the moving message and the reading station. Some work has been begun on the use of fluorescent inks in a relative-amplitude code which could be picked up and analysed at a distance without the need for close registration. Different fluorescent inks would have to be combined with varying areas to give a fluorescent amplitude-spectrum appropriately floodlit. The pick-up system requires selective photocells for decoding.

"LOCK-ON" IDENTIFIERS

The human eye has little difficulty in reading a moving message. The eyeball moves to keep a message in register whilst it is read. Electronic devices can do the same. For example, the Optronscope made by the Optron Corporation of Santa Barbara, U.S.A., will automatically lock onto a light mark. It uses a cathode-ray-photo-multiplier servo-system. Similar devices can be built using image-converter tubes. So far these devices have not, to my knowledge, been used for automatic lock-on code reading, but they could probably be adapted for this purpose.

PRACTICAL EXAMPLES OF AUTOMATIC STORES

Practical examples of automatic stores are almost entirely to be found in the U.S.A. The following six examples illustrate the main developments.

9,000 Cases a Day

One of the most advanced automatic stores system in the world is that due to the Alvey-Ferguson company and installed in the Colgate-Palmolive Co. distribution centre at Kansas City, U.S.A. This system uses punched cards, electronic controls and live storage racks. It picks an order a minute, with a daily throughput of 9,000 cases. Since this distribution centre supplies Colgate-Palmolive products throughout the entire mid-west of the U.S.A., speed and accuracy of order-fulfilment are essential.

The main claims for the system are that it gives close control over capital tied up in stock, safer handling, reduced labour costs, and is fully integrated with the company's data-processing procedures.

About 80 per cent of the throughput is handled entirely automatically. Punched cards instruct the storage racks when to release which products into the "conveyorized" dispatching system. Three types of storage and order-picking are involved. In the knowledge of the relative demands for the company's products, the goods are divided into 72 items (80 per cent of the total volume) which are the most active, 130 slower-moving items and 35 live storage racks. The slow-moving items are placed into manually-picked live storage racks, and the very slowly moving items are stored on shelves. The three methods are closely co-ordinated. Manual picking is done close to the central control point. The procedure is as follows (Fig. 13.2)—

1. A set of punched cards for automatic picking, and a list for manual picking, are prepared by the stores office. These papers are dispatched to the central control point. Each punched card of the order can call for up to 99 cases of any one item, and a maximum order would involve 72 cards, one for each line of automatically dispensed items. This paper-work also nominates the truck dock number.

2. At the central point the operator selects a "tote" box which carries a code design so that photo-electric scanning cells on the route will ensure that it eventually gets directed to the correct truck dock. The tote box thus finds its route automatically, and is placed on one of two accumulating conveyors which merge with the lines from the automatic racks, a signal light indicating which of the two is available.

3. The controller places the cards for automatic picking into the card reader, and, while these are being read, he assembles any manually picked items and places them behind the tote box on the conveyor. The card-reader reads, sorts and memorizes the cards at a hundred a minute, and scans an average order in about ten seconds. This information is stored in a memory and fed in the proper sequence to the gates at the end of each automatic rack line.

4. There are three vertical levels in the automatic racks, each leading to a conveyor running across the face. As the impulses from the card-reader reach the lane gates, they release the required number of cases from the lanes to the conveyors. These three conveyors lead to a common point where their contents are accumulated for each separate order. Since the racks can feed out about fifty cases a minute to the three conveyors, close co-ordination is needed to make sure that each train of automatically picked goods reaches the merging points in time to follow the tote boxes and manual items from the manual conveyor. This timing problem is solved by having each conveyor from the automatic racks empty into one of the two accumulating conveyors. These empty at the proper time into the main conveyor, which takes them for stencilling, and then proceed to one of six lines to the truck docks. Since

each powered belt along the face of the rack empties into one of two accumulators, a second order can be picked whilst the first is being processed. At the truck docks, telescoping gravity skate wheel conveyors extend into the truck bodies for fast loading. The system is designed to handle cartons ranging from $5 \times 7 \times 6$ in to $18 \times 18 \times 8$ in.

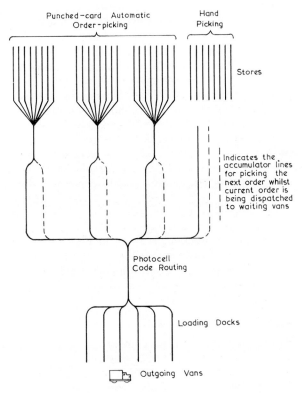

FIG. 13.2.   ORDER-PICKING SYSTEM AT COLGATE-PALMOLIVE

Order-picking with Cartoned Goods

The Mathews Conveyor Co. has done much pioneering work in the U.S.A. on automatic storage, particularly in order-picking cartoned goods. Two installations are particularly well publicized, one at Gallo Sales Co. in San Francisco and the other at Jerseymaid Milk Product Co. in Los Angeles.

SIXTY-SIX VARIETIES

This system consists of a bank of sixty-six roller conveyor storage lines in a three-deck arrangement with one type of product per line. At the lower end of each inclined line is an electrically controlled escapement which will allow one case at a time to flow onto a belt conveyor at right angles to the gravity conveyor. There are altogether three conveyors, each corresponding to one level of the three roller conveyors. The three output belts converge vertically and discharge onto a wide chain-driven live roller conveyor which converges the flow horizontally so that the final result is a single conveyor line flowing to the truck door.

The whole system is controlled by an operator at a control console. He makes up the orders for the various commodities by means of two banks of switches, one for quantity and the other for type. When he has put the order into the control panel, he presses an "order complete" button, so causing the cases to be counted out of the storage lines automatically. While this is happening the operator can be setting up the next order on the control panel.

The system contains 5,000 ft. of conveyor, and stores about 4,000 cases. The system puts out at an average of 1,000 cases per hour. Each order has to be allowed to clear the conveyor system before a succeeding order can be released. Very-slow-moving commodities are kept on static racks near the operator, so that he can place them on the output conveyor while automatic dispensing proceeds.

The input to the system is loaded at the upper end of the gravity roller lines by a crew of four men taking product from bulk pallet loads. The same crew also operate the order-picking systems. One man is at the console. The other three are at the output end, stacking goods on pallets ready for the dispatch trucks.

SUPERMARKET PACKAGED PRODUCE

The system at the Jerseymaid company at Los Angeles operates in a frozen store at $-60°F$ ($-50°C$) and is handling produce packaged for a supermarket. In some ways the system may be regarded as a natural development of the Gallo Sales system described above: the order-picking is done by punched cards.

Until automated, this store handled 500 case an hour. Now it handles 2,000 cases an hour, and a step up to 3,000 cases an hour is visualized. The company handles 350 different frozen-food items, of which 120 are in the automated system and account for 70 per cent of the total volume of goods passed out.

The roller conveyors are interesting mechanically. A length of conveyor is set within another frame on rollers, and a rotating crank gives an 8-in. reciprocating travel. By this means a conveyor velocity of 60 ft./min. is reached without danger of smashes between cases.

Data-processing is based on an I.B.M. 604 electronic calculator and punched-card system. A card is originated for each type of item, and up to ninety-nine of any item can be included on the card. The cards are stacked and fed to a reader which originates electrical pulses and opens the release mechanisms. Thus orders are dealt with in item sequence. I visited this installation in 1960, and was very impressed by the rate at which cases went to the waiting trucks. The limitation of the sytem appeared to be the speed with which the truck loaders could operate.

FIG. 13.3.   AUTOMATIC ORDER PICKING AT COLGATE-PALMOLIVE
(*Courtesy: Alvey-Ferguson*)

The automatic system is topped up by manual effort based on bulk supplies in pallets, with low-level warning signals. One man operates the control system from an office at the end of the truck-loading bay, so that he can see the output end of the system.

Handling Electric Motors

So far the automatic stores described have been limited to those with automatic order-picking, the stocks being topped up manually from static bulk storage.

The "Retriever" storage system, designed by Triax Equipment Co. of Cleveland and installed for the Reliance Electric and Engineering Co., is particularly interesting because it can automatically insert goods into stock and take them out again. The system is applied to the handling of electric motors in the ¾ to 30 h.p. range. An automatically programmed handling machine is set in motion by means of push-buttons and places a crated electric motor into an assigned storage compartment. It will retrieve the motor from the same location.

There are 4,800 motors stored in 5,000 sq.ft. of floor area, about double what was obtained before this automatic system was installed. The 4,800 compartments are arranged along both sides of four parallel gangways (*see* Fig. 13.4) to a height of 21 ft. Each gangway

Fig. 13.4.   Stores Retriever System at Reliance Electric and Engineering Co. Cleveland by Triax Co.

(Courtesy: Triax Co.)

has its own retriever. A powerful roller conveyor at right angles to the four gangways integrates the system.

The data-processing system has foreknowledge of item location. Paper-work coming into the stores gives (*a*) location identity by gangway, (*b*) side of gangway, (*c*) vertical column number, and (*d*) height. To operate the system the stores attendant presses buttons corresponding to this information at the head of the appropriate gangway. The retriever then travels down the gangway, guided by floor and ceiling tracks to the required column position. It turns right or left, and rises to the compartment specified. Extraction is by means of a horizontal platform which slides into position under the pallet. The system then repeats all its operations in reverse, until the motor is out of the gangway and automatically deposited on a table next to the coupling conveyor. Here the operator attaches any relevant papers, and presses a button to transfer the motor onto the output conveyor.

Motors are put into stock in a similar way. The general control technique is to use limit switches to define all points of change of direction, the limit switches being activated by push-button programming on the control console.

Very simple paper-work is used. It is claimed that the automatic stores can operate within one minute of receipt of an outside order. The simplicity is obtained by keeping all location tags in the order office, attached either to inventory papers or kept in an "empties" file. The paper work for incoming goods is sent to the stores controller together with an "empty" location tag giving location instruction, and after the motor has been stored the tag is sent back to the office with the paper receipt. On outgoing orders the inventory will show location: a location tag is attached to the shipping papers, and after the motor has been extracted the tag is sent back to the office for the "empties" file.

This system thus has the advantage that no particular zone is used for the storage of particular products. Space utilization is therefore high. Goods are always being sent in to use up empty space. This "random storage" idea may well be worth more consideration in connexion with the general economics of automatic storage.

Dealing with Non-packaged Goods

The system I shall now describe was invented by Donald Gumpertz and is made by Industrial Electronic Engineers Inc. of North Hollywood, California. It is also licensed in Britain to Solartron—John Brown Automation Ltd. It is essentially an order-picking system. The first installation is at the Brunswig Drug Co., Los Angeles.

The system differs from those I have already described in that it can handle non-packaged goods such as individual bottles, and the whole of an order is dispatched almost simultaneously. Handling at the Brunswig Drug Co. is preceded by considerable data-processing on an I.B.M. machine, which operates through the following stages—

1. The incoming order (often telephoned) is typed on a preliminary invoice.

2. Punched cards are already available covering (*a*) the customer's name and address, and (*b*) each item stocked in the warehouse.

3. Based on the above information, new cards are automatically punched for each type of item on the customer's order, and the pack is sent to the stores control area.

4. The cards are put into a reader. A memory system issues impulses to the discharge chutes, "instructing" them to operate.

Because of the combination of a high-speed card-reader and the memory system, the goods are effectively dispensed in parallel, and fifteen seconds is a typical time for the delivery of an order to the output conveyor. It is claimed that 2,000 orders can be dealt with per day.

Individual chutes hold 1,800 different items, accounting for 50 per cent of the total volume handled by Brunswig Drug Co. (involving 34,000 items). Each supply chute holds about eight hours' supply of goods. The products range from razor blades to napkins, and may be contained in jars, bottles, tubes or multiple packs. Each chute is angled at 20°. At its end there is a counting and dispensing device (electrical), which issues a warning when the chute is nearly empty. The main collecting conveyors take the goods along to a diverter gate by a control bridge. The goods are held there until a packing station is empty and available, and until the order is complete. The paper work to accompany the goods is dropped on to the conveyor at the control bridge, and the whole passes forward for packing.

General Merchandise Co. System

One of the economically most successful automatic stores is that run by the General Merchandise Co. of Milwaukee for mail orders. The company's president forecasts a saving of $250,000 a year, with a reduction in warehouse personnel from 200 to 20 (*see* Fig. 13.5). This installation is again for order-picking, but operates by choosing articles of same type against several orders at once, later sorting the products by customer's order. This involves a principle we have not yet discussed.

A clerk converts the incoming order into a punched card and the cards are collated into batches of 400 orders. The card stack is fed into an I.B.M. Ramac (random access) installation which checks availability, cost and location and then produces a picking card for each item. At this stage the 400 orders are subdivided into four groups of a hundred, and the whole of each group is dealt with at one time (*see* Fig. 13.6).

Each picking card for a given item (one card per customer) also carries a temporary code-number, from 1 to 100, identified with a particular customer, and the stacks of cards are given to manual pickers who select groups of like items irrespective of customer. These groups are then treated by attaching the picking cards (with sticky tape) to the item. The cards reveal the customer's identity in terms of the code-numbers 1 to 100.

The group is released to a conveyer for sorting by customer identity. At the end of this conveyer the goods are placed by hand into a pan conveyer, so arranged that the customer's identity-number is clearly visible. The pans pass a girl scanner, who presses buttons corresponding to the number she sees. This operation activates the memory of a computer so that, when the pan reaches the correct destination point (1 to 100), a signal is given to tilt the pan, which dumps the goods into the customer's "tote" box.

FIG. 13.5.   GENERAL MERCHANDISE CO. ORDER-PICKING SYSTEM
(*Courtesy: Speaker Sorting Systems Inc. and General Merchandise Co.*)

It is claimed that the system can deal with 100,000 items per day, and errors run about $\frac{1}{2}$ per cent. Transit time for an order to be received and processed in this way is $2\frac{1}{2}$ hours.

The analogue computer which remembers the destination for the particular customer is a rotating magnetic disk geared to the dis-

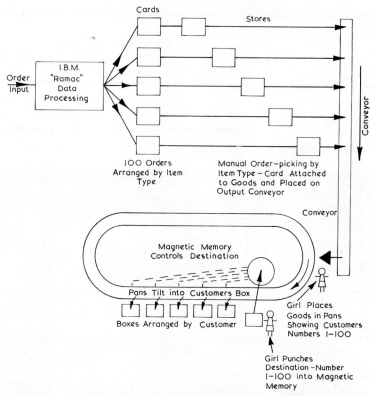

FIG. 13.6. GENERAL MERCHANDISE CO. ORDER-PICKING SYSTEM

tributing conveyor. The distributing conveyor consists of two loops, each 350 ft. long, each operating as a distinct system with its own destination-recognition girls who are each operating at a rate of one item per second. An intermediate memory between the girl's push-button operation and the magnetic-disk memory ensures that the latter is activated at a modular point, so that the corresponding ultimate tipping of the pan is also at modular register with its station.

Miscellaneous Features

In general, the foregoing descriptions cover the principal features of existing automatic stores. These are mainly order-picking systems. But there are many automatic stores in the U.S.A., and some of them have different detailed features. The following are three worth noting—

Diana Stores Corporation, New York. An automated clothing warehouse supplying 208 chain stores. Uses monorail conveyors with ferris wheel elevators, all goods being in trays. A command routing conveyor system is programmed by telephone-type dialling by the input operator.

Food Machinery and Chemical Corporation. An installation for a West Coast refinery handles incoming and outgoing cases of canned motor-oil by means of stacking and unstacking robots, in association with conveyor belts.

H. & J. Heinz Co. at Pittsburg. An input conveyor system in the works counts cases until a pallet load is signalled. The "pallet train" is then command-routed on conveyors to the correct warehouse locality, where it is palletized and automatically elevated to upper floors if required. Advantage is cheaper continuous belt conveying while keeping product in pallet volume.

ORDER-PICKING AS THE MAIN ATTRACTION FOR AUTOMATION

The foregoing practical examples of automatic storage systems in the U.S.A. focus attention on order-picking as the sector which has attracted interest for automation. This conclusion is also agreed by most of those concerned with the supply of the hardware for automatic storage schemes.

Why is this? The labour content in a store is more or less directly related to the number of times a storekeeper has to visit a given location, and the larger the store the more this is true. Imagine a manufacturer who makes a million articles annually, spread over a thousand different products, so that the average movement is a thousand of each article per annum. If he is making so many different products it is certain that he will not be in continuous production on all lines simultaneously. A typical production policy would be to make 20,000 articles a week, spread over 200 different products, so that all products were made every five weeks. If each product were put into storage once a day, he would store 200 different products in batches of twenty per day.

Thus the storekeeper visits 200 locations a day, or 50,000 locations in the year (assuming a five-day week and fifty working weeks in the year). This is a rough relative measure of the input aspect of his stores labour costs.

But such a business implies that all products are in constant demand—otherwise the manufacturer would not make all his product lines so frequently (a batch every five weeks). It would be reasonable to assume that an everyday order involves 500 out of his thousand varieties, and that there will be many such orders, perhaps twenty a day. So his storekeepers have to visit 20×500 or 10,000 stores locations a day, something like fifty times more than the number of locations he has to visit when putting the stores into stock. The figures above are hypothetical, but they are typical of my experience on stores work.

One can generalize as follows: *there is far more stores labour involved in order-picking than there is in input stock placing.* Furthermore, stock input can usually be spread evenly to suit the labour available, whereas order-picking has often to be quick in order to meet transport according to schedule.

The above example also shows the wisdom of the General Merchandise Co. system in Milwaukee, where orders are picked by product type rather than by customer.

Taking the above into account, and considering other aspects of the stores examples quoted, I suggest the following rough guide when approaching an automatic stores study—

1. If a data-processing system is available (e.g. punched cards with sorters), there is every advantage in making this do the maximum possible work if it will save costs on other automation. In particular, it should be employed to arrange the order-picking to involve minimum motion by either stores labour or mechanical handling devices.

Where a great variety of *heavy* goods is involved, entirely mechanized random-location stores (on the lines of the Reliance Electric and Engineering Co.'s system) ensure maximum use of mechanized capacity.

Where there is a tremendous variety of goods, say 20,000 different articles or more, with a corresponding number of storage locations, mechanization of the store istelf would appear to be out of the question. But there is a great deal to be said for processing the orders in batches, so that order-picking is by product type and not by customer. Such a system reduces the labour of hand-picking, and a semi-mechanized system for order-sorting (on the lines of the Milwaukee system) can give extremely favourable results.

2. In those cases where the stores input labour movement will about equal the order-picking labour movement, there may be a case for the total automation of the stores on both input and output sides. I cannot myself visualize exactly what sort of business could be based on such a balanced situation, but it might exist where all products are made simultaneously and there are bulk deliveries. Such a business would be one with a few product lines, say up to twenty, where the input and output flow patterns are very similar. This might apply to potato crisps, cereals, soap and other branded specialities.

3. In general, bulk input to order-picking systems appears to be best dealt with by means of palletized static stocks, manually or semi-manually loaded into the automatic system on receipt of low-level signals.

SEMI-AUTOMATION OF SUPERMARKETS

A "supermarket" is a large retail store where goods are picked by individual customers. The tremendous developments in this field have been in the U.S.A., and no doubt the pattern of development will be followed throughout the world in due course. The object of a supermarket is mainly reduction of labour costs, and considerable thought is constantly being applied to see how further automation can make supermarket more efficient and effective.

One of the major problems still to be solved is loss of goodwill if customers spend excessive time queuing at the exit where the goods are costed, checked, packed and paid for.

The following are three approaches to this problem. They are systems already in operation.

Keedoozle. The customer inserts a special key in a slot below the display of the desired item of goods. This causes a code to be punched in a tape in the key. The result is a sort of do-it-yourself punched card. The key is taken to a check-stand where the punched tape is removed and put into a tape reader. The reader activates a chute carrying the required goods from a warehouse behind the scenes, and thus serves the customer.

Auto-serve. The customer tours the store, picks up punched cards at merchandise displays, and takes his collection of cards to the check-stand. There they are run through a reader, and the goods are dispensed from chutes. The operation can be automatically costed and totalled.

The gun system. The customer is given a coded key. He inserts this into a door behind which the goods are displayed, so opening the door, and removes the goods. The act is automatically recorded on a tape inside the customer's key (a special sort of key with an integral tape gun). At the check-stand the tape is removed and used to compute the customer's bill.

As mentioned earlier, it rarely pays to mechanize stores input, but it does pay to automate the order-picking. This is done free by the supermarket customers (who also like to handle the goods), so there is little economy of money or time to be achieved by mechanical handling. The main problem remaining to be solved is therefore rapid check-out.

Clearly there are many possibilities in automatic identification and costing. It may well be that the ultimate solution will react on packaging techniques: if all goods were offered in packs of identical geometry, it would not be difficult to mark a price on them for automatic reading.

CHAPTER 14

SORTING AND TRAFFIC AUTOMATION

In the analysis of principles given in Chapters 3 and 4, I described *sorting automation* as a major branch of the subject, mainly in relation to processes having a random input of materials. The most characteristic random-input processes are traffic situations such as the public mail, railway goods, distribution and road transport systems. In each of these the destinations and origins of the moving materials are not predetermined by the carrying system, and the system as a whole has to adapt itself to deal with its load. It is necessary to differentiate between a rail system, which is described by its timetables, and a road system, which is random.

A study of random transport systems indicates that they can be divided into two groups—

Group 1. Each moving item has a specific and declared destination. The automation problem is to recognize destination labels and take appropriate routing action.

Group 2. The moving items have undeclared destinations and volition. The automation problem is statistical—how to avoid traffic jams.

In this chapter I shall deal with the approach to each of these problems, illustrating Group 1 with the case of the public mail, and Group 2 with developments in automated road-traffic control.

THE PUBLIC MAIL

The public mail is a remarkable example of a random-input process. The destination of each letter or parcel has to be recognized, and the items must be progressively resorted and rerouted through a network of sorting offices and distributing facilities. The magnitude of the problem is immense, and behind the scenes there is tremendous activity to ensure that letters and parcels arrive on time.

The problem has been a focus for automation studies and developments for many years past. I shall describe some developments in connexion with the British Post Office.

Some years ago an organization known as the M.B.P.E. (the Manufacturers of British Postal Equipment) was brought into being at the suggestion of the Post Office. It organized a demonstration of automated postal operations at Eastbourne in July 1960. The range of equipment included sorting machines, coding systems, conveying systems, stamp-cancelling systems and segregating and facing systems.

Sorting and Coding

The G.P.O. has been collaborating with the Thrissell Engineering Co. on letter sorting. Their machine presents incoming letters to a human operator. He reads the addresses, and by pressing buttons on the console immediately in front of him can route them to any one of 144 separate boxes. The speed of sorting depends entirely on the speed at which the operator can work. A skilled operator can deal with between seventy and a hundred letters a minute.

The letters are automatically fed to a viewing window. The operator can press any one of twelve keys with his left hand, and a similar set with his right hand, the permutations available being 144. This causes the letter to be moved into a "waiting" compartment whilst the next letter comes up into the reading position. While the previous letter is in the waiting compartment, the destination chosen is "remembered" electronically, but if the operator feels that he may have misread the address he can cancel his previous route-choice by pressing a key. As the second letter is read and coded this causes the previous letter to be dispatched into a conveyor. The electronic memory now transfers its information into a mechanical memory, which signals the various mechanical diverters. They first direct the letter to one of five levels, and then to the appropriate final dispatch compartment.

The system still requires a human operator to read the address in each sorting station, and this may have to be done several times on the route. The Post Office has looked into ways for automating here too. One method is for the original sender to inscribe a code word on the envelope. This is put into artificially readable form at the first sorting office, and the letter automatically finds its way through subsequent sorting offices.

The Thrissell Engineering Co. have developed a machine which requires initial presentation to a human operator. He types a code corresponding to the address. The code consists of the first three and the last two letters of the address (Nottingham would be coded NOTAM). As the operator types, the letters are electronically converted into a binary code. Meanwhile, the letter is being automatically clamped against a backing plate. A strip of phosphorescent-coated paper is fed across a gap between the plate and a set of heated code-bars. Solenoids are energized to make the bars strike the coated paper and transfer phosphorescent marks to the envelope. The letter is then released into a conveyor, where it is passed over an ultra-violet lamp and "read" by a photo-multiplier system. This automatically checks

G

the code on the letter against the information fed into the machine from the operator's keyboard. If all is correct, the letter is fed into a multiple conveyor for automatic sorting.

Size Segregation

A machine, developed by the G.P.O. and manufactured by the Mechanical Automation Division of Elliott Bros. (London) Ltd., forms part of a system handling letters at a rate of 72,000 an hour. The machine grades the letters by size, facing and stacking them for sorting in the manner already described, without the tedious manual

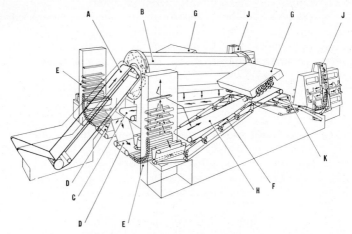

FIG. 14.1.   MAIL SIZE GRADING MACHINE

  A. The feed conveyor receives raw mail from the bags and feeds it to the segregating drum at a uniform rate.

  B. The segregating drum where normal letters and post-cards are separated from thicker items.

  C. The discharge conveyor removes the mail ejected from the drum.

  D. The cross conveyor splits the stream of mail emerging from the discharge conveyor into halves and transports it to the separating towers.

  E. The separating tower breaks up bundles of mail, splits the ensuing stream again and extracts very large letters.

  F. The stepped conveyors are provided to ensure letters settle on their longest edge prior to extraction of wide letters and sorting for length.

  G. The wide-letter extractor for removal of wide items (over 6 in.) from the letter stream.

  H. The aggregating conveyor by which large letters are carried to the manual clearance area.

  J. The stacking unit where letters are sorted and stacked according to length.

  K. The reception area for packets and large letters, often replaced by conveyor.

(*Courtesy: Elliott Bros. (London) Ltd.*)

operations normally associated with such processes. The system is shown in Fig. 14.1. There is an input conveyor which receives raw mail from the collecting bags and feeds it to a segregating drum at a uniform rate. The drum (*see B* in Fig. 14.1) is formed of overlapping slats and is inclined downwards. It rotates slowly, and letters or post-cards escape between the slats to be conveyed away. Thicker items are meanwhile moved down the drum to fall out of the lower end and be conveyed away. The letters and post-cards fall onto a belt and are carried to separating towers in two streams. Letters travel upwards between pairs of rollers spaced at wide intervals. The rollers allow items which are short in the direction of travel to roll across the top of the rollers and drop outside them. Items of mail which are sufficiently long to span the longest of three such gaps are taken from the top of the tower and fall through chutes to conveyors. The shorter letters, emerging from the roller gaps at intermediate levels of the separating tower, are divided between two trough conveyors. The system can be considered as equivalent to a series of sieves, in which smaller letters can escape through smaller openings.

Letter Facing

The above machines merely separate bulk mail into different size-categories in preparation for recognition and stamp cancelling. G.P.O. engineers have worked on a number of alternative techniques for "recognizing" the position of the stamp on mail, and a machine has now been designed. Letters coming from the grader are manually placed in the input of the facing machine, which presents them one at a time to a scanner. A signal is transmitted when a stamp carrying phosphorescent material passes the scanner, and the position of the stamp is automatically found before the letter passes to an inverter. Here the letters are handled, automatically and individually, according to the stamp-position information, and are rearranged so that the stamp is always in the same position. The machine also cancels the stamps, date-stamps the letters, and separates first- and second-class mail. The system deals with between 16,000 and 40,000 letters an hour, depending upon the size group being handled.

Postage Stamps for Automation

Stamps for automatic recognition have been developed by G.P.O. engineers in collaboration with Harrison and Sons Ltd. Original experiments were with electrically-conductive graphite lines on the stamp, but more recent work has been done with phosphor lines. The over-printing ink is transparent, containing an organic phosphor which does not alter the appearance of the stamp. Exposure of the ink to ultra-violet light causes an intense phosphorescent glow for some seconds. This can be detected by appropriate electronic equipment, including photo-multiplier tubes.

Parcel Sorting

Letters are rather more easily handled than parcels, since the latter have considerably more variable shape, size and weight. Many systems are being developed for package-sorting by railways and other parcel distributing organizations. I shall turn to the U.S.A. to describe one such.

A system for package sorting has been installed at a terminal of the Railway Express Agency in Long Island City, New York. It was designed and built by Nelson Laboratories Inc. of Hyattsville, Maryland, in collaboration with the Railway Express Engineering Division. The purpose is to take incoming parcels from road trucks and sort the parcels for reshipment by road to fifteen destinations. One of the main features of the system is that it automatically "recognizes" the different size of parcels and modifies the mechanical handling equipment accordingly.

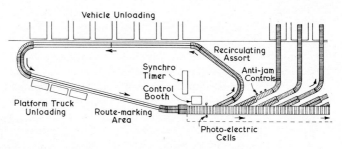

FIG. 14.2.   PACKAGING SORTING SYSTEM AT RAILWAY EXPRESS AGENCY, LONG ISLAND CITY, NEW YORK

Goods are deposited from the incoming trucks on to a loop conveyor (Fig. 14.2). The conveyor is of aluminium slats connected together by a roller chain and riding in Micarta runways on a steel frame. Each slat has a drawer slide on which is mounted a sliding bar with a triangular boot projecting above the conveyor. For segregation these sliding boots are made to move transversely to the direction of conveyor travel, to cause a parcel to be deposited onto a branch system.

The goods travel round to an area where the addresses are read by human operators who mark the packages with a code corresponding to one of the fifteen possible destinations. The marked packages then travel to the human router, who punches the coded destination on a keyboard. The package next moves to a photo-electric system which measures the length of the parcel. This determines the length of the side thrust required to divert the package into its appropriate destination conveyor. These two pieces of information, the destination code and the size, are transmitted to the "brains" of the system, a Pratt and Whitney "Synchrotimer."

FIG. 14.3.   SYNCHROTIMER MEMORY IN WHICH ROUTING INFORMATION IS MECHANICALLY STORED UNTIL PACKAGE REACHES PROPER SEPARATION BRANCH

(*Courtesy: Nelson Laboratories Inc.*)

The Synchrotimer, shown in Fig. 14.3, is an electromechanical memory. It consists of a number of wheels which rotate synchronously with the package conveyor. One complete rotation corresponds to one cycle of the distributing conveyor. Arranged round the periphery of the Synchrotimer wheels are pegs which can be pushed either way in their bearings by solenoids. The particular wheel to be used is selected according to the destination code, and the number of pegs pushed through the wheel is selected according to photo-electric information on package size. The Synchrotimer revolves with the conveyor motion, and the pushed-through pegs eventually work a limit switch which actuates the sliding boots on the conveyor slats. The number of boots is settled by the number of pushed-through pegs (*see* Fig. 14.4). Thus the extent of the side thrust is effectively predetermined by the preceding measurement of package size.

Not only is the number of pushing boots appropriate to the size of the package being handled, but also the extent of the sideways motion is such as to form an effective angle equal to the angle of the second diversion conveyor. Consequently the goods are handled in a smooth manner throughout.

Fig. 14.4.   Package Being Pushed Off Conveyor Belt by Sliding Boots
(*Courtesy: Nelson Laboratories Inc.*)

Sensing fingers under the output conveyors raise an alarm if there is a jam. They bring into operation the full loop circulation system, so that further incoming packages continue to circulate round the primary loop until the jam is cleared. This does not stop the whole system, but only diverts packages from the particular path which is jammed.

AUTOMATIC CONTROL OF ROAD TRAFFIC

One of the principal problems of our civilization is to cope with increased traffic on the roads, and the possibility of some sort of automation is engaging the minds of traffic engineers in all the main countries of the world.

Traffic lights have been automatically controlled for many years. In general they have been confined either to single crossings, with vehicle-operated road-strips regulating the lights, or to traffic streams in which green-light waves are made to progress in a direction favouring the densest flow. Unfortunately, these two concepts are mutually exclusive, since one favours a single intersection whilst the other favours a whole road or area. Therefore much effort has been devoted to designing more comprehensive traffic-light systems with some form of central control, either regulated by the current traffic pattern or by some variable programming system based on historical knowledge of traffic in the district.

At the present time (1962) there are two outstanding installations in the world which merit some detailed description. The first system is in Los Angeles, U.S.A. There traffic volumes are monitored by radar, and a central computer selects a range of alternative programs. This installation is based on techniques used in the Baltimore traffic-light control system, but as it is a later model it also has a few more modern features, including radio control of local lights from the central computing station. The second of these advanced systems is in Munich, Germany, and was introduced in 1958. It is based on central programming of traffic lights, with minor adjustments based on televisual observation.

The Los Angeles System

The Automatic Signal Division of Eastern Industries Inc., Connecticut, has been in the traffic-light-control business for many years. In the past it has developed some quite sophisticated local-crossing light-control systems allowing a great deal of flexibility and local alternative programming. In the Division's latest system (*see* Fig. 14.5), such local variable-program traffic-light controllers are integrated into an entirely automatic centrally controlled system, with full closing of the loop and selection of an optimum program.

It is assumed that there will be certain roads or road crossings where the traffic flow is representative of quite a large part of the surrounding road system, and which can therefore be established as traffic-monitoring sampling points. For example, transferring the problem to London, one could be reasonably sure that a traffic-monitoring point established about Bond Street would give a good representative idea of the traffic over the part of Oxford Street between Marble Arch and Oxford Circus.

It is further assumed that, if one can set the traffic-light system for maximum flow at the sampling point, then nearby lights co-ordinated with the lights at the sampling point will also give optimum flow.

At the sampling point the traffic is separately monitored for flow rate in both directions. The first decision required from the central computer (to which this flow information is fed) is with regard to the direction in which the green-light wave must progress to favour the heaviest traffic. It is also assumed, in general, that applying the green-wave system to several adjacent intersections will produce a better traffic flow than allowing any decisions to be made at an individual intersection.

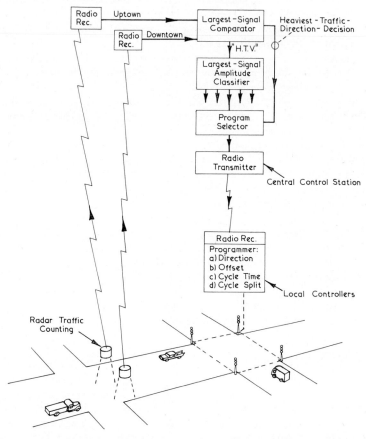

FIG. 14.5.   LOS ANGELES AUTOMATIC ROAD TRAFFIC LIGHTS

The principal rules for computer decision are—

1. The direction of the green wave must favour the heaviest traffic.

2. At individual intersections the total time for the cycle green-orange-red-green must be divisible into different ratios of green and red in order to give more green time to the heaviest traffic direction at the intersection.

3. The total length of the cycle green-orange-red-green must be variable. When traffic is not heavy, this total time can be short, to let odd vehicles through in each direction, and also to give pedestrians as many opportunities as possible to cross the road at the intersection. Correspondingly, when traffic is heavy the cycle time should be long, to give time to the large fraction of the traffic held up behind the lights to pass.

4. The period of time between the appearance of green lights in a green-wave arrangement ("offset time") should be variable. When traffic is thin, vehicles will be travelling near to the legally permitted maximum speed. Then the offset time should be relatively short. When traffic is heavier, the offset time should be somewhat longer. The correct choice of offset times is more complicated than one might imagine, for traffic flow is not maximal at the highest vehicle-speed. At higher speeds vehicles have greater distances between them for braking. It has been calculated in the U.S.A. that maximum traffic flow in a system takes place at about 22 m.p.h., at which speed drivers do not mind moving with very little separation between vehicles. There is also one special case: when traffic is very congested and it is desirable to reduce the offset time to zero, so that all traffic lights in a system move to green or red simultaneously.

These four factors, green-wave direction, cycle split, cycle time and offset time are the main variables to be worked into an automatic traffic-control system.

In the Los Angeles system the problem is divided into two. All alternative programs for the four variables are stored in local inter-section controllers, whilst all program choices are made by the logical system of the central computer, based on radar-measured traffic-flow data. The system (essentially a logical juke-box system of the kind described in Chapter 8 and shown in Fig. 8.3) has the components which are listed below, and which are connected together as shown in Fig. 14.5.

1. Two radar traffic-counting detectors working on the Doppler effect and transmitting impulses back to the central station through a radio link.

2. Radio link.

3. The two sets of pulses are separately added over a fixed time period, converted into an analogue magnitude and compared in a bridge circuit to determine the heaviest direction of traffic flow.

4. The heavy traffic direction and its magnitude having been determined, these values ("h.t.v.") are used for all further decisions. They measure the bottleneck.

5. The h.t.v. is fed to a signal classifier which selects a relay function unique for this range of traffic flow-rate. In turn this relay function transmits a frequency, uniquely associated with this particular h.t.v. over a radio link to the local controllers at the traffic intersection. Reception of this particular frequency calls into operation a particular matrix programmer, which selects the appropriate local programs for cycle time, cycle split and offset time.

The system is an excellent example of what is effectively a logical juke-box computer. It illustrates the value of such a system when applied to problems to which there can be no exact answer, but only an answer which will give reasonable statistical optimization. There could be no exact optimization of a road-traffic-control problem unless each vehicle-driver were to declare in advance his intended destination. Without this information a road-traffic system must always have an appreciable degree of uncertainty. It would

G*

appear to be most satisfactory to devise a system which contains a limited number of possible traffic-light programs and to select these according to current traffic-flow measurement. Nevertheless, such a system is a data-controlled process on two counts: (*a*) by virtue of the traffic engineering knowledge crystallized in the alternative program combinations at the local controllers, and (*b*) by virtue of the data coming from the radar traffic-flow detectors and closing the loop *via* a logical decision as to which is the heaviest traffic direction and what is the classified group rating of the traffic in this heaviest direction. These two decisions and classifications are economic computery in the ideal sense—they involve effective decisions with a minimum of hardware.

Since this system is the end product of many years of experience on local traffic controllers, the equipment has many safety features, alarm devices, and the possibility of emergency manual and entirely local operation. Juke-box computer systems lend themselves to the maximum incorporation of past operating and engineering experience, progressive integration under central control, and ultimately (as in the present example) to full closing of the control loop through the medium of automatic logical functions.

Operational Experience

The Los Angeles installation covers about seventy traffic intersections on two main boulevards. It has two monitoring points, each with two radar detectors for two-way traffic-flow measurement. The system ensures that the green-wave direction favours the morning downtown traffic rush, gives longer green signals during this period, and adjusts the offset time for the likely average speed. In the afternoon the characteristics are automatically reversed by the traffic-measuring apparatus. Away from the times of densest traffic, the system tends to go into balance, with some automatic readjustment of the cycle split to give relatively more time for cross traffic than for main boulevard traffic.

Unpredictable traffic conditions, as during holidays and week-ends, are automatically recognized, and the system adjusted accordingly. The radar detectors also give information on the traffic flow, which is monitored and recorded. The figures are studied for occasional readjustment of the range of choices in the local programmers, and the Los Angeles Traffic Department is continuously analysing the information in a separate computer.

During a visit I paid to the installation in November 1960, I discussed the practical results with the traffic engineers, and although they had not yet compiled sufficient statistics over a full operating year to give an exact answer, the improvement in flow appeared to be considerable—of the order of 50 per cent—and the city was planning considerable extension. This provisional view was confirmed in several discussions with private citizens who had driven over the system before and after its installation.

One very strong impression I received at this installation was of the very small amount of equipment involved. With the completely automated version there is no need for the comprehensive central traffic-light-monitoring facilities that are in evidence elsewhere. This latest form of the system has the advantage that existing traffic lights can be used by the addition of a single local controller with radio reception, so that extensive rewiring is not required. Alternatively, the central control can be coupled by means of a pair of telephone wires using a tone-coding system, with filters to select the appropriate local program.

The Munich System

The centralized traffic control system in Munich is similar in many ways to the Los Angeles system. It is based on the selection of prepared local operating programs, but the loop is closed by human operation or by means of a timed automatic program change.

The system (Fig. 14.6) consists of—

1. Controllers at each traffic intersection, containing a range of alternative programs for cycle time and offset.

2. A multicore wire transmission system from the local controllers to the central station.

3. A system of traffic pads giving traffic flow data to the central system.

4. A central station consisting of:—

    (a) Push-button programmers for setting green waves.

    (b) Push-button setters of cycle time.

    (c) A variable programmer for automatically resetting central programs according to a daily time clock.

    (d) A television monitoring room with sixteen screens coupled to 36 cameras. This gives "bottleneck" traffic information to—

    (e) A human controller who can extend the green-light time at an intersection if required for clearance.

    (f) An information-and-traffic-engineers' calculation room, in which are displayed the traffic counters, and from which information can be sent to the traffic controller to indicate that some change should be made in the programming.

The system is therefore one in which a degree of central programming, based on experience, is supplemented by human intervention from an operations room collecting information on current traffic conditions. The central control man can either intervene temporarily by remote control, or he can set a new program.

The system also has a large display board (Fig. 14.7) showing the condition of all the city's traffic lights. The local controllers have a push-button system which enables a local policeman to take over any crossing and operate it manually. If he does so, the fact is shown by a special warning light on the display board. There are telephones for conversation between the local policeman and the central controller.

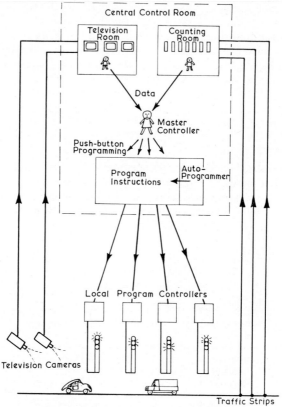

FIG. 14.6. MUNICH CENTRALIZED ROAD TRAFFIC SIGNALS CONTROL SYSTEM

Many detailed refinements are incorporated, arising from know-how gained over the years. One of these is a traffic-light fault-detector with central display. If a fault is announced, the police flying squad is called into action by radio-telephone. Another feature is that at night, or other thin traffic times, all the lights can be made to "wink" amber, so that all cars proceed over all crossings with discretion. The system is particularly suitable for dealing with such emergencies as may involve ambulances or fire engines or police cars, since an all-green route can be quickly programmed and observed by television.

In comparing this installation with the Los Angeles system one has to bear in mind the different original problems. The Munich system grew out of an experiment with the central square in the city, which has a tremendous number of alternative traffic paths. Simple traffic-counting for closed-loop control might well not have sufficed for the problem, and some degree of human supervision might be essential to deal with awkward situations. On the other hand, for cities whose streets are laid out in a regular grid, as is typical in America, radar sampling at a few points would appear to be adequate for accurate diagnosis of the traffic situation and completely automatic regulation.

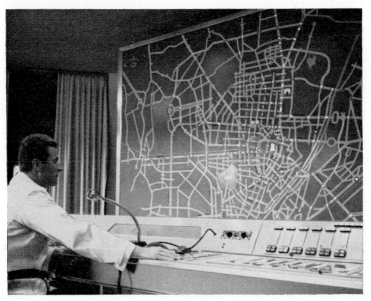

FIG. 14.7.   MUNICH CENTRAL TRAFFIC LIGHTS CONTROL ROOM
(*Courtesy: Signalbau Huber of Munich*)

Traffic Identification and Location

All transport systems, whether air, road or rail, are increasingly developing techniques for the automatic identification and location of vehicles. There are two main systems available at the moment for such purpose: that developed by the London Transport Executive (called "Teletrac"*) for monitoring the movement of buses; and an American system (called "Tracer"*) for monitoring rail wagons, and possibly aircraft on runways.

* Manufactured by General Precision Systems Ltd.

The "Teletrac" System

"Teletrac" is a registered name, covering only the optical scanner that is used. A code plate is mounted on the moving vehicle, and the optical scanner "interrogates" the plate as it passes the light beam of the scanner. The resulting pulses are fed into a data transmission and handling system, and thence on to a suitable display medium.

The code plate carries red and white reflectors that form a binary digital code, easily changed by using a different mask. The size of the plate is determined by the number of binary digits required.

A light source and optical system projects a narrow slit of chopped light across the path of the moving body. The light beam reflected by the code plate travels back through the same optical path and is focused on two photocells, one of which is sensitive to white light, and the other to red light only. The outputs of the cells are demodulated and fed into the "interrogator," which stores the code number of the passing vehicle.

The transmission system uses solid-state logic units throughout, and is designed to operate over standard G.P.O. telephone lines. The stored information at any interrogation point is held until that particular interrogator is triggered from a central control unit. Then the stored information is transmitted and the local interrogator is cleared for further information. The method of handling the received information at the control centre is governed by the subsequent display method or control required.

The system is extremely flexible in that the values of the different parameters can be easily interchanged. For instance, the maximum permissible speed of the moving object can be increased by increasing the space between adjacent reflectors. The range of speeds over which any particular system will operate is in the region of 40:1. With a a rate of 250 binary digits a second, and with a digital word length of eleven binary digits, up to fifteen interrogation points can be used on one transmission line, with the provision that each interrogator is sampled every second. Using this binary-digit rate, a transmission line can also be used for simultaneous speech without having to adopt frequency modulation equipment. If speech transmission is not required, the rate can be increased to 1500 binary digits a second, with resultant increase in information by increased multiplexing, increased word-length, or increased frequency of transmission.

The "Tracer" System

In this system there is an electromagnetic inductive coupling between the vehicle and the interrogating equipment. There are three functional units. They are the *interrogator*, the *response block*, and the *central office equipment*. The response block is powered from the interrogator aerial loop, and sends back a coded signal to the interrogator which uniquely identifies the particular response block. The interrogator translates the coded response signal to audio frequencies, so that it can be placed on a communication channel and relayed to the third unit, the central office equipment. The central office equipment accepts the signal from the communication channel, decodes it, and provides an output which is readily adaptable to any displaying, recording or computing device. The decoded information identifies the vehicle being interrogated, the time of its passage, and the point at which it passed. The interrogation sequence, from origin in the interrogator, through the response block back to the interrogator and to the central office equipment, is as follows.

The transmitter section generates a carrier frequency and a set of modulation code frequencies. The carrier and code frequencies are precisely generated in individual oscillators, and combined to make up the modulated interrogator signal. This composite signal is fed through a power amplifier which drives the interrogator loop with a constant current that keeps an inductive field constant in spite of metal rails, vehicles, or changes in weather. This inductive field energizes the response block when it is passed over the interrogator loop. The inductive loop is an extremely efficient aerial, so there is no appreciable electromagnetic radiation and subsequently no interference with or from radio communication systems (coupling between the response block and the interrogator loop is strictly inductive). The passive response block has a tuned pick-up circuit which couples signal energy from the interrogator loop when the block is in the inductive field. This signal is modified within the response block to establish the unique code, and then returned to the interrogator receiver at frequencies different from those sent out by the interrogator transmitter. The return signal from the response oscillator is picked up by the interrogator loop and fed through a narrow-band filter and receiver.

The equipment is designed to work with separate power and response signal loops, in order to make the equipment flexible. For example, separate receiver loops can be used for simultaneous interrogation of parallel tracks by one interrogator, and hence give a more economical set of equipment for interrogation of parallel tracks. The receiver section has no output until a strong response signal is obtained; at this time it switches an automatic gain-control circuit in to maintain a constant output level, and switches the output into the audio filter and line amplifier. The output from the line amplifier contains groups of audio frequencies that make up the uniquely coded signal which identifies both the response block and the interrogator location. This output of audio frequencies, essentially a digital signal, is sent through a communication channel to the central office equipment.

CHAPTER 15

AUTOMATED MECHANICAL HANDLING

It is almost impossible to separate problems of mechanical handling from problems of automation, since data control almost always has to be imposed with the aid of some mechanical handling. In previous chapters I have described a number of automated processes with dominant mechanical handling features. Thus in Automatic Inspection (Chapter 11), Automatic Assembly (Chapter 12), Automatic Storage (Chapter 13), and Automatic Sorting (Chapter 14), a major characteristic of the system has been automated materials-handling, Mechanical handling is probably the biggest single factor in productive and distributive industry, and the scope for automation in this field is immense.

But I have defined automation as development into data-controlled process, so I shall not deal with simple mechanized conveyors. These merely constitute a continuously available service for transfer of a product between positions.

In this chapter I shall therefore devote myself to *automated* mechanical-handling, which involves principally automated conveyor systems using some degree of data processing, either in programmed operation or to acquire some self-homing characteristics.

SOME POSSIBILITIES OF AUTOMATED CONVEYANCE

The main developments in automated conveyors appear to fall in the two groups: (*a*) systems to ensure that various materials and components are brought together at the right time for assembly, and (*b*) self-routing systems, where the destinations of products on a given conveyor may be different, and the system is programmed so that they find their way correctly.

Feeder Conveyor under Punched-card Control

Both of the above two main groups (synchronized and self-routing) are coming into operation in motor-vehicle factories. There, the aim is to manufacture components relatively independently of hour-to-hour final-assembly commitments on the whole vehicle, but with the ability to call on a supply of components adequate for the daily assembly schedule. The general schematic diagram of such systems is shown in simplified form in Fig. 15.1.

As an example, take a vehicle which has a single type of chassis

197

but which can use three alternative engines, two alternative back axles, and two alternative front suspensions. The essence of the problem is how to make up a schedule of vehicle-types for production on the main conveyor line while ensuring that the correct components meet the main assembly line at the correct time.

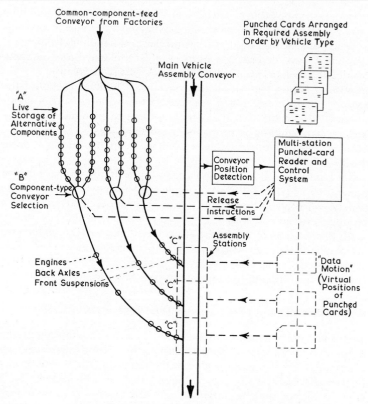

FIG. 15.1.   PUNCHED-CARD CONTROL OF CONVEYOR ASSEMBLY SYSTEM FOR MIXED RODUCTS (VEHICLES)

The starting point for a system of this type is to have punched cards, each of which represents a certain vehicle-type, and on which are punched codings for the particular subassemblies to be used, such as different types of engine. Then the production schedule for the day can be represented by a pack of punched cards arranged in the required order of production and these will be fed itno a "multi-station" punched-card reader. There are several ways of arranging this, but in principle they all consist of a travelling punched-card reader. This is sometimes arranged on a miniature conveyor which is an analogue of the main assembly conveyor, so that as the vehicles travel down the assembly line the punched cards move in synchronism in their miniature duplicate travelling card-reader, probably in some control room. An alternative arrangement is an electronic "memory." The original punched-card information is made to travel around the memory in synchronism with the movement of the main assembly conveyor. This sort of system can be used to call components on to the line at the correct place and time. The movement of the conveyor belt itself signals to this command system to "move up one." There is synchronization between *conveyor motion* and *"data motion."*

In order to supply such an assembly line with components or sub-assemblies, it is usual to marshal alternative components in a fully mechanized set of conveyor sidings (*see A* of Fig. 15.1) so that each siding contains only one kind of component. These sidings may well have buffer capacity sufficient for their infeed to be only in rough statistical balance with withdrawals, so that shops do not have to make components in exact synchronization with the main assembly demand.

The first operation is to start reading of the punched card some minutes in advance of the motion of the main assembly line. Time has to be allowed for components to arrive at the main assembly line, and this card-reading establishes the marshalling sequence by calling up components according to card procedures at the buffer-stock outlet at *B* in Fig. 15.1. The components are then automatically routed in the required order to waiting stations at the main assembly line (*C* in Fig. 15.1).

As the main assembly line begins to move, each assembly station works a limit switch which causes the waiting component to be released at the required moment. The main card-reader continues to marshal components in the correct order. Note that the punched cards do not necessarily control the motion of the main conveyor (the reverse is usually true), but they marshal components.

If the main assembly conveyor is a short one, with few stations, there is no need to have a travelling punched-card reader: an incoming card can simply set going the correct sequence of component feeding for all stations simultaneously for a given vehicle-type. But if the assembly line is extensive, this would involve undue accumulation of waiting components at the later stations, and the mechanical handling system is cheaper if a travelling system is used. A further advantage of this arrangement is that the travelling punched-card system is a true analogue of what is happening out in the shop, and it can be "interrogated" concerning progress.

A system working broadly (but not exactly) on these principles has been installed at the Longbridge works of the Austin car factory, the equipment having been supplied by George King Ltd. of Hitchin. Four main assembly lines are automatically fed with chassis frames, rear axles and front suspensions, engines and bodies. The sub-assemblies are brought to the main assembly department from feeder works over 1,000 ft. away, and first go to live storage where they are arranged for correct sequence marshalling to the assembly line stations.

Electronically Controlled Conveyors

Webb Conveyors and Automation Ltd., a member of the Elliott-Automation Group, recently announced the development of an electronic control for overhead conveyors, one which opens up further possibilities in the realm of mechanical handling. The system permits the use of a standard overhead conveyor, without any of the special mechanical attachments which are normally associated with selective handling equipment. It can be adapted to deal with virtually any number of pick-up points and delivery stations.

A typical system, now in course of manufacture, will serve thirty machines. Each machine must be fed with any one of seventy different raw materials. On long continuous runs some machines use the same materials for several weeks, whilst others change their feed every few hours. The flexibility of this particular system is such that feed variations of this kind can be made in less than two minutes by a single operator at a central control console. The thirty machines are fed with raw material from an overhead chain conveyor, carrying fifty 100-lb. bottom-emptying buckets moving at a speed of 30 ft./min. The conveyor passes under pneumatically-operated gates, which control the discharge of materials from the seventy 1-ton bunkers, and proceeds over the machines in a continuous circuit. Each machine has its own hopper, fitted with a minimum-level detector. Pneumatically operated ramps, mounted over the hoppers, are raised automatically to engage buckets carrying materials called for by the particular machine. The contents are emptied into the hopper, and the bucket completes the conveyor circuit before being blown and wiped clean automatically. This installation handles six tons of material an hour, which, with a few minor modifications, can be increased threefold if required.

Here is an illustration of the method of operation. Number 27 machine, on a continuous run, consumes a present minimum quantity of material. A signal is sent to the control console, where it is held pending the arrival of an empty bucket at the appropriate bunker. Discharge is initiated by the console as soon as an empty bucket arrives, and the appropriate material is then conveyed to the machine that has called for it. An important point to note is that the operator can change the feed to any machine during normal shift-working without affecting any of the other machines. The procedure simply involves changing a plug from one socket to another, while the control centre goes on monitoring the supply of material to all thirty machines. Visual indication is provided for the operator's guidance, and shows clearly which machines are calling for materials and what materials are in process of transit.

Mechanized Self-routing Conveyor systems

The above illustrates the essential principle of automated, data-command, conveyor systems. An alternative form of automated system is the self-routing type, in which the goods being carried take along with them their own routing instructions. This implies that the goods being conveyed, or their container, must issue some form of identifying signal which can be read by an interrogation station. Often the signal is given by mechanical fingers which can be set manually to form a destination code; when the article reaches an interrogation station set with the same code, the article is stopped or diverted.

Fig. 15.2.   Self-routing Conveyor System in a Tailoring Factory
(*Courtesy: Valida Maskiner, Sweden*)

A typical system is that made by Valida Maskiner of Sweden. The example shown in Fig. 15.2 is installed in a tailoring factory. An operator can route goods, placed in a tote box on a common conveyor to any other operator in the shop. This is an all-mechanical system, and the "data programming" is done by pressing one of two button-arrays (*see* Fig. 15.3) to give a total of about fifty destination codes. As the photograph shows, a finger emerges beneath each button that is pressed. When the two fingers meet a preset obstruction, a mechanism, powered from the main conveyor, diverts the tote box to the station siding.

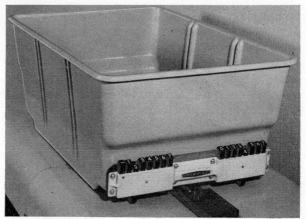

FIG. 15.3.   DETAIL OF PAN DESTINATION SETTING ON ABOVE
(*Courtesy: Valida Maskiner, Sweden*)

New developments in self-routing conveyance include systems which will automatically decode punched cards that are carried on the travelling goods, causing them to be diverted at the chosen station. Other systems use magnetic-tape labels or phosphorescent codings.

DRIVERLESS TROLLEYS

The driverless trolley-tug is a new development in flexible mechanical handling under data control, and one which can be installed in a works with the minimum of erection cost and disturbance. The trolley-tug finds its route at command, and is particularly suitable for moving batches of goods. The tug follows a wire laid $\frac{1}{2}$ in. below the floor surface. The wire carries an alternating current of $\frac{1}{6}$ amp. A small voltage is induced in two sensing coils underneath the tug, and this is amplified by a two-stage transistor amplifier to operate the steering motor. The latter is connected to the steering wheel through reduction gearing.

As long as the tug remains on its correct course the voltage induced in either of the two sensing coils is low and no steering control is exercised. Should the vehicle deviate from its intended course, the voltage induced in one coil will increase sufficiently to operate the steering motor and turn the tug back on course. As soon as the tug is back on course the steering motor is automatically switched off.

If the current in the wire fails, or the tug wanders off course, the starter relays are de-energized and the brakes applied. Joined to the front of the tug by four springs is a bumper. This is fitted with a micro-switch that will open a circuit and de-energize the interlocking relay to stop the tug if an obstruction is met.

For controlling a number of tugs on a variety of routes, the track is divided into blocks as in railway practice. The track is normally de-energized, or "dead," and only the section of track over which the tug is passing, or about to pass, will be "live:" a dead block will always exist between any pair of tugs.

Each tug has an electric program unit which controls the selection of routes in accordance with a prearranged sequence of stopping points. They are chosen simply by pressing numbered switches. The stopping points accord with the sorting arrangements for the respective cartage posts, etc. The tug is halted at these points by means of counting coils that are buried in the floor and energized by the main track current. Thus the program unit is kept informed of the position of the tug in the circuit.

Installation at British Railways

The latest manifestation of British Railways' modernization program is an installation of five E.M.I. "Robotug" driverless trucks now working continuously on inwards-goods handling, from 6 a.m. daily, at the Wolverhampton Goods Station.

This scheme results from two years' study and experiment by British Railways and E.M.I. Electronics Ltd., with an installation of two "Robotugs" at Newton Abbot Goods Shed. The aim of the Wolverhampton scheme is greater efficiency—the movement of a larger tonnage with less manual effort. An attempt has been made to combine all the best features of earlier schemes of mechanization for sundries traffic. The goods station will be filled with 48 wagons, loaded with inward sundries, at the start of each working day. At present an average of 86 wagons is discharged every day, for delivery by road to Wolverhampton and surrounding districts.

The "Robotug" system has several advantages over conventional manual goods-handling. No marker or driver is required, and the savings in wages pay the capital cost of the equipment within a few months. The extreme flexibility of the system enables it readily to meet fluctuations in traffic.

Preliminary sorting helps the cartage checkers: packages are received in unit loads from a slat conveyor, instead of singly, and the checker is also able to load his vehicle in accordance with delivery requirements, thus reducing handling.

The system is completely automatic and inherently safe. Any fault that may occur, either in the tugs or the control system, results in the stopping of the tug or a particular section until the fault is put right. If there is a complete stoppage, owing to current failure or any other reason, the tugs (which are battery-operated) can be controlled by a driver or pedestrian: a walking-stick tiller is fitted to the steering pillar in a matter of seconds.

CLASSIFYING CONVEYORS

A particularly interesting conveying automaton for a special purpose is the "Classomat" system, made by Polymark Ltd for laundries and dry cleaners (*see* Fig. 15.4). In this the identification of the customers' goods throughout the production process is perhaps the main problem.

The machine consists of a 5 ft. "primary" belt conveyor, inclined at approximately 30°, followed by a number of short conveyor sections. These are separately driven, but form a continuous conveyor, running at a speed of 300 ft/min. Any one of the sections can be made to pivot, or tip up, at an angle of 60°; an operator does this by depressing the appropriate key on a keyboard by the machine. As the section, or "flap," opens, it stops driving, and any article that has been fed along the conveyor drops into the opening uncovered by the flap. The item is then deflected into trolleys or bins placed beneath.

The operator marks each garment, and, while it is still being held, the primary belt takes the trailing end up the inclined belt. The operator then depresses the appropriate classification key which opens the desired flap. Then the garment is carried up the incline and falls into the correct classification bin.

The advantages of automatic classifying with the "Classomat" are—

1. Classifying, as a separate job for one operator or more, can be abolished.

2. The incorporation of automatic classifying into the operator's job increases her productivity by 10 to 15 per cent.

MISCELLANEOUS DEVELOPMENTS IN AUTOMATED MECHANICAL HANDLING

There are many new developments afoot in automated mechanical handling, perhaps particularly for the movement of goods in steel-works. One example is a system which will be capable of handling steel billets in the forging process, where it is necessary to inch the product into the press and turn it at the same time. This type of application is likely to involve radio control of the handling system, so that the operator can move about freely.

Radio control of cranes is common on the Continent and in the U.S.S.R. A small, portable, controlling transmitter is held by the operator where the goods are being lifted. He can see exactly how he wants the lifted goods to be placed.

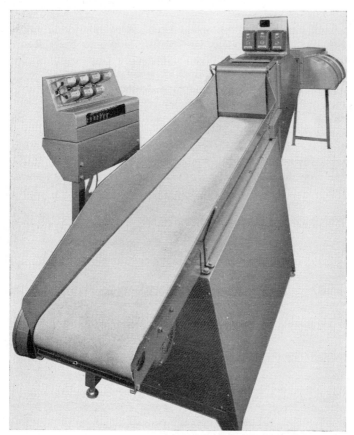

FIG. 15.4.   CLASSIFYING CONVEYOR FOR LAUNDRY INPUT SYSTEMS
(Courtesy: Polymark Ltd.)

Another important development is in gantry cranes for steel-works. They can now be programmed to go to within an inch or so of any place in the area covered. One of the problems here is to locate the precise position of the crane hook, since the distortion of the whole gantry under load may be considerable, and position control with reference to the wall side rails and the cross beam is not sufficiently accurate for some applications.

CHAPTER 16

AUTOMATION IN THE STEEL INDUSTRY

THE steel industries of the world have made remarkable strides in automation. In particular, The British Iron and Steel Research Association has carried out an automation research program on behalf of the whole British industry for several years.

Automation of the steel industry divides into two sectors, the prime steel-making process and the later forming ("mechanical working") process. I shall not deal with the former as it is highly specialized, but automation of mechanical working, e.g. forging and rolling, involves control principles of considerable interest to other industries. The basic flow diagram is shown in Fig. 16.1.

The considerable increase in the output of the industry since the

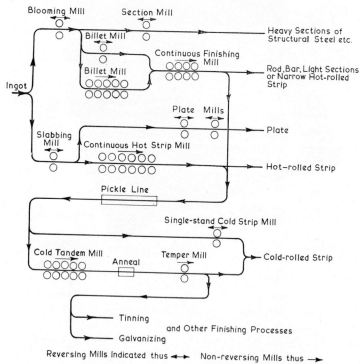

FIG. 16.1. THE FORMING PROCESSES OF THE STEEL INDUSTRY

(Courtesy: English Electric Co. Ltd.)

206

war has been accompanied by improvements in quality, range of product, and operating efficiency. This, to a large extent, is due to the great advances in automation.

Among the many ways in which the specialized controls designed for the steel industry bring benefits are—

(a) They allow faster processing, so directly increasing the potential output without a commensurate increase in capital outlay.

(b) They allow production in larger units, e.g. coils of strip weighing fifteen to twenty tons, with a proportionate reduction in non-productive handling time.

(c) By automatic detection and control of the factors affecting the quality of the product, a consistent high standard is obtained which could not be achieved by manual control. Not only is the percentage of reject material reduced, but the user is provided with a product of a quality previously unattainable.

(d) There is a reduction in the manpower requirement per ton of product, permitting increased production without an increase in the labour force.

(e) There is an improvement in working conditions, for operators' controls can be remote from heat and foul atmosphere, and the danger of injury is reduced.

(f) By greater efficiency in the use of electrical power and gas supplies, the cost of these per ton of product is reduced.

CONTROL OF SCREW-DOWN DRIVES ON PRIMARY ROLLING MILLS

"Primary rolling mills" reduce heated billets in thickness and increase them in length. There are two kinds of primary mill. One is the "reversing" type, in which the billet is passed backwards and forwards between one set of rolls. In tandem mills the squeezed billet is passed through a series of pairs of rolls, each set with a reduced gap between the pair. In reversing mills means must exist to close the roll gap progressively.

The British Iron and Steel Research Association has developed a series of prototype devices for the control required, as reported in a paper read to the Iron and Steel Institute in February 1959, and entitled "Remote Position Control of Screwdown Drives of Primary Rolling Mills." This basic work formed the foundation of a commercial development program by the English Electric Co. Ltd., who have now produced a standard range of equipment for rolling-mill control on the following lines—

Automatic Programming Equipment

The English Electric automatic programming equipment uses a number of standard units according to the functions required. Components in each unit include uniselector switches for storing programs, relays for local sequencing and interlocking, and resistors for the production of output reference signals. The basic unit for a hot reversing mill (*see* Fig. 16.2) can store a maximum of fifty

FIG. 16.2.   CONTROL CABINET FOR STEEL REVERSING MILL
(*Courtesy: English Electric Co. Ltd.*)

programs, and each program controls fifteen passes. When the number of stored programs, the number of passes, or the number of output settings required exceeds those provided by the basic unit, additional small standard units may be incorporated in the equipment. Additional facilities include plug-boards which allow new or experimental programs to be accommodated, and these can be selected in the same way as normal programs. The units are normally supplied without built-in programs, so the temporary plug-board system can first be used to settle a particular program. When this is satisfactory it can be permanently wired into the system. The individual units are as follows—

Selector Unit. The required pass schedule or program is selected by switches which are identified in terms of the dimensions and physical properties of the ingoing piece and the required dimensions of the outgoing piece. Actual screw-down position, manipulator position, mill speed, etc. are not present, so the amount of switching required to select a program is kept to a minimum. Thus it is quite reasonable to include switches for temperature, type of material and other factors which may cause the program to vary.

The setting of the appropriate selecting switches causes a motorized uniselector contained in the selector unit to "home," and this in turn causes the homing of program-storing uniselectors in the function control units and fine-setting units; an arrangement which ensures maximum use of all program-storing uniselectors.

The selector also contains a ratchet-type uniselector which scans, pass by pass, the wipers of all the motorized uniselectors, homed by the motorized uniselector in the selector, thus ensuring correct selection of programs and passes.

Function Control Unit. This unit comprises input and output motorized uniselectors; a terminal board to facilitate wiring-in of programs, together with the highly accurate resistors associated with the reference for these devices; and the relays necessary to control and sequence the unit.

Large Programming Unit. This unit comprises a program-storing uniselector, with programs and passes controlled from the selector unit, and is complete with terminal board as before. The output of this unit, however, is fed into the function control unit in such a manner as to control the output uniselector, and thus the output signal from this unit. Each large program unit therefore doubles the storage capacity of the function control unit for one function. Depending on the external connexions, either the number of stored programs or the number of passes per program can be increased. Any number of these units can be included in equipment to increase the capacity as required.

Fine-setting Unit. As before, a program-storing uniselector, controlled from the selector unit, is included together with a terminal board for program wiring. In this instance the output comprises fifteen relays, signalling in four binary digits. The signal is fed into the function control unit in such a manner as to increase the number of possible settings from fifty to 750. The unit can also be used in place of a function control unit where only fifteen outputs maximum are required, and where this output can be in the form of operation of relay contacts instead of an electrical signal. Mill speed is an example: relays control the speed-setting contactors.

Sequence Control Unit. This unit comprises all the relays and ancillary equipment required for automatic sequencing. It is controlled from photocells, timers, etc. It will be largely non-standard and will depend upon the requirements of the installation.

Plug Boards. Each plug board can handle one function. It is complete with fine setting facilities, and is controlled and selected from the function control and fine-setting units.

Draught Control Unit. For hot-reversing-mill screw-downs an alternative type of setting equipment is available. An initial screw-down setting is made by means of coarse-and-fine-setting switches. For example, in a mill with a 60-in. lift the coarse-setting switch would be calibrated in six steps of 10 in. and the fine switch would be calibrated in twenty steps of 0·5 in. Thereafter, the operator has control of the "draught," or reduction per pass, by means of push-buttons, or self-resetting switches. Normally there would be twelve push-buttons, each calibrated in terms of a total required draught, and operation of any one push-button would cause the distance represented by this button to be subtracted from the original setting determined by the two switches. The interlocks are arranged so that, when one push-button is operated, subsequent operation of any of the push-buttons has no further effect until the signal is cancelled either manually or by operation of the mill. Subsequent operation of any push-button then subtracts the corresponding distance from the remainder, and there is cumulative subtraction, pass by pass. Operation of a further push-button resets the screws to the original position determined by the two switches (which can be preset during the draughting for an edge pass or for a new program).

The calibration and number of setting switches and push-buttons is flexible, and can be varied to suit individual application.

PUNCHED-CARD PROGRAMMING OF ROLLING MILLS

Where a very large variety of information has to be stored the punched-card system offers very attractive possibilities.

If the standard business card is used, a single card will not store information sufficient to meet the requirements of many mill systems. This difficulty can be overcome by adopting the normal business-machine procedure of storing the information on a number of cards and reading these cards in rapid succession. The information for a program is stored on the necessary number of cards. The cards are read by a standard card-reader, and the information is fed from this into an intermediate "memory" which stores the information taken from the cards for as long as necessary. The individual speed- and position-control systems are referred to this intermediate memory for information.

The intermediate memory system, which can be quite a complex transistor network, is not needed when all the information for one sequence can be stored on a single card. The individual control systems are then referred to this card for information. In such systems the card can either remain static and be read by a matrix of photo-cells, or it can move so that each line or pair of lines is read in succession by a line of photocells.

In many mills it is necessary to use a specially large card to store all the information required for each program. Fig. 16.3 shows a

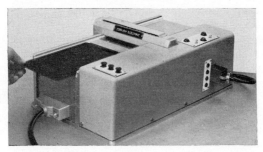

FIG. 16.3.   PUNCHED-CARD READER FOR STEEL-MILL CONTROL PROGRAM
(Courtesy: English Electric Co. Ltd.)

card-reader of the type in which the card is moved pass by pass beneath two rows of photocells. The information for more than one program cannot be accommodated in this type of card-reader. On the other hand, the fact that a single card stores all the information for each program makes it much easier to accommodate and select cards. The cards immediately required can be kept near the operator, who can readily select the card for a particular program.

HOT-STRIP MILLS

A typical modern hot-strip mill may consist of four horizontal roughing rollers and six finishing rollers, which normally reduce slabs approximately 3 in. thick and 16 in. wide to coiled sheets 0·064 in. thick. Each stage is individually driven, and the final speed is up to 3,000 ft. per min. Special problems arise from the change in speed as the material enters and leaves the rolls of each stage. Since the one piece of material is being simultaneously reduced at several points, the roll speeds have to be controlled to within close tolerances.

Small inaccuracies may cause stretching of the material between stages, or the formation of loops which can build up and fall over. The consequent double-thickness entry not only damages the mill rolls, but also causes the following material to pile up. Rolling is better when the strip is not being stretched.

Unlike a cold mill, which accelerates with the material in the mill from almost zero speed, a hot continuous mill is run at a fixed speed, and material enters the rolls with the stages running at this speed. Hence there must be good control of stage speed, inter-stage looping and recovery after the impact of the initial drop. The setting-up procedure for the mill must be simple and flexible, so that rolling programs may be changed quickly, easily and confidently. Furthermore, during actual rolling the stage speeds should be adjustable to allow for variation in slab temperature and for stretch in the mill housings.

The control of the roughing stages is straightforward, since the strip is travelling slowly. It is thick and strong, and there is considerable distance between the stages, so the piece leaves one stage before it enters the next.

For the finishing stages, however, higher rolling speeds require additional control, and two systems are used.

1. Grid-controlled mercury-arc rectifiers connected in parallel banks supply the main busbar system for the motor armatures. The supply is adjusable over the range 360–600 volts and is held constant against changes in load or supply voltage by a magnetic amplifier control on the grids of the rectifiers.

2. The speed of the individual motors is controlled through the mill-motor fields, in order to obtain both accuracy and a fast transient response. Slack is also taken up during rolling, and stage speed settings are trimmed to correct any initial setting-up errors made by the operators.

The automated features are of a negative-feedback kind, to control either at constant load or constant speed, irrespective of fluctuation of reactions from the process.

FORGING CONTROL

The manipulation of hot steel billets between the squeezing operations of forging presses has been studied for some years by The British Iron and Steel Research Association. A paper in the *Journal* of the Iron and Steel Institute (February, 1959) by Chant and Seredynski described an experimental development on a 200-ton forging press at Sheffield (Fig. 16.4).

The press is controlled through a solenoid-operated pilot valve. The controlled motions of the billet manipulator comprise: longitudinal movement of carriage, raising and lowering, and rotation.

Hydraulic motors were chosen for the drives on account of their better torque/inertia ratio. A single motor-driven pump with bag-type accumulator supplied all motions and the gripping jaws.

FIG. 16.4.   EXPERIMENTAL FORGING PRESS FOR AUTOMATED BILLET MANIPU-
LATION
(Courtesy: British Iron and Steel Research Association and Iron and Steel Institute.)

Because of the nature of the solenoid-operated hydraulic control valve, essentially an "on/off" device, the control circuit was made on/off also. A polarized relay is connected between the sliders of two potential dividers, an input potential divider on the control desk, and an output potential divider, chain-driven by the press cross-head. Displacement of one or other of the potential dividers causes the relay to operate in the appropriate sense, and its contacts complete the control circuit through further relays to move the press crosshead. On the downward strokes, when forging, the crosshead is retarded more at the end of its stroke (owing to the resistance of the ingot) than at the end of the upstroke, and different amounts of velocity feedback are necessary for the two directions.

The manipulator is moved longitudinally by a floor-mounted motor, geared through a long rack and pinion. Like the press, the manipulator is controlled by solenoid-operated hydraulic valves. The control system is basically similar to that for the press, with potential dividers to give input and position feedback signals, and a tachogenerator driven by the motor for velocity feedback. In this case, however, error detection is by means of electronically operated relays.

Normal forging practice requires progressive withdrawals of the

H

ingot from the press in successive equal or approximately equal amounts. The controls are arranged so that, after preselection of the length of each withdrawal (1 in., 2 in., 3 in., or 4 in.), successive operations of a push-button cause successive withdrawals of the chosen amount. In addition "tens" and "units" switches are used to set a position to which, after sufficient withdrawal, the manipulator may be returned by operating a "reset" button to begin the next pass.

Rotation is provided by a gear-type hydraulic motor mounted on the forward end of the peel. The control system in this case is very similar to that for the longitudinal motion, power to the hydraulic motor being controlled again by solenoid-operated valves. The only real difference lies in the means by which angular position is detected, and here synchros are used instead of potential dividers.

Press, longitudinal, and rotational controls have been linked in an automatic sequence, the relays which control any motion having to start the next motion. For example, at the end of a forging downstroke a relay is operated to begin the upstroke. Contacts on this relay are arranged in parallel with the starting button of the rotational and longitudinal movements, so that each forging stroke causes one step of longitudinal movement and one of rotation, giving a spiral forging pattern.

The savings due to this mechanization of forging have not yet been measured, but it has been estimated that the time saved could be as much as 25 per cent during a forging operation. Further savings are possible by being able to forge to closer limits, necessitating less subsequent machining. The control achieved is sufficiently promising to justify further work aimed at fully automatic and programmed operation of the forging process.

MEASUREMENT IN THE STEEL INDUSTRY

Measurements of process variables in the steel industry are principally concerned with metal widths and thicknesses, with load measurements, and with the speed of moving materials.

Width Measurement

Metal widths are usually measured either by mechanical sensing elements or by photo-electric means. The British Iron and Steel Research Association have developed a photo-electric system which determines the position of each edge of a steel strip and takes these two positions into account to determine the strip width. This method is only suitable for wide, slow-moving strips, but for fast-moving strips with considerable lateral shake they suggest the use of another photo-electric system. In this the strip partly interrupts a light beam so that the residual width of the beam is an inverse measure of the width of the strip. The advantage of this method is that it is unaffected by shaking of the strip, and only has to respond quickly enough to deal with *width* of the strip, which is the desired measurement. The actual technique employed is shown in Fig. 16.5. A single beam

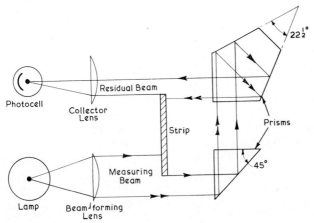

FIG. 16.5.   BASIC OPTICAL SYSTEM FOR WIDTH MEASUREMENT OF HIGH-
SPEED STEEL STRIP
(*Courtesy: British Iron and Steel Research Association and English Electric
Co. Ltd.*)

of parallel light is partly intercepted by one edge of the moving steel strip, and the escaping light passes through two prisms. The second prism reverses the beam, which illuminates the second edge of the steel strip before falling into a photocell. The ratio of light change to strip-width change is kept high by using a single beam in this way, and no balancing system is required (as it would be if there were two independent light sources for each edge of the strip). The general accuracy of measurement with this system is to 0·005in. with a time of response of 0·1 second. Shaking of the strip is self-cancelling. Means are taken to stabilize the sensitivity of the system by using a comparison light beam and amplifier.

This system is the subject of patents and is being developed to the commercial stage by a British firm. It would appear to have many non-contact measuring applications outside the steel industry.

Thickness Measurement

The two main methods of measuring the thickness of metal sheet in rolling mills are nucleonic and mechanical. A typical commercial thickness instrument is that made by the Pratt & Whitney Company. This mechanical system has a pair of rollers between which the strip passes and the separation of the rollers by the strip is magnified by electrical means to give a discrimination sensitivity of 0·0001 in. The gauge head is freely suspended, and $\frac{1}{2}$-in. vertical motion is possible without affecting the measurement. A linkage ensures that the roller axes are always kept perpendicular to the motion of the sheet. The final output is an electrical signal which can be used for control.

Speed Measurement

Nucleonic and mechanical gauging techniques tend to be too coarse in the face of the increased speed of strip and sheet mills, and the requirement for closer control of thicknesses. There is, therefore, a tendency towards a method of measurement in which the speeds of the incoming and outgoing steel sheet are compared, since this can be correlated with the reduction in thickness. It is now being required to measure variations of 1/10th per cent, either in thickness reduction or speed-increase after reduction. The British Iron and Steel Research Association have developed a technique for measuring the velocity of random surface markings on the sheet by photo-electric means. Two slits of light are projected onto the steel sheet, some inches apart, in the path of travel, and the "surface noise" thrown up from the sheet surface is collected by two photo-cells. The "noise" from the upstream photocell is put into a magnetic-tape-delay system which can be varied by varying the distance between magnetic recording and pick-up heads. The memory of the upstream noise is put into an electrical circuit together with the noise from the downstream photocell, and the reading gives a peak when the set delay-time is equal to the time taken for the steel sheet to pass between the two photocells. The delay setting can be kept at the peak-reading position by a servo-system, and the distance between the two magnetic heads is then a measure of the speed of the sheet. The accuracy of reading is considerably greater than the 1/16th in. width of the optical beam slits, and shifts 1/200th in., the velocity can be measured to an accuracy of one part in $200 \times 15 = 1:3,000$ or 0·033 per cent, and this is a far finer measure of thickness-reduction than can be achieved by nucleonic or mechanical gauge methods. Such accuracies have been achieved experimentally, and it seems practicable to build a commercial system to an accuracy of at least 0·1 per cent.

CHAPTER 17

AUTOMATED INTELLIGENCE SYSTEMS

In Chapter 7 you saw that one of the major advances towards automation in the chemical industry was in the adoption of centralized
control rooms of the sort illustrated in Fig. 7.2. A necessary preliminary
step towards automation of complex processes may well be to gather
together all the vital control strings in one place. Such central intelligence or operations rooms became highly developed for all three
fighting services in the last war. Another, more up-to-date, version is
the control room of a large international airport.

Whilst the chemical and oil industries are particularly advanced
in this technique, and are now moving a step further towards computer control as described in Chapter 8, other manufacturing industries in Britain have not made appreciable use of this technique.
But there are significant developments in the U.S.A.

This chapter will be devoted to describing the possibilities of
central automatic intelligence systems for manufacturing industry.
Examples will be quoted from the aviation field.

INDUSTRIAL DATA ACCUMULATOR

The General Electric Co. in the U.S.A. has devised a system known
as an industrial data accumulator ("I.D.A.") which automatically
collects facts from the shop floor and puts them into a temporary
memory for interrogation as required. Typical facts are the answers
to questions like: "which machines are filling what orders for parts?"
and "how many pieces have been produced?" and "what employees
are working on which machines?" and "a piece-part worker changes
his job during a shift—this may mean two different pay-rates—how
much does he earn at each?" All these questions are of the sort constantly being answered in a conventional industrial system by progress
clerks, planners, time clerks, and shop supervisors generally. Normally they divert much activity into writing on pieces of paper, and
supervision is so much less effective.

The aim of the I.D.A. system is to relieve supervisors of their
clerical duties, enabling them to be constantly in touch with their
men and machines for the duties which only they can do effectively.

A schematic diagram of the system is shown in Fig. 17.1. From
this it will be seen that the system bridges the gap between the shop
floor and a computer. The I.D.A. collects all the facts needed for

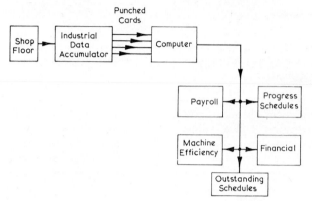

FIG. 17.1.   SCHEMATIC DIAGRAM OF INDUSTRIAL DATA SYSTEM

payroll and production control. The main collected facts are a record of work performed by each worker, production time, and down time. Hours and piece-work by each employee are fully identified with regard to pay rates. At the release of a button in the I.D.A. system, all this information is recorded on I.B.M. punched cards. The cards are then processed in a "Univac" digital computer, which makes up the payroll and gives reports and comparisons for the planning of future production and the information of the management.

Shop-floor Transmission

Communication from the shop floor to the central I.D.A. room is by means of a "machine box" on each machine. The box—

    1. Sends an impulse to the control room each time the machine operates: each impulse turns counters in the control room, giving production totals.

    2. Carries red and green lights which tell the operator and foreman whether or not the machine should be operated.

    3. Has a dial switch which permits the operator to call for any assistance he may need: a recorded message pages a foreman, electrician, etc., according to the switch position.

    4. Has a down-time switch which is operated by the foreman with a key: this turns on red lights on the box and also in the central control room, and starts a down-time count in the control room; and

    5. Permits the foreman to talk with the control-room operator through a portable telephone.

Control Room Equipment

The central I.D.A. control room contains—

    1. Counters that accumulate operating time, down time, and units produced: a subtracting counter shows how many pieces are yet to be made on an order.

2. Equipment identifying employees on the machines: when a man moves from one machine to another, his identifying plug is moved to the panel of the new machine.

3. Equipment noting pay rate, which varies with the employee, the operation, and several types of irregular circumstances: the codes for pieceworkers are set on two dials, and some special circumstances can be entered by means of a wired plug with contacts that can be adjusted to give a variety of number patterns to the card-punching machine.

4. Lights that show whether the machine is operating or on down time.

5. A push-button that permits the controller to make an I.B.M. card at any time: this records all data present in a machine panel, and sets all counters and dials to zero.

The I.D.A. system can continuously create punched cards for subsequent data-processing, and use the classifying and collating techniques of high-speed business machines. In addition it provides a constant communication system between the shop floor and central control, and can reduce down-time, speed up production, and reduce the surplus factor on the number of parts normally made when using conventional progress systems.

DATA-TRANSMISSION SYSTEM

The "Collectadata" system of Friden Inc. is a general-purpose system for data-transmission between different parts of a factory and a central data-processing office. The system consists of an arrangement of two types of instrument—

The Transmitter takes punched cards and transmits the information on them to a central punched-tape recorder. The transmitter has eighteen dials which can be adjusted for adding variable numeric data. Thus if a punched card is accompanying a production order for a hundred items, the fact that only ninety-five items have been made can be transmitted by putting the punched card into the transmitter and setting to "ninety-five" dials to a "work completed" column.

The Receiver accepts the transmitted data from the peripheral punched-card transmission unit, and punches a tape which can be processed in a conventional business machine directly, or translated into punched cards for processing.

The prime use of the system is for factories where production control is by punched-card and where constant progress information is required at a control centre. Control circuits permit several transmitters to share the same cable. If the line is engaged on another transmission a warning light comes up, but automatically reads the local card when free.

Typical applications of this system are—

Production Control. In a punched-card production-control system the order card can be stacked in a loading rack, and when the job is started it can be punched into the transmitter to record the commencement. Material receptions at a goods-inwards department can be similarly recorded for central action, and the progressive movement of material through a factory can be continuously followed. At the end of the day all punched tapes can be processed to produce for control staff up-to-date reports on schedule progress, shortages, lost orders and other vital matters.

Production Time Recording. A standard "time code emitter" can be added to the receiving unit. This records time information as well as other data such as job movements, work starts and completions, etc., and the information can be used subsequently for labour and job-costing calculations.

Inventory Control. A daily record can be kept of stock movements by using a master card for each stock item, the figures being entered by setting dials. Thus stock records can be brought up to date daily, after the central tape has been processed.

DISPLAY SYSTEM BUILT FROM STANDARD UNITS

The "Productograph" system (Farrington Instruments Corp., U.S.A.) is constructed on a standard unit basis (*see* Fig. 17.2). A central control display receives production information (countings and timings). The display consists of numerical and linear Gant-chart counters, plus a lamp display to indicate machine states such as "on operation" or "down time," and causes of failure to operate. Communication of machine state from the shop floor is by means of a multi-push-button box attached to each machine. In addition there is a telephone system, and conversations are automatically recorded on a magnetic tape for checking.

Totalizers record the total number of parts produced in a machine or factory, and also a classified break-down of operating and down times. This analysis may be automatically recorded on a graphical bar recorder, which is continuously charting the production and down-time of each machine, together with down-time reasons.

This highly standardized unit system, which is independent of the use of punched cards and other data-processing devices, has been widely used on the Continent, particularly in Germany.

SYSTEM FOR STEELWORKS

Whilst the previously described systems are suitable for general-purpose flow of information from a shop floor to a central information centre, there is a special problem in the steel industry, where it is essential to keep exact progress records of material movements.

This is because steel billets of varying metallurgical composition can easily lose their identity after heat treatment, and serious processing mistakes can occur unless an exact tally is kept of material identity and position. The British Iron and Steel Research Association have devised an experimental system called the "Tallimarker" for this purpose.

FIG. 17.2.   "PRODUCTOGRAPH" AUTOMATIC SHOP-PROGRESS SYSTEM

It has the following functions—

Information Input. Push-buttons feed in numerically coded information about material at various positions in the steelworks.

Information Store. The information store accepts all incoming data at a central point and stores it in readiness for display at the next operation station after a billet is transferred there, and also for central progress information.

Information Display. The display stations tell an operator about the new billet he is receiving, so that he can process it correctly.

So far this system has been developed to the level of a full-scale model capable of dealing with billet flow through four successive operations. There would appear to be no reason why the system could not be used on a punched-card basis to reduce the danger of an operator keying incorrect information.

H*

ELECTRONIC SYSTEM FOR AIRLINE SEAT RESERVATIONS

A contract was placed in April 1961 by the British Overseas Airways Corporation with Standard Telephones and Cables Ltd. for the supply and installation of an electronic system which will provide ticket-selling offices throughout the U.K. and Europe with up-to-the-minute information on the availability of airline seats on all flights operated by B.O.A.C. The system will also give information on the flights of other airlines associated with B.O.A.C.; in each case the information will be available for flights over a period up to twenty weeks ahead.

Initially, a central magnetic-drum store of flight information in Airways Terminal, London, will serve about a hundred sales personnel using special keying sets within the Terminal Building. Later, the system will be extended, using telegraph circuits, to various points in London, including London Airport. Further extensions over standard telegraph channels will be made to large centres in the United Kingdom, such as Birmingham, Belfast, Manchester, Leeds, Glasgow, and then to a number of cities in Europe.

The system affords great scope for additional geographical expansion, and can be developed to perform other essential reservation functions. These extra facilities include the reporting of sales and cancellations over long distances, automatically and at high speed. When this stage of development has been reached the numerical "inventory" of seats sold on each flight will be made within the system. This development will necessitate changes only in the central equipment, not in the keying equipment being initially supplied.

The existing manual methods by which the space control centre promulgates seat-availability information to all selling offices are expensive in manpower and excessively slow in processing. With the new system, the availability information is given automatically in a few seconds. In the initial phases booking will be by telephone or teleprinter. The "status" information will be up-dated in the central magnetic store by control clerks. In the later phases, this up-dating and seat inventorying will be automatic. Seats will be booked by a single push-button.

The total system is shown schematically in Fig. 17.3. It has four main sectors: the sales clerk's desk set, the control clerk's desk set, the supervisor's console and the information store.

Sales Clerk's Desk Set

Each sales clerk within the system has access to a push-button unit for interrogating the computer store. He has a set of "flight

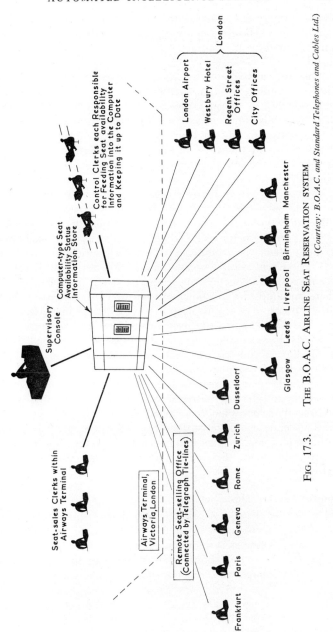

Supervisory Console

Computer-type Seat Availability Status Information Store

Control Clerks each Responsible for Feeding Seat availability Information into the Computer and Keeping it up to Date

London Airport
Westbury Hotel
Regent Street Offices
City Offices
} London

Seat-sales Clerks within Airways Terminal

Airways Terminal, Victoria, London

Remote Seat-selling Office (Connected by Telegraph Tie-lines)

Frankfurt Paris Geneva Rome Zurich Dusseldorf

Glasgow Leeds Liverpool Birmingham Manchester

FIG. 17.3.   THE B.O.A.C. AIRLINE SEAT RESERVATION SYSTEM

(Courtesy: B.O.A.C. and Standard Telephones and Cables Ltd.)

plates"—thin metal plates with standard flight information printed on both sides. These plates are supplied periodically from the control centre, and show the pattern of flight information for twenty weeks ahead.

When the clerk receives an enquiry he selects the appropriate plate, which contains details of related flights, and inserts this into the desk unit. Notches in the plate operate micro-switches in the unit and identify the plate and the side which is being studied. The clerk then presses buttons on his desk unit corresponding to the departure and arrival points on the sector of the route in question. He also presses buttons corresponding to the date and class for which a booking is required.

Having thus set up the interrogation formula, he presses his ASK button to send the interrogation code at high speed to the central processing equipment. There the information store can indicate one of three conditions for each flight on the flight plate: "open for sale," "request" (i.e. where limited seats only are available) and "waiting list." These replies show up as a pattern of lamps on the clerk's unit: green, red/green together, or red respectively. A fourth condition, where no lamps are lit, indicates that for various reasons the flight is not for sale. The status of up to ten flights per interrogation on a given plate can be brought up for consideration by the clerk simultaneously. For example, where ten flights go to a common destination on the day considered, the seat-availability situation on these ten flights will be presented simultaneously.

The mode of interrogation is extremely simple, and enables the sales clerk to offer alternative accommodation where that originally required by the passenger is not available. Seat availability on adjacent dates is ascertained merely by depressing the new date button. Details of the transaction are then sent by telegraph to the appropriate space control unit, where they are converted into orthodox punched-card records.

Control Clerk's Desk Set

The control clerks in Airways Terminal are responsible for keeping the status information for all flights up-to-date in the magnetic-drum store. These clerks note incoming bookings and cancellations. When a flight is fully booked, or booked up to a predetermined figure, they change the status information in the drum store accordingly.

The control clerk's key set is similar to that of the sales clerk, but has additional buttons for feeding the magnetic drum of the information store with "coloured light" status on any or all of the flights on any flight plate. By pressing his ACT button, the control clerk cancels the existing information in the drum store and "writes-in" the new status information so that the sales clerk's interrogation will always yield the correct answers.

The system permits the control clerk to revise flight status in approximately one second, and from this moment the revised information is available for any subsequent interrogation throughout the network. The ability to re-open a fully booked flight on which a number of cancellations has been encountered represents one of the most substantial benefits to B.O.A.C. from installing this system.

Supervisor's Console

The supervisor's console contains keys which enable him to initiate any of twelve different computer programs. Two programs have been described: these are initiated by the sales clerks and control clerks when they press the ASK and ACT buttons. The supervisor's equipment includes a key set for amending and checking information stored in the drum.

The other main programs initiated by the supervisor are: automatic daily up-dating of availability information as each day's flights become redundant: storage of address and the "open for sale" condition when new flights are included: verification of the positions and alignment of information on the drum store.

Information Store

Two drums constitute the information store. The drums have 1,000-bit positions on 320 tracks. This method of storage allows simultaneous reading and writing on many tracks. Flight status records are written along drum lines each of which consists of a number of track positions along a common angular position. The length of a record is therefore determined by the number of tracks which it occupies.

GROUND-MOVEMENT CONTROL AT LONDON AIRPORT

The ground-movement control system at London Airport was installed by Standard Telephones and Cables Ltd. An essential feature of this control system is that the flying control officers and the ground-movement control officers at the control desks are provided with remote-control equipment so that the patterns of airport guidance lighting can be programmed to meet the requirements of a particular aircraft.

A special type of indicator board known as the "Mimic" (Fig. 17.4) displays a miniature diagram of the airport. Small lamps depict the services which have been selected.

The movement of aircraft on the runways and taxiways of the airport is controlled by red and green lights which indicate to the pilots of the aircraft the routes to be used. As the red and green lights are not visible on bright days, "daylight route indicator boards," fitted with powerful white lights, are set up at the side of the routes for daytime use. Some idea of the extent of airport illumination can be gained from the fact that over 7,000 lighting fittings are in use at London Airport.

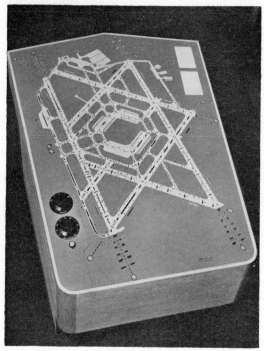

FIG. 17.4.   RUNWAY DISPLAY SYSTEM AT LONDON AIRPORT
(Courtesy: Standard Telephones and Cables Ltd.)

TUNNEL CONTROL AT LONDON AIRPORT

In order to give access to the central area of London Airport without disturbing aircraft movement, it was necessary to construct a tunnel about half a mile long from the Bath Road. The tunnel is of twin construction, to provide inbound and outbound pedestrian paths and cycle tracks, flanking inbound and outbound dual carriageways for motor traffic. Each of the latter is capable of carrying 2,000 vehicles an hour.

Since the tunnel is the only road artery to and from the central area, it was essential to have an efficient system of protective devices to ensure freedom from congestion and accident.

Standard Telephones and Cables Ltd. supplied all the tunnel control equipment; lighting, traffic lights, fire alarms, ventilating fans, water pumps, traffic counting pads and a central control room (Fig. 17.5).

The "Fire and Control" points, eleven in each tunnel, are spaced along the length of the tunnels and comprise fire alarm and telephone boxes with push-button control. Fire alarms are indicated in the tunnel control room in the airport fire station.

FIG. 17.5.   THE CONTROL ROOM AT LONDON AIRPORT FOR SAFETY IN THE
UNDER-RUNWAY ROAD TUNNEL
(Courtesy: Standard Telephones and Cables Ltd.)

The push-buttons give control of "stop engines" signs in the tunnel, flash red lights at the entrances, and bring the traffic lights to red, should there be a blockage in the tunnel owing to accident or other emergency. The "Stop engines" signs are displayed if a column of traffic, standing with engines running, should overload the atmosphere with carbon monoxide beyond the extracting capacity of the ventilating fans. A system is also used to control the number of vehicles in the tunnel by means of red and green lights, in order to prevent congestion.

CHAPTER 18

INDUSTRIAL PROBLEM-SOLVING BY COMPUTER

ELECTRONIC computers were originally designed for scientific calculations, but with the passage of time their use has been extended
to a great number of other tasks, of which the following are typical—

Accounting and similar business operations.
Computation in connexion with producing the programs for
automatic machine tools.
Solving engineering design problems.
Solving traffic distribution problems.
Solving process problems.

In this chapter we shall be concerned with the last three of the
above, since these have a close bearing on the automation of manufacture, design, and distribution.

In Britain, over the last five years or so, the principal computer
makers have established machines which can be used for a fee.
A considerable number of standard computer programs has resulted,
each for solving a standard problem. This chapter will only give a
broad survey of the sort of calculation that can be handled by
digital computers and computer centres.

It is noteworthy that the Cement and Concrete Association at
Stoke Poges has established with the computer manufacturers a
considerable number of computer program specifications related to
problem-solving in structural design. We may expect this lead to be
followed by other trade and research associations concerned with
specific industrial facets.

SOME CIVIL ENGINEERING PROGRAMS

The Ferranti Company, together with outside experts, have produced
a range of computer programs for civil and structucral design problems of which the following are typical.

Solution of Grid Frameworks. An example of a grid framework is
the steel work for a bridge or a roof: the finished assembly is a box-
like structure of connected struts and ties. The engineering calculations
for this type of structure can be extremely complex when great
numbers of steel sections are involved. The original program for this
type of structure was written in 1952 by R. K. Livesley for the Ferranti Mark I computer at Manchester University, and a similar

program was written in 1958 by M. Rooney (then at Babcock and Wilcox Ltd.) for the Ferranti "Pegasus" computer. This program has been written to determine the stresses in a frame having not more than eighteen joints and fifty-six members.

Stressing of Swept Multi-web Structures. There is a program, which runs to thirteen closely spaced pages of mathematical equations, which enables one to determine quickly the stresses in swept multi-web structures.

Beam Sections. A program exists for the solution of design pro- blems in large-span bridges using beams of varying section.

Composite Beam and Slab Structures. Numbers of computer programs have been designed to solve stress problems in beams and slabs arranged in different combinations, including skew conditions.

STUDY OF LOAD ON POWER SYSTEM

In a complex system for electrical power distribution, such as the British "grid," where many power stations feed into a transmission network, it is a complicated problem to predict exactly the values of the voltages, currents, and transmission losses in the system. This information is very important in deciding which power station's load to vary in order to minimize transmission losses, bearing in mind the relative generating efficiency of the various stations.

A Ferranti computer program exists to solve these problems. It can be applied to a system having up to 120 transmission lines, thirty-three junctions, twenty-one electrical generators, and thirty-two load zones. It is of interest to note that the time taken by the computer to come to an initial solution of such a problem is about fifteen minutes, and successive variations of such a problem can be carried out in fifteen seconds.

A "CUT AND FILL" ROAD PROGRAM

"Cut and fill" is the name given to the problem of deciding which road levels will minimize the earth burden transfer required for embankments and cuttings. It is very important to keep to a minimum the earth-moving on such projects, and computers are now brought to bear on the initial calculations. (A corresponding program has also been written for the I.B.M. 650 computer.) The program has been compiled on the assumption that the road route has been chosen and surveyed at regular intervals to give information on the terrain. The computer examines the terrain information, interpolating where survey information does not exist, to decide whether there will be an embankment or a cutting. The end point of the program defines the volumes of earth to be moved. The cost of such computer calculations is of the order of £8 per mile of road.

SOLVING COMPLEX PIPEWORK PROBLEMS

The English Electric Computing Centre at Kidsgrove, Staffordshire, provides a postal computing service for solving problems on the design of pipework systems. At the time of writing it has already completed its thousandth study of this nature. Design problems handled have included those concerned with complicated pipeline systems intended for carrying gases and liquids at high temperatures and pressures in such installations as oil refineries, chemical plants, and heat exchangers for nuclear and conventional power stations and ship installations. The computer programs take into account the stresses and distortions introduced by temperature and pressures at pipe joints. Formerly these involved a great deal of laborious calculation, but the large electronic digital computer has completely changed the outlook for these probelms. The repetition involved in flexibility calculations both for individual pipe-sections and for complex branches makes this work ideally suitable for a digital computer. This enables designers to apply much more rigorous methods of mathematical analysis. The most complicated pipework stressing problem solved to date by the English Electric Company has dealt with a system having ten anchor points, two loops and twenty-three branches, and the solution took about four hours of computer time.

LENS DESIGN

The design of optical lenses is essentially a mathematical problem, and lends itself ideally to electronic computation. In 1957, Taylor, Taylor and Hobson, Ltd., installed a National-Elliott 402 digital computer entirely for the company's optical lenses. This is an outstanding example of improvement in product quality by resort to computer design. The design of a lens involves a mathematical cut-and-try approach, and the speed of a computer permits rapid and progressive refinement of the design factors. In order to check progress in design, between thirty and forty light-ray paths have to be calculated. This used to take a girl about five minutes a path, and the computer takes about one second.

Whilst at the present time lens design in a matter of successive approximation, it may be that an analysis by a computer of its own final calculations will indicate some new method by which the computer itself can design the whole of the lens quite automatically. The position of lens design is rather similar to that of shipbuilding as described in Chapter 10, in that a few years of use of computer techniques could possibly lead to a fundamentally different approach to design optimization.

The use of the digital computer for design work for lenses is typical of a whole range of product-design problems which now have to be carried out by laborious successive approximation. Another example is gear design, including hypoid-axle design for motor cars. Very much time can be saved on many of these design problems by the use of standard digital-computer programs.

LINEAR PROGRAMMING FOR SOLVING TRAFFIC DISTRIBUTION PROBLEMS

Great economies can sometimes be made by the application of computing techniques to distribution problems, such as how best to use transport facilities. The mathematical theory covering the optimization of distribution is called *linear programming*, and it takes this name because the mathematical solution involves a series of linear equations. The answers produced by linear programming are economic answers, i.e. how to arrange loads or distribution in transport systems in the cheapest way. Applications for which mathematical methods are available include—

Most economic storage of goods in warehouses, allowing for transport and handling costs.

Most economic production batching in terms of order forecasts, production facilities and work-in-progress capital.

Optimizing production and blending procedures in oil industry.

Allocation of vehicles in traffic systems, based on statistical records.

Problems of loading and booking which *cannot* as yet be solved by linear programming are those where an individual item has a sequential requirement, i.e. machine-shop loading with sequential operations on a given part, and where the sequential aspect is a variable facility which could have been alternatively loaded with other parts.

Computer services for linear programming problems are furnished by the English Electric Co. and Leo Computers Ltd.

AVAILABILITY OF DIGITAL COMPUTER SERVICES IN BRITAIN

In 1961 there were seven computer companies offering some problem-solving service on digital computers. They were—

British Tabulating Machine Co. Ltd.

A "Hec" computer at the Hollerith Computing Centre, 36 Hertford Street, London, W.1.

Elliott Brothers (London) Ltd.

Two "402" computers at the Computer Division, Borehamwood, Hertfordshire.

English Electric Co. Ltd.

Two "Deuce" machines at its Nelson Research Laboratories, Stafford, and one "Deuce" machine at its London centre, Marconi House, Strand, London, W.C.2.

Ferranti, Ltd.

A "Pegasus" computer at its London Computer Centre, 21 Portland Place, W.1.

I.B.M. United Kingdom Ltd.

An I.B.M. 650 computer at 101 Wigmore Street, London, W.1.

Leo Computers, Ltd.

A Leo II computer at Elms House, Brook Green, London, W.6.

Typical fees for the hire of computers are £35 per hour, more or less, depending upon the complexity and speed of the particular computer. The practical cost will depend upon the time required for programming by the computer-centre staff. If the problem to be solved is one for which a program already exists, then the cost of the operation may only be a few pounds, but if a new program has to be written for the solution of a complex problem, the cost may be of the order of hundreds or thousands of pounds.

ANALOGUE COMPUTERS IN DESIGN STUDIES

Generally speaking, digital computers are particularly suitable for design studies, either on static structures (such as bridges or lenses), or for solving problems involving a considerable number of sequential stages. For dynamical solutions involving time as a variable, the analogue computer is particularly suitable. Here are two typical examples.

Analogue Computer and Chemical Plant Design

One of the most comprehensive analogue-computer studies yet applied in Britain to chemical-plant design was the collaborative study between Laporte Industries Ltd. and E.M.I. Electronics Ltd., made on the latter's "Emiac I" analogue computer. This work referred to the Laporte hydrogen peroxide plant installed at Warrington in 1958, and the studies were carried out to determine design factors.

One aspect concerned the determination of the desirable target points of the many negative-feedback controllers to be used, and particularly to avoid settings which might set up interactional hunting between the controllers. A second aspect concerned study of the capacities of the various vessels in the system to deal with surges and flow variations, especially those involved under starting-up and shutting-down conditions. The main mathematical problems involved were to produce mass-flow equations which could be fed into the computer. Many of the data were theoretical and obtained from the drawing board, and these were supplemented by some information gleaned from a small pilot plant. In general this study was more of a control-system-checking operation than a prime design matter, but was considered successful in contributing advance knowledge of how the full-scale plant was likely to behave when installed. The cost of pioneering this study was £3,500 and a similar repeat venture would probably cost less than half this sum.

Analogue Computers in Automobile Design

Although analogue computer studies have been used in the United States for a number of years as an aid to producing improved suspension systems to suit widely differing road conditions, British manufacturers have, by and large, been conservative in their approach to new methods of studying design problems.

Commenting on this caution, an analogue-computer expert has said: "We in electronics know that with experience gained in simulating guided missiles, and similar problems, we can be of great assistance in speeding up the advanced design of suspension systems through the combination of computer techniques and practical track testing. There are, of course, difficulties in adequately defining the complex non-linear behaviour of the component parts of such systems, but we are confident that, given the right co-operation between both industries, the result would be of great impetus to motoring safety and comfort."

Experience gained in the guided-weapons field, where the problems are in some respects similar, has shown that, by combining computer-analytic studies with experimental work, the most rapid advances in development can be achieved. E.M.I. Electronics have developed their own analogue computer to deal with such problems. Known as the "Emiac II," it is already widely used in aircraft, nuclear and commercial fields to solve problems beyond solution by conventional methods. Analogue computers have the important advantage that they enable the operator to take liberties with time, speeding it up or slowing it down at will. By stating the problems in terms of an equation based on the facts as far as they are known, one may explore the unknown and add greatly to basic knowledge.

An outstanding example of a car whose designers have used computer techniques is the Citroen DS19.

CHAPTER 19

MISCELLANEOUS APPLICATIONS

THE previous chapters in this book have been concerned with practical automation, in each case more or less naturally associated with some industry. In addition to these applications there are many miscellaneous applications which are of general interest because of some technique which may be applied to other industries. Because of their miscellaneous nature it is not possible to make a very connected story out of them, so I shall deal with them at random. They include—

A coal-mining robot.
Automatic cheque-reading.
Punched-tape control of carpet weaving.
Punched-tape knitting of fully-fashioned garments.
Automated teaching.
Automated road-surveying.

COAL-MINING ROBOT

The British National Coal Board's research establishment at Isleworth, Middlesex has recently produced an automatic coalminer. One of the main technical problems of such a machine is sensing the difference between the coal seam and the underlying rock, since it is economical to cut the coal as near as possible to the rock face without cutting into it. The technique devised for this uses gamma radiation from an isotope, directed towards a coal face and scattered back to a Geiger-counter pick-up which differentiates between reflexion from coal and rock. (The sensing principle is illustrated in Fig. 11.6 and described in Chapter 11 on Automatic Inspection.) The machine will sense coal-thickness to an accuracy of half an inch up to four inches total thickness.

The first coal-winning machine to be fitted with this equipment is the "Midget Miner" (*see* Fig. 19.1) at New Lount Colliery. This machine cuts 2 ft. 3 in. of coal from a nominally 2 ft. 7 in. seam. It moves on two skids, in each of which the coal-sensing element is mounted as close as possible to the two cutting heads in the machine. The main body of the "Midget Miner" is coupled to the skids by four hydraulic jacks which steer the machine in the vertical plane. The operator is provided with two meters which record the thickness of the coal floor, and from whose indications he controls the machine's

FIG. 19.1.   THE "MIDGET MINER" COAL CUTTER FITTED WITH NUCLEONIC
AUTOMATIC COAL SENSING AT NEW LOUNT COLLIERY
(*Courtesy: National Coal Board*)

movement. Experience so far shows very great improvement. Accidental cutting into the rock face is avoided, the cut faces are smoother, and less dirt is shipped out with the coal. The next stage is to design an automatic system which will link the gamma sensors with machine movement.

AUTOMATION IN BANKING—CHEQUE READING

Automation of banking is almost entirely in the clerical sphere, but some of the techniques used for automatic reading and character recognition are of great significance for general industrial use, and may one day be applied to the automatic identification of articles in factories. The problem in banks is how to deal with myriads of cheques so that they finally finish up at the originator's bank, or at least in his corresponding central account. This is a good example of sorting automation, and the detailed problems concern (1) the automatic handling of cheques, and (2) the automatic identification of cheques.

The automatic handling has been satisfactorily solved by a mechanical system which will handle mixed cheques between 6 and 8 in. long and from 3 to 4 in. wide. No doubt in due course this problem will be further simplified by using one cheque-size and a single paper-thickness and consistency.

Whilst it may one day be possible to read the handwriting of different individuals automatically, the short-term practical technique is to operate a numeric code. The most advanced system is that developed by the Bank of America. This relies upon a type form known as "E13B" (Fig. 19.2) which has now been adopted as a standard

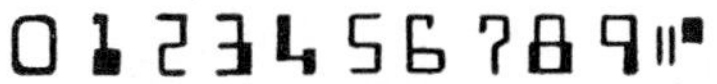

0 1 2 3 4 5 6 7 8 9 ⑪ ▪

FIG. 19.2. "E13B" CODE FOR MAGNETIC CHARACTER READING ON BANK CHEQUES

by the American Bankers' Association. "E13B" character markings could be "recognized" either optically or magnetically, but the latter is the preferred technique since it is unaffected by creases, pencil marks and cancellation stampings. The characters are printed with an ink containing fine magnetic particles, and when the characters are sensed by a magnetic reading head of the sort used in tape recorders, an electronic wave-form is produced. The scanned areas may be divided into squares like a crossword puzzle, and the presence or absence of magnetic ink in a particular square then gives the clue as to the character coded.

The system is not true character-recognition. The printed characters are deceptive—all they do is give out a minimum of coded magnetic impulses, though decorated to look like a conventional number for human reading when required.

TEXTILE AUTOMATION

Punched-tape Control of Carpet Patterns

Axminster carpets are woven on a grid of seven to the inch in each direction, and complicated carpet can use up to 36 colours at any one time. The problem of yarn spool selection was formerly a laborious matter, and it took several months to train operators to do the work. The Birstall Carpet Co. of Yorkshire has installed a Homfray machine, which is an electronic version of the original automatic setting machine developed by the Magee Carpet Co. of Bloomsburg, Pennsylvania. It uses a special punched paper tape to position the yarn at a rate of a thousand yarns per minute. The designer is restricted to a total of fifty colours per carpet, of which he may use 36 colours in any one row at a time. The selection of the order of the yarns on the setting machine is controlled by the paper tape made from examination of the original pattern. The finished machine operation is as shown in Fig. 19.3 and the total programming technique is as follows—

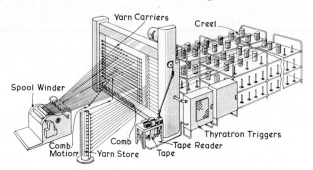

FIG. 19.3.   PUNCHED-TAPE PROGRAMMING FOR CARPET SPOOL PREPARATION
(Courtesy: Control Engineering and Birstall Carpet Co. Ltd.)

1. Each row of the carpet is broken down into "colour shots." There will be 252 such shots in a 36-in. row, and the programming must arrange for one of the thirty-six colours permitted in each row to be presented at the appropriate colour shot. An enlarged master diagram of the colour shots is first prepared for each row: this is the design "blueprint."

2. A 6-in. paper tape is arranged to have thirty-six possible punchings across its width. The holes punched are a code for the colour selection, and the rows lengthwise down the tape represent successive colour shots. A simple cursor enables a human setter to read from the "blueprint" and key in the corresponding punches. (Note: If the original blueprint had been magnetically coded as described in the previous section on banking automation, there would seem to be no reason why the preparation of the punched tape could not be automatic.)

3. A punching in a spare 37th row of the tape marks the end of a row of 252 colour shots.

4. The tape is processed through a counting system which records the number of shots of like colour and thus assesses the total coloured-yarn demand.

5. The tape is then inserted into the reader of the Homfray setting machine. This consists of three sections: a reservoir of spools of different colours, the colour selection system, and the final mixed-colour spool winder. This machine is of complexity comparable to that of all textile machines. The punched tape controls the selection of yarn colours and arranges that they are sequentially collected on the spool winder.

Tailor Knitting

The Macqueen tailor-knitting system is a highly automated arrangement designed to produce three-dimensionally fashioned knitted garments such as ladies' dresses.

The system is a most advanced example of almost complete automation in an important sector of the clothing industry. It is a good illustration of the possibilities of automation, for garments made by it can be high-quality fully-fashioned products with no waste of material. The knitting machine itself is only one part of an integrated system which includes special equipment right back to the fashion design stage. In many ways the system is closely analagous to the Ferranti machine-tool-control system described in Chapter 9, but for a totally different end-product.

After the garment has been designed, the essential working instructions are transferred first to squared graph paper and from this on to rolls of chart paper. One roll is for control functions, and either one or two further rolls are for the patterning. The information provided includes the stitch length, the course length, the nature of the yarn, and other technical information. The rolls of coded chart paper are fed into a tape perforator desk where they are optically projected on to a screen in front of an operator who punches a keyboard to create a $5\frac{1}{2}$ in. wide perforated plastics tape.

This tape is then put into a code reader associated with a master control cubicle. The reader decodes and amplifies the instructions to feed up to eight individual machine-control cubicles, which in turn can control eight individual knitting machines.

On the knitting machine itself, at every position on the tape where there is a hole, a corresponding needle is selected to knit and the stitch length is similarly controlled.

The travel of the knitting cam-box across the machine is limited to the length of the particular course being knitted, so that the cam-box does not have to traverse the whole width of the machine for each course. This restriction of movement is estimated to save an average of 35 per cent of the total knitting time when knitting an average dress.

The total capital costs of a six-machine unit using this system are estimated at £130,000. In spite of this high cost, the break-even point compared with previous methods is something under fifty per cent of full load. The average time to knit a fully fashioned dress is about fifty minutes, and it is claimed that the system could show about ten to fifteen per cent savings over present methods.

AUTOMATED TEACHING

The electronic "Autotutor" made by U.S. Industries Inc. is typical of several modern devices aimed at the speeding-up of teaching.

A 35 mm film is back-projected on to a screen so that the picture faces the pupil. The picture presented to the pupil is one page of a lesson. At the end of the page are questions, each with a set of numbered answers. Only one of the answers is correct. When the pupil has decided which he considers to be the correct answer, he presses his chosen-numbered button and the next frame is projected. At the top of the new page the pupil is told that he is either right or wrong. The matter lower on the page takes his lesson further, or tells him how he went wrong, and then sets him further questions. Since the "pages" (frames) of the film are in a scrambled order the pupil is unable to go forward until he has given correct answers to all the questions. Matters are so arranged that he is not even able to go back to a previous page and learn by trial and error. The machine examines without leaving any possibility of cheating. Furthermore, by measuring the time taken to progress through the film "book," the machine can give an automatic intelligence rating based partly on speed and partly on the number of mistakes made. It is claimed that this method of teaching is better than direct methods because at no time can a pupil get out of his depth. Progress can only be made as fast as the pupil can assimilate knowledge. The device is being adopted by U.S. military and other Government authorities for rapid teaching of routine.

ROAD SURVEYING AND CALCULATION AUTOMATED

In both Canada and America there is considerable activity towards automation of road surveying and route calculation. It is considered in some quarters that these methods may reduce the time involved in highway planning by thirty to fifty per cent. Typical developments are on the following lines—

1. Electronic surveying instruments such as the "Tellurometer" measure distances accurately over the range 500 ft to forty miles, over any type of terrain. This microwave system has an accuracy of 11 inches in forty miles, and the receiver and transmitter do not have to be in visual communication with each other. By the use of helicopters an immense amount of territory can be quickly surveyed.

2. A Canadian invention known as "Auscor" is a device for facilitating the production of ground elevation contours from overlapping aerial photographs. It works at a speed up to a hundred times faster than existing manually-operated steroscopic plotting machines. It takes position elevations from aerial photographs almost instantaneously, and can plot cross-sections in a matter of minutes.

3. The "Phonotrix" process combines the outputs from an automatic plotting machine to produce a punched tape from which an I.B.M. 650 computer finds optimum road routings, i.e. routings requiring minimum earth-burden removals for a range of maximum permissible gradients.

AUTOMATION IN PRINTING

The printing industry is perhaps the most mechanized of all industries, since it is engaged in mass production for very-high-volume throughputs. With black and white printing of newspapers and magazines, the techniques of mechanization have been adequate to ensure product quantity and quality. With the coming of colour printing, the problems of quality and registration have required the development of new techniques. Incorrect colour is very readily detected by a reader. Two techniques of automation will be described here, both the product of J. F. Crosfield Ltd. They are known under the trade names of "Scanatron" and "Autotron" respectively.

Making Colour Plates

For colour printing it is necessary to make either three- or four-colour photographic separations through special colour filters, and from these separations the various types of printing surfaces are finally prepared. The physical limitations of the colour filters and the colour sensitivity of the photographic emulsion introduce serious colour and tonal distortions. These, together with deficiencies in the printing inks themselves, and the allowances which have to be made for the various etching processes, all combine to make the initial photographic separations unsuitable for use in their original or uncorrected state.

To compensate for the irregularities, and also to provide the under-colour removal which is necessary when a black printer is used, each of the negatives has to be retouched by hand. This is a highly skilled and laborious job, often involving many hours of hard work, and the quality of the result always depends on the manual skill, judgement and experience of the individual retoucher. Such has traditionally been the practice ever since the introduction of colour printing by the half-tone process. In the modern age the answer to this very complex problem is the electronic scanner. The scanning time is only ten minutes for a 17 in. $\times$ 12$\frac{3}{4}$ in. positive. The total time for making a set of four scanned positives of full size is only fifty minutes: similarly, for a three-colour set, forty minutes. A four-colour set measuring 10 in. $\times$ 8 in. takes less than thirty minutes.

A cathode ray tube (like a television tube) is used. A tiny spot of light scans the face of the tube in a series of very close parallel lines. There are over a thousand lines to an inch, and they overlap so that in the final corrected positive there is no detectable line structure whatever.

The cathode ray tube [see (1) of Fig. 19.4] is mounted horizontally and a mirror (2) turns the light beam through 90°. The light is then split into three beams by means of the lenses (3), so that three images of the cathode-ray-tube face are produced in position (4) in exact register with the three separation negatives. As the spot moves over the face of the cathode ray tube the whole picture area of all three negatives is covered simultaneously and in register.

In the centre position an unexposed plate or film (5) is placed in emulsion-to-emulsion contact with the negative. Were the light spot on the cathode ray tube of constant brightness, then a normal contact positive print would be made from this negative. By varying the brightness of the spot, however, one can impose the required correction, and obtain a positive still that has the sharpness of a contact print.

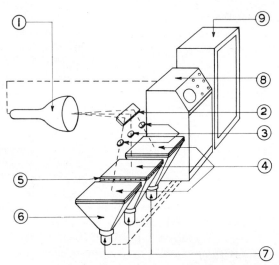

FIG. 19.4.   "SCANATRON" SYSTEM FOR COLOUR PLATE MAKING

1. Cathode ray tube	6. Light integrators
2. Mirror	7. Photomultipliers
3. Lenses	8. Electronic computer
4. Separation negatives	9. Power supply cubicle
5. Corrected Positive	

In each of the outside positions the negatives are in contact with a piece of glass. Beneath all three negatives are reflecting cones (6) which ensure that the light over the whole area of each negative is evenly reflected on to its corresponding photocell (7).

Because the separation negatives have density values corresponding to the red, green and blue values of the original picture, the light falling on the photocells and the electrical currents they produce correspond to the colour values of the original picture. The three currents are then fed into a computer (8) where they are amplified and combined. The resulting voltage modifies the brightness of the cathode ray tube so as to introduce the required correction into the contact positive in the centre position. In this way a single light source both scans the negative and produces the positives.

Colour Registration in Printing Presses

A typical colour-printing-machine layout consists of five printers, the first for black printing and the remainder for four-colour overprints. The problem is to ensure that the four colours are in correct longitudinal and transverse position. I shall describe one out of a number of alternative ways of carrying out the process. In this the first printing-roll puts registration reference marks on the side of the paper, as shown in Fig. 19.5. The horizontal mark is to control the longitudinal register and the inclined mark is to control the transverse register.

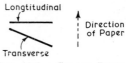

FIG. 19.5.   COLOUR REGISTRATION MARKS

A scanning head contains a lamp, and a very small motor which drives a rotating disk carrying eight lenses. These cause two spots of light to sweep across the edge of the paper 480 times a second. When the spots pass the edge of the scanning-unit window, there is a change in the illumination of two photocells. A motorized magnetic switch is coupled to the printing mechanism. When the impulse from this switch synchronizes exactly with the photocell signal for the horizontal mark, then the printing is in correct length register. When the signals from the two photocells are simultaneous, then the paper is in correct transverse register. Any differences from the ideal longitudinal or transverse register give rise to time lags between the three sources of signal (one magnetic and two photo-electric). These differences are measured and used for correction. Length register is corrected by negative feedback to a compensating roller which shortens or lengthens the paper between two printing units, and side register is corrected by negative feedback to a motor operating a leadscrew and a sideways guidance mechanism.

CHAPTER 20

AUTOMATION AND RELIABILITY

PROBLEMS of reliability will become increasingly important in schemes for automation. Where there is semi-automation, of the kind in which partial break-down of automatic working on one process can be compensated by increased output on a parallel process, reliability may not be of such vital importance, or at least of no greater importance than the reliability of any important machine. Furthermore, in some partial-automation schemes, it is often possible to deal with a break-down by supplementing with human labour and treating the matter as an uncomfortable but temporary emergency.

In more advanced schemes, which are beyond "the point of no return" to temporary human labour, the question of reliability becomes paramount. This is particularly so when an automated operation is at some bottleneck in a factory, where failure threatens to close down preceding and subsequent processes.

These are not new problems, and they have already exercised the ingenuity of engineers, particularly in the aircraft industry, where failure of automatic equipment could have disastrous consequences.

RELIABILITY SCIENCE

As a result, a new sort of science is being developed—a science of designing for reliable operation. The principal features of such design are as follows—

1. It always ensures that a given automatic function is carried out as simply as possible, with the *minimum* number of a given type of component.
2. It provides facilities for rapid diagnosis of incipient and developed faults.
3. It allows for rectification of faults as an operational routine.
4. As far as possible, it incorporates more than one degree of freedom in the system—if part of the equipment fails then its functions can either be rapidly taken over by other equipment or the system can adopt emergency procedure.

The rest of this chapter will be devoted to clarifying further the implication of the above reliability-design features.

SIMPLICITY AND THE THEORY OF SYSTEM RELIABILITY

Any functional system, whether an automated one or just some kind of machine, derives its functions from the effective interplay of its component parts. Thus system reliability is a function of component reliability.

All components can be divided into two sorts: (a) *vital* components, and (b) *non-vital* components. In our own bodies the heart and the liver are vital components, since their failure causes failure of the whole body, the "total system," whereas many bodily tissues and duplicated organs (such as the eyes and ears) are non-vital components, whose failure may be inconvenient but not mortal.

Thus the reliability of an automated-system depends on the reliability of its *vital components.*

In this book we have so far managed to avoid mathematics. But there is a very simple mathematical principle of such importance that it is desirable to introduce it here. This principle is—

System reliability $= R = r_1 \times r_2 \times r_3 \ \ldots\ldots$

> where r_1, r_2 etc. are the reliability measures of the vital components, each lying between 0 and 1.

If a system is made up of three vital components whose individual reliabilities are 0·9, 0·85, and 0·7, then the system reliability is: $0·9 \times 0·85 \times 0·7 = 0·6$. Such a system would be likely to operate for only sixty per cent of the time. If all vital components have the same average reliability the formula becomes—

$R = r^n$

> where r is the average component reliability and n is the number of components.

In the following further discussion I shall use this simple formula in order to arrive at correspondingly simple but very important conclusions. In Fig. 20.1, this formula has been worked out for a

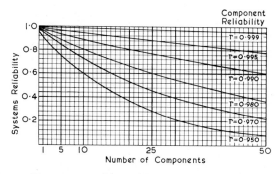

FIG. 20.1.   DEPENDENCE OF SYSTEMS' RELIABILITY ON COMPONENT RELIABILITY AND NUMBER OF COMPONENTS

I

variety of vital-component reliabilities and numbers of components. From the graph it will be seen that—

1. As the component reliability falls away from a very high value, such as 0·999, the system reliability decreases rapidly with the number of components. A system of 25 components, each with a reliability of 0·970, has a system reliability of only 0·47, so would operate correctly for less than half its time.

2. As the result of the above a reliable system must: (*a*) have components of very high individual reliability, *and* (*b*) use the minimum possible number of vital components.

The above is common sense, but practical working-out on such principles is far from obvious. Consider in a little more detail just what is meant by a "vital component."

Take as an example a "black box" for sequencing functions. Suppose that it has the following components and component reliabilities—

1 uniselector switch	$r = 0·9999$
6 relays	$r = 0·995$
100 resistances	$r = 0·99999$
200 soldered joints	$r = 0·9998$

The black box's reliability will be—

$$R_{bb} = 0·9999 \times 0·995^6 \times 0·99999^{100} \times 0·9998^{200}$$
$$= 0·9999 \times 0·97 \times 0·999 \times 0·992 = 0·962$$

From the above you see that the six relays are the weak link in the system. You can probably forget about all the other components, provided that you take steps rapidly to diagnose failure of relays and to replace them. But if you make them plug-in units (for replaceability), with four contacts on every relay, each with a contact reliability of (say) 0·98, then this new factor itself introduces a weakness measured by the factor $0·98^{6 \times 4} = 0·61$. This is a far greater weakness than all the others, and the introduction of plug-in units is thus a retrograde step.

Now what can you do when, by introducing rapidly interchangeable components, you introduce serious unreliability into the system? If you are an electronics designer you may try to find more reliable relays, or you may duplicate relays, but if you are an *automation user* you should insist on being supplied with figures for the *total black-box reliability*, together with figures for suspect vital-component reliabilities incorporated in the black box.

RELIABILITY OF BLACK-BOX AUTOMATION

An automated system is usually made up of black boxes. Assume that an automation user has been provided by his supplier with reliability figures for individual black boxes, and now wishes to assess his total automated-system's reliability. He has first set targets for such reliability, and a reasonable objective might be 0·999, which will give one shut-down hour per thousand hours worked.

Assume also that the system as originally contemplated is made up of six black boxes as shown in Fig. 20.2, having individual relia-

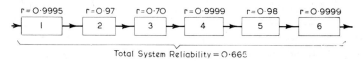

FIG. 20.2.　　　EXAMPLE FOR SYSTEMS SPARE PARTS STUDY

bilities as shown. The user first calculates the total system's reliability by multiplying together all the individual black-box reliabilities, and this gives a figure of 0·665, or 335 shut-down hours per thousand hours worked. That is not nearly good enough. Clearly the system's unreliability is associated with black boxes 3, 2 and 5, in that order, and something must be done about them. Yet if nothing can be done inside the black boxes, there is no choice but to go for a policy of parallel duplication, or even triplication. One may call this a "spare parts policy."

SPARE-PARTS POLICY CALCULATIONS

In order to simplify the mathematics, let us define black-box reliability as the ratio of the number of useful hours worked to the total hours of installed existence. We shall not suppose that a black-box repaired is good for a new lease of life and that repairing time can be forgotten. This is partly because electronic equipment often deteriorates just as rapidly on a shelf as in use. A spare part brought in has also some probability of failing.

The situation is rather like the throwing of two dice. The probability of throwing a double on a nominated number is a very small but it *can happen*. If a black box has a low reliability, say below 0·995, then not even duplication will guarantee continuous operation, although it may make it probable.

The probability formula which I use, and which may be considered pessimistic, is based on the assumption that spare equipment will fill in a proportion of the down time equal to the reliability figure for the failed equipment. Thus if the reliability of an original black box is r, the fraction of its life spent uselessly is $1 - r$, and the spare black box recovers $(1 - r)r$ of this. The system reliability of duplicated black boxes will be—

$$R = r + (1 - r) = 2r - r^2$$

This means that a duplicate system with two black boxes of 0·9 individual reliability will have a system reliability of 0·99. Similarly the reliabilities of systems based on triplication and quadruplication are given by the formulae:

$R = 3r - 3r^2 + r^3$ for parallel triplication

$R = 4r - 6r^2 + 4r^3 - r^4$ for parallel quadruplication

Consider again the example in Fig. 20.2, where the aim was to achieve a system reliability of 0·999. We found that three black boxes (Nos. 3, 2 and 5) made this impossible. Now we can see how much multiplication will be required. The figures are shown in the table below.

STAGE RELIABILITY

WEAK LINK BLACK BOXES	EXTENT OF SPARE PARTS		
	0	1	2
No. 2	0·97	0·9991	0·99998
No. 3	0·70	0·91	0·973
No. 5	0.98	0.9996	0·99999

Adequate total-system reliability could be achieved by duplication of black box 5, by triplication of black box 2, but even quadruplication of black box 3 is not enough to give the component reliability of 0·9998 that is necessary to achieve a system reliability of 0·999.

PRACTICAL LIMITS OF "SPARE PARTS"

We thus discover that a system reliability of 0·999 (one hour's breakdown in a thousand) can be achieved in a six-unit system if the average black-box reliability is not less than 0·9998.

In my view it is not practicable to go further than duplication, and, as a rule-of-thumb guide, any black box with a reliability of less than 0·9998 should be ruled out. This means that the black boxes must be very reliable indeed, and that any shaky components or technique must be eliminated from consideration at the start.

VITAL-COMPONENT RELIABILITY AND PREVENTIVE MAINTENANCE

The ideas of vital-component reliability and "limited" component-life are not the same. By preventive maintenance a vital component with an average life, of say, 200 hours, can be made to give reliable operation in a system expected to run continuously for a thousand hours or more. The user need only know the suppliers' figures for "guaranteed minimum life" or for "trouble-free period before servicing," and work these times into his planned-replacement and servicing routines.

RAPID DIAGNOSIS OF FAULTS

A well-conceived automation system will have built-in facilities to detect declining performance and actual failure, and also to diagnose faults rapidly and indicate the corrective action required. The usual system is to make the system do a "dummy run" periodically. Thus a machine-tool control-system may periodically be requested to go back to the datum point $x = 0$ and $y = 0$. Independent dimensional sensors can then check that the operation was correct. An automatic inspection machine may periodically be checked against a sample with known properties. An alarm can then be raised if the signal does not correspond to the known figures. Such procedures will often indicate trends to failure so that they can be rectified in time, but do not give diagnostic information. Diagnosis requires separate instruments to perform additional functions. Some diagnostic functions may be very complicated, but what is important is that they shall not increase unreliability in the main automatic system by increasing its complication. It does not much matter how complicated the diagnostic system is itself, providing that it is conceived as a *separate system*. We have already seen in an earlier example how the introduction of "plug-in" units for rapid maintenance can introduce more unreliability than it can help to alleviate, and this can also apply to the introduction of diagnostic systems.

All this is simply a question of arranging the circuits in such a way that the diagnostic apparatus never becomes a vital part of the main system. One simple measure is to bring check leads in the main system out to a multi-way socket, and to connect separate diagnosing apparatus to this point when required.

RELIABILITY FACTORS—THE NEED FOR A NATIONAL TESTING STATION

The unreliability of many of the components and systems at present available for automation is notorious. There are very few British suppliers to whom one can go and ask for "vital-component reliability" figures, so it is usually impossible to forecast the reliability of a system. That is why I have seen a great deal of automation hardware in factories under dust-sheets—virtually reduced to scrap. This is a major problem and one which I have discussed with many engineers in user industry. They are rather bitter about it, and are all agreed that British suppliers must be prepared to issue certificates of performance, with reliability information. Nobody is looking for perfection in all this, but one does expect a black-box manufacturer to be able to say: "This equipment will do so many hours between servicing, and for continuous performance you should replace such and such items, at these times." It is essential that manufacturers be able to specify the conditions under which the apparatus will give *continuous service*, apart from specified maintenance and replacement schedules, and they must be able to do this as a result of their own experience of testing the equipment.

The British armed forces are largely protected from these problems because the specifications of their electronic equipment call for evidence of such testing, and the Government's military establishments are provided with their own testing facilities to ensure that the specifications are met. But generally the British electronics industry does not go nearly far enough in this respect.

What is wanted is a National Testing Station, and a generally accepted set of British Standard Specifications for electronic equipment used under industrial conditions. We already have the station in the National Physical Laboratory—the remaining need is for some realization of the urgency of the position, and a little more organization.

EMERGENCY ALTERNATIVE WORKING

With the best design in the world, an automated system will still creak and break down occasionally. To meet this emergency one needs some plan of action. The seriousness of the situation can be at one of two levels: failure may be either temporary or extended.

Time is required either to rectify a fault or to change over to stand-by equipment. Providing that there is some slack in the line, one of these things can be done without embarrassing consequences.

If the failure is "temporary," the usual technique is to forecast the time likely to be required for rectification or change-over, and provide a reservoir to absorb production, plus a small safety allowance, from the working part of the process. Thus it if is forecast that a fault will take ten minutes to clear, a fifteen-minute production accumulator might be allowed for. An implication is that the rectified process must be able to accelerate enough to re-absorb the temporary accumulation, and free the reservoir for a future fault. A number of American automated systems are arranged on these lines. They have product accumulators between each automated section, and each section can work (say) ten per cent faster than the average speed of the line.

The second type of failure, extended failure, requires emergency procedure if production is not to be stopped. This may take several forms, of which the two most obvious are manual assistance and by-passing. Just what can be done in this way depends upon the nature of the process, but a great deal can often be accomplished where there has been sufficient forethought.

All this implies that there should be built into an automated system the very maximum number of *degrees of freedom of operation*. The people who have probably studied this matter more than any others are the aircraft designers and operators. Pilots simply *must* be able to land their aircraft safely, in spite of break-down of machines, weather, or landing systems. The whole philosophy of aircraft control is to preserve a maximum number of degrees of freedom of operation, so that if one procedure is threatened by failure, another system can be brought in.

WORKED EXAMPLE ON A SYSTEM HAVING FOUR DEGREES OF FREEDOM

Take as an example a punched-card weighing system intended to handle packages in a cycle time of ten seconds, as shown in Fig. 20.3. The system has to run 24 hours a day. The weighers are known to have a reliability of 0·97 and a day-time fault-repair requirement of ten minutes (when the maintenance staff are on duty), but they cannot be repaired at night

The system (Fig. 20.3) was designed as follows—

1. The single-weigher reliability of 0·97 was considered to be too low, so duplicate weighers were specified, giving two degrees of freedom and a calculated reliability of 0·999. (From formula: $R = 2r - r^2$).

2. Since some of the weigher faults would be of short duration, an approach reservoir with capacity for fifteen minutes' production (150 cases) was provided for. The weighers were designed to handle an eight-second cycle, so that

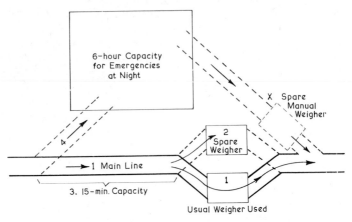

Usual Weigher Used

FIG. 20.3.   AUTOMATION SYSTEM WITH FOUR GRADED DEGREES OF FREEDOM

they could recover a ten-minute break in fifty minutes. This procedure granted a third degree of freedom to the system.

3. If a serious fault were to occur on the night shift, when no appropriate maintenance man was about, the second weigher was to be switched on. The probability that this second weigher would break down was one in a thousand, or one night in four working years. Arrangements were made to divert production to a spare area, if necessary, using manual labour for stacking, until the day shift came on. This unusual occurrence might lead to an accumulation of, say, six hours' production, of 2,160 cases, a pile 20 ft × 25 ft × 4 ft. Corresponding floor space was reserved. Such a back log was considered too great to be recovered by the day shift's automatic weighers, since it would take 6 × 5 = 30 hours, so a spare hand-weigher was specified at X in Fig. 20.3. This would operate on a thirty-second manual cycle, so that the lost weighings would be recoverable over eighteen hours. So a fourth degree of freedom was obtained for emergency working.

Such expensive precautions may only be justified at bottlenecks in flow-production factories, but at these points they are essential.

CONCLUSIONS

At the present time in Britain progressive electronic automation is retarded partly owing to lack of confidence in reliability. In some cases this lack of confidence is fully justified, and a theoretical reliability survey would reveal that many systems simply could not work round the clock. This shortcoming can be rectified by two main steps: (1) users insisting that system reliability is studied at the time when schemes are designed, and (2) suppliers determining vital-component reliability figures for the guidance of users. This latter step could involve the setting up of something like a National Testing Station or equivalent organization.

CHAPTER 21

AUTOMATION ECONOMICS

THE range of practical examples given in the previous chapters is adequate evidence that data-controlled processes are making headway on an increasing scale. But whilst the techniques are of considerable technical ingenuity, and of great interest to those who earn their living in technical positions, decision whether to go ahead with an automation project must ultimately turn on economic factors.

The popular conception of the savings to be made by automating may be that they are in terms of labour, but in most cases this sort of economy is by no means the principal one. Considerations such as improved service to the customer, increased reliability of operation, etc., may be more powerful. In this chapter I shall discuss the general arguments, and also some arguments which may apply only to special instances.

THE COST OF AUTOMATION

The cost of automation will fall under the following headings: (1) preparatory studies; (2) design; (3) equipment and installation; (4) trouble-shooting; and (5) maintenance.

Preparatory Studies

Preparatory studies for automation projects require a thorough conventional work-study to find the costs of operation by *current* techniques. It is a fact of experience that this almost always leads to proposals for improving existing methods. A final determination of the best way of carrying out a process using existing methods will inevitably raise the competitive standard for the automated version.

This is a particularly common result of work study on the possibility of installing date-processing equipment for office procedures. By the time that an existing system has been streamlined and simplified to make it suitable for automation, there may be no case left for continuing with the latter. This need not be an anti-climax, and may be considered as a good reason for studying automation possibilities.

In any case, therefore, the technical *end-point* of work study on existing methods will be simplification and clarification, to define a *starting point* for automation. Let us call this conceptually simplified process the *optimum existing procedure*.

Stage two of study consists of finding what the optimum existing procedure requires technically if it is to be automated. One cannot generalize about this stage of study, except to say that it will differ very greatly according to the different industries and problems involved, and may range over any of the techniques described in the previous chapters.

The project will involve not only technical proposals but a thorough appraisal of the five types of cost described earlier, for comparison with the costs of the optimum existing procedure. The general point which should be emphasized is that a project should not commence with technical studies but with *work study*, related to the user's general objectives. It may well be desirable to call in management consultants or others highly skilled in work study, to ensure that there is no attempt to automate some outdated type of procedure, and that the enterprise is founded on the best possible and most simplified specification.

At this stage it will not normally be necessary to go into exact details of design. It is usually sufficient to make a broad financial assessment.

Design Costs

Assuming that the first study hurdle has been passed, the next problem is that of project design and its costs. These costs will cover—

1. Preparation of an exact specification of requirements.
2. Engineering design of equipment (and this may have to include an allowance for some experimental work if some uncertain features are involved).
3. Process modification design, to ensure that the process will be responsive to the data-control features.
4. Installation design.

In considering automation design costs, notice is often taken of only the second of the above four expenditures, but the other three sorts of cost may be formidable, and are an important part of the economic equation. Indeed, the costs involved on the third factor, process modification, may sometimes well outweigh all other costs.

This may be a good place for me to encourage potential automaters to be prepared to pay separately for the first item above, the requirements specification, sometimes known as the "system cost." At the present time, in both Britain and the U.S.A., users of automated systems are not willing to pay for the preparation of the requirements specification, and they expect an equipment-supplier to recover the cost of his considerable preparatory work in the value of the equipment contract. In doing this the users get very bad value, since the equipment supplier is then bound to make the equipment costs as high as possible to recover his expenses. In such circumstances the buyer must not be surprised to find that everything is gold-plated, including the bill.

Providing that the user makes clear the extent to which he is willing to pay preparatory costs, he will almost always save considerably on the total project cost. Modesty forbids me to suggest that the best procedure of all is to employ automation consultants for this stage of the work.

For the purpose of economic studies on automation projects, all study costs and design costs should be lumped together with the later costs of equipment, installation, etc., and treated as a total capital sum.

Equipment and Installation Costs

Equipment costs are simply a matter of tender, but the cost of installation by the user should be forecast as accurately as possible.

Trouble-shooting Costs

On no account should the economic assessment omit an allowance for "trouble shooting" or "debugging" after installation. Debugging can be a major operation, as those who have installed data-processing equipment have discovered. Under this heading allowances should be made not only for the time involved but also for scrap and loss of output.

Treatment of Total Costs

When the above costs have been assessed and added, the sum has to be referred to management for permissible "write-off" of the capital represented. A fairly conservative policy followed by average firms is to expect to recover this capital cost by savings over three years if single-shift working is involved, or over five years if multi-shift work may be involved. Such decisions will turn on current government policy on tax allowances, process obsolescence possibilities, and possible process overload requirements.

The general effect of such a policy is to favour automation prospects for the process industries. They often work round the clock, and savings after the write-off period are correspondingly greater for a capital investment. This is to some extent confirmed by the fact that it is the process industries which have in the past been more progressive in automation, although a second contributory factor is the greater ease which which such industries can mechanize fully by fluid-pumping techniques.

The costs of capital installation for automation are incurred for three classes of gear—

1. The automating nucleus itself, which may be some data-processing system.

2. Machinery for all associated materials-handling, so that the whole process can be responsive to the data-control system.

3. The links between the control system and the process, particularly the various forms of sensing device and data-controlled actuator.

In practical cases it will often be found that the costs of the second item, materials-handling mechanization, far outweigh other costs, particularly in piece-and/or-assembly manufacturing (as distinct from fluid process) systems. This is because it is much more expensive to mechanize the transport of parts and assemblies than the transfer of fluids and powders. You can well imagine how much more expensive it is to mechanize the movement of automobile bodies by conveyors than to pump the same tonnage of fluids along a pipeline.

THE POTENTIAL SAVINGS OF AUTOMATION

The potential savings of automated systems fall under the following headings—

Labour savings.
Plant utilization savings.
Increase of maximum plant capacity.
Space savings.
Product quality and scrap savings.
Savings due to progressive optimization.
Benefits of progressiveness.

Labour Savings

Providing that the initial work study has been correctly done, it should be relatively straightforward to compute labour savings, compared with probably increased maintenance labour in an automated system. It is my experience that very few automated projects can stand the economic test on labour savings alone. Economic justification is much more likely to be found from other points of view.

Plant Utilization Savings

In general, the major savings to be made by installation of an automated system will be in terms of increased plant utilization. The reason for this is quite simple. A data-controlled plant receives its instructions from some programming device, and, providing that the programs have been correctly prepared, the plant can go into operation as soon as an appropriate "start" button has been pressed.

Thus on a highly automated plant there should be a minimum of "setting-up" time. The production plant can be used to a maximum for its designed purpose, i.e. *to produce*, and not be standing idle whilst preparatory and intermediate setting and adjusting are being done by hand. This is also the major saving to be made with data-controlled machine-tools, but it applies equally well to such other forms of automation as chemical batching.

In order to make an accurate assessment of these savings it is essential that a most accurate work-study be done on existing techniques, preferably by means of clocks which record actual current, plant-utilization time over a considerable period. The results, when compared with the forecast for an automated plant, will often prove decisive. Considerable savings are often to be made in this way, even in processes which apparently do not have a well-marked manual setting-up operation, even in an automated plant which does the exact equivalent of the former manual operation. For example, a series of tests showed an average saving of 16 per cent on cycling time after a batch chemical plant had been converted to automatic sequence control. This saving was made up of many small time-savings: the operator had had to turn control valves by hand, and did not always catch the "previous process complete" stage as smartly as possible.

There is always a tendency for operators to go off for tea breaks or other interruptions at precisely the time when plant has completed one stage and is in a stable state, this being a safe time to leave it for a few minutes. An automatic batching and sequencing system gets on with the next job immediately the previous stage is finished, without idle time. It is found in practice that, whereas a manual plant may give, say, four batches a day, the same plant with automatic control may well give five batches in the same period.

Increase of Maximum Plant Capacity

The effective maximum capacity of an automated plant should be considerably higher than that of the equivalent manual plant because

1. There is no accumulation of small dead times and setting-up times, as described above.

2. Labour may not be available to run a manual plant on overtime, double shifts and triple shifts.

3. The quality of supervision on shift work varies greatly (it is a common experience that night-shift output is well down on day-shift output, owing to inferior night supervision).

Taking all these factors into account, I believe an automated plant can have an *effective maximum* output up to even twice that of the equivalent manual plant.

Space Savings

The total space occupied by a process plant depends partly upon the volumetric requirements of the plant itself and partly upon the space required for accessibility. In many cases the automated version of a manually controlled plant will occupy considerably less floor-space because accessibility need not be taken into account to anything like the same degree. It is true that some accessibility will be required for maintenance, but the various data-controlled actuators involved can be tucked away in relatively inconvenient positions, since there is no need for accessibility at a fixed operating height.

Furthermore, in some automated systems (e.g. an automated conveyor system), the whole process can be put up in a roof space having only minimum emergency-access arrangements. In general, much better use can be made of the height of a building. This is particularly true of automatic storage systems, wihch may go up to forty feet in height or more, with entirely mechanical handling.

A second saving is that no space need be allowed for casual dumping of products. The process should be designed for true continuity and mechanization of all handling. Thus an automated plant should be a very clean plant. Savings in this sector will also include the value of work-in-progress in dumped and forgotten material.

Product Quality and Scrap Savings

Perhaps the second-most important economic factor after increased plant utilization is improvement in quality control. The savings will fall into the following categories—

　　1. Increased value owing to increased average quality of product.
　　2. Automatic inspection will—
　　　　(*i*) increase goodwill by protecting the customer against delivery of imperfect products,
　　　　(*ii*) save assembly costs and other subsequent wasted work, because unsatisfactory items are rejected early, and
　　　　(*iii*) reveal process trouble earlier, so that it can be rectified with less cost in scrap labour.

The above factors are extremely difficult to evaluate in preliminary discussions, and yet they represent major reasons for automating. Hence a very considerable economic dilemma, since boards of management are very loth to take decisions when given only broad indications and reasons which cannot be accurately assessed as to profit or loss. It would appear that there is no simple answer to this problem, only a hope that a growing climate of opinion and experience will make management more progressive. Perhaps some firm in an industry more progressive than the rest will go ahead, and the performance of its pioneering plant may set standards which the more cautious brethren will feel obliged to follow.

Savings Due to Progressive Optimization

The philosophy behind automation is that of "robot control," and implicit in this concept is that the robot will continue to carry out its instructions day in and day out without loss of vigilance and performance. This is a great deal more than can be said for existing manually controlled plants, especially where a high degree of supervisory skill is required. Their operations are subject to deterioration owing to increased age of staff, staff changes, illness, and the many errors and omissions that arise from human fallibility.

One of the major advantages of automated systems is that they remove the fear of this type of insiduous deterioration. The benefits falling under this general heading are probably threefold.

1. The general easing of management nerves when it is known that manufacturing and other instructions will be accurately kept: managers turn into "program deciders" rather than general nursemaids.

2. The fact and the knowledge that product quality is not likely to vary because of such minor inconsistencies of human procedural control as are extremely difficult to locate and pin down. The savings under this heading are of all those interminable inquests which involve taking countless opinions and end up with somebody saying, "Forget it!"

3. The rigid control provided by a data-controlled system provides a stable background of plant performance against which to introduce technical changes aimed at further improvement of output and product quality. At the same time it is possible to introduce such changes at short notice with immediate benefit. This saves the long palaver usually involved in training operators and supervisors in new procedures.

Altogether the above factors represent a very considerable potential benefit in the running of a productive or distributive organization, but they are extremely difficult to assess in advanced studies and economic equations. The best argument that I know in attempting to convince people of these management and control advantages is to take them to a *partially* automated factory. Those who have experience of such units, for example one with 90 per cent of the operations already mechanized and automated, will know to their sorrow that it is the residual 10 per cent of manual buffering which causes almost all the problems in the plant, and which tremendously reduces the effectiveness of the 90 per cent automation. In particular it will be found that if the 10 per cent of human activity is in inspection and quality control, the automated plant may be kept idle for half its time whilst human evaluations and decisions are made.

The Benefits of Progressiveness

So far, in dealing with the potential savings to be obtained by the installations of automated systems, I have concentrated on those factors which can be logically understood to confer direct financial benefits, even though these may be very difficult to assess in advance.

There is one other benefit to be obtained whose value it is quite impossible to forecast in advance, and that comes under the general heading of *Progressiveness*.

This is really bound up with general morale in a factory, and particularly among the intermediate younger level of a technical staff. Although they may realize that their jobs could be threatened by increased automation, they, nevertheless, also realize that this is the direction in which the world is moving, and that failure to move with the times represents a certain sort of individual failure. I have come up against this situation on many occasions, where intermediate staff in an organization were ready, keen and briefed to proceed with automation studies and installation, but were unable to convince management clearly about the financial benefits of such changes.

When staff have suffered for a considerable time from inability to get some action under these conditions, there arises a progressive sense of frustration which seeps through considerable areas of the organization. Such a frustration complex, which is extremely common in British industry, inevitably results in staff either giving up the whole effort as a bad job and settling down to await their pensions, or seeking more enterprising employers elsewhere. The basic technical urge to automate is simply the natural expression of the creative spirit in people under modern industrial conditions. It must find its outlets. As more highly automated plants come into operation in a country, they set the target for the competitive spirit amongst young engineers and industrial scientists.

Whilst a great number of people may be content to work just in order to earn a living, the best and most progressive people work to have technical fun, to satisfy their sense of adventure and creativeness. These are the pioneers who take a country forward and create wealth for the future, and *we frustrate them at our peril.*

CHAPTER 22

AUTOMATION AND LABOUR

LABOUR is deeply concerned with the implications of automation. There is no use in glossing over the fact that automation of certain industries may involve a net reduction in the number of workers employed. In other industries automation may so stimulate productivity and market outlets that the net effect may be to increase the number of workers involved. In a third category the effect may be to leave the total number of workers unaffected, but change the emphasis on the sort of work which they do.

Although the effects of automation on labour cannot be simply assessed, it is most important that the workers involved be generally briefed about their prospects, so that the necessary readjustments can be made relatively painlessly and in an atmosphere of intelligence and understanding.

Since the broadest effects of automation will be to increase productivity and total work, there is no reason whatsoever why the world at large should be afraid of automation. It is clearly a major factor, which can lead to increased material prosperity and cause a gradual but progressive reduction of the working week, with increased leisure for all. The whole problem is how to organize for automation and reap its benefits whilst at the same time dealing fairly, intelligently and sympathetically with the interests of the individual human beings concerned.

The interest of human beings must be paramount. If the transition is correctly guided there is no reason why a single person should resist the change or be caused to suffer.

In this chapter I shall consider the various problems involved. They come under the following headings—

1. National outlook for labour.
2. Possible implications in specific jobs.
3. Role of the unions.
4. Technique adopted by individual firms.
5. Role of the Government.

EFFECT OF AUTOMATION ON NATIONAL EMPLOYMENT

The overall national effect of correctly organized automation is to increase productivity, expressed either as a single annual value or as value per worker. There is simply no doubt about this, as we can see from developments in the United States of America. The U.S.A. has the most highly automated industry in the world, and also the highest productivity and average standard of living. Progressive automation and productivity form a closed circle, in which one factor must stimulate the other. Increased productivity involves increased average wealth per worker, and this necessitates the payment of increased wages to provide the purchasing power to soak up the productivity. Increased wages *per se* threaten the economic stability of a business, so it has to mechanize and automate even further to reduce the manual content per unit of productive value. This, in turn, increases productivity, wages, and automation incentives. All this is as it should be, and is one of the really desirable spirals. The effect on a nation is generally to increase standards of living and reduce the length of the working week.

We have seen this happen all over the world as a direct consequence of increased mechanization and productivity, and there appears to no limit to it. By the end of the century it would not be at all surprising if the working week were reduced to about twenty hours. If you consider this forecast exaggerated, compare conditions in 1900 with those of today, and you will concede that these things are at least probable.

Furthermore, the advances over the last sixty years have been made in spite of the tremendous expenditure on armaments and the disastrous effects of two major "hot" wars and one "cold" war. Actually, the wars are not entirely irrelevant to this progress. The techniques for increased productivity are simply the application of science and brains to industry, and it is a horrifying comment on human nature that the big advances in applied science are made in times of hot and cold war. This is true of the present time, and the major developments in computers, electronics, and servo-mechanisms are taking place in the military field: but the same techniques are being made available for the peaceful purposes of productivity. It is a great pity that only actual war, or the threat of war, will make a nation loosen the strings of its money bags to finance technical development at full speed.

Now what is the effect of this development on labour? We can be sure that, on the *average*, the worker will be considerably better off, and that he will have more leisure in which to spend his greater income. There will also be two sectors of industry where even more workers will be employed than before. These will be (*a*) the automation supply industry, particularly in electronics, and (*b*) the operating and maintaining of automated installations.

Indeed, if countries can obtain economic access to all the increased raw materials required for the increased productivity that comes with increased automation, there could be an actual increase in total employment, particularly over the extended transition period during which industry is being so re-equipped.

Another positive aspect of the situation should be that, as the undeveloped nations of the world see more of the standard of living in the industrialized nations, they will increasingly strive to bring their own standards of living into line. It is my view that they can achieve this only with packaged automatic factories, bought from the more advanced countries. Only such factories incorporate packaged management and supervisory skills. Lack of these skills, after all, is the bottleneck for backward countries. Such packaged automatic factories could be a major export from Britain, and we already have the makings of such a business in our current exports to the U.S.S.R. There is no reason why this sort of export should not be applicable to other countries such as China, India, and the newly self-governing countries of Africa.

At the moment this may not appear to be feasible, owing to the problem of deciding who is to finance such export operations. But it appears very probable that the industrialized and wealthy nations will simply have to provide the money to equip the undeveloped countries in this fashion. Already there is very considerable capital aid coming from the wealthy countries, and all the indications are that this aid will be greatly increased, out of compassion or simply to keep the peace.

All this is very relevant to the position of labour, since these are reasons why productivity must increase for export purposes. High employment and high total productivity go hand in hand.

It may even be worth considering what sort of automated plants of packaged factories Britain may export in the near and more distant future. We can see what the near pattern will be from what is happening in Russia, a country with a low standard of living, which is making great efforts to secure a rapid increase in its standards. We may also consider as relevant the fact that the newer self-governing territories, such as India, have clearly expressed their intention to be self-supporting industrially. Thus the first generation of exported plants will be for heavy industry, particularly steel and cement plants and the like, and these will be rapidly succeeded by machine-tool-making plants and other factories for making vital productive equipment like spinning and weaving machinery.

The undeveloped countries are much more likely to concentrate on increased production of necessities, rather than the luxuries of the west, and the most basic of all necessities is food. Large sectors of the undeveloped nations are threatened periodically by famine, and these threats increase with the current rapid increases of world population. Does automation have a place to play in this problem? Clearly it does, and one sees a future full of prospects for the export of automated plants for processing fertilizers, taking nitrogen from the air, taking fertilizer from the sea, hydroponic cultivation, irrigation, sea-water de-salting, making food from plankton, and using solar energy.

Perhaps in twenty years' time plants like these will be our major capital exports, and it is not too early now to plan for such inevitable developments. In all of them automation will be of the first importance, and all are related to the vital future of labour in Britain.

I should like to stress these basic points with particular reference to Britain. Employment in Britain depends upon the country's ability to export. Increased automation increases productivity, and thus the demand for imported raw materials, which can be paid for only by increased exports. The external world is moving towards self-sufficiency in consumer goods, and Britain must look more and more to the export of capital goods to pay its way and to increase its affluence.

But the capital goods of the future will be automated capital goods, automated producing plant and factories, and we shall only have the know-how to make these if we automate at home. So the British worker has a direct, positive, and vital stake in the rapid advance of automation in Britain, and we may be sure that a great number of workers will be required. Thus, *overall*, we need not fear that automation will adversely affect the net national fortune, nor the fortune of individuals in such a progressive nation.

EFFECT OF AUTOMATION ON LABOUR
IN INDIVIDUAL FIRMS

Whilst the outlook for a nation which is progressive in automation is pretty cheerful, and can only be increased average wealth, shorter working hours, and the ability to help nations less well favoured, the implications for individual industries and firms will, nevertheless, vary very greatly. I have already indicated that in certain cases employment will be increased, and that these will be the electronics and capital goods industries. But there may be three sectors of labour where net employment may be reduced, as follows: (1) unskilled and semi-skilled workers in mass production; (2) highly skilled craftsmen in the engineering industries; and (3) clerical workers.

Semi-skilled Workers. The semi-skilled workers of industry are mainly engaged on such activities as assembly, testing, inspection, packing, storage, and labouring. All these six categories are, in my view, potentially threatened by modern automation. The main job of labourers, for example, is to move goods about a factory, and this is increasingly being dealt with by mechanical handling systems. This trend also leads to cleaner factories, since goods are not dumped on the floor to anything like the same extent, and automated factories can be quickly cleaned up by means of semi-automated devices.

One of the most difficult production jobs to automate is assembly, which involves particularly effective human faculties for recognition and positioning, but automatic assemblers are now coming on to the market and will in due course displace some labour, both male and female.

A sector where more rapid developments may be expected is inspection and testing. Britain may be expected to follow the present American tendency to automate these functions, with important gains in improved product quality.

Another threatened redundancy sector is in packaging. There are many products which are rather difficult to pack automatically, but the considerable developments in this field will progressively displace packaging workers. The remaining main concentrations of labour in such industries as food, proprietary medicines, etc., is in the packaging sector, and strenuous efforts are being made to automate all these activities.

This also raises a side issue—the present calamitous necessity, in an otherwise highly mechanized production line, to employ semi-skilled workers who must keep pace with the automation. Some of the jobs are incredible to witness. They include packaging, handling, inspection and machine feeding. It is quite common to see girls feeding parts into a machine at the rate of one cycle a second, and doing this for forty hours a week for years on end. The scene is reminiscent of what one imagines went on in the worst periods of the nineteenth century. Such jobs, where a worker is sandwiched into a flow line and has to keep pace with a rapidly cycling machine, must be eliminated in the name of national self-respect.

"Automation sandwich" jobs must also be eliminated for economic reasons: one or two people become vital to the continuity of a plant in which great capital sums are tied up, and the efficiency of plant utilization is greatly reduced by these few manual workers. Often these jobs can only be described as horrifying, and their elimination from such industries as pottery, paper-carton making and the engineering industries is a "must."

Engineering Craftsmen. The popular idea that automation is particularly for mass-production industries such as motor-car manufacture, etc., should have been thoroughly dispelled by the earlier chapters of this book. In my view there are many jobs at present being done by craftsmen, particularly in the engineering industries, which will in future become automated. They are jobs that can be done by data-programmed equipment. Typical among these jobs are toolmaking, ship-plate flame-cutting, and batch chemical processing. The reason for the change is that a data program can be made to include the most minute and accurate details of procedure, and can be made to control machines and processes even beyond the accuracy which we expect of the craftsman. Take toolmaking as an example. All tools are made to a drawing, and if this drawing is codified on to a punched or magnetic tape and processed through a computer the result will operate a machine tool to much finer accuracy than any craftsman. Furthermore, the same data-programmed machine tool can be adapted to inspect the result of its own workmanship automatically in far less time than a man can do it. With these new methods there is simply no room for the craftsman. The robot brain provides the accuracy and, indeed, permits many things to be made which cannot be made at all by the best craftsmen: for instance, jet turbine blades. The time appears to be coming, over the next twenty years, when the great majority of the craftsman's machining and fitting operations will be replaced by data-controlled machines. However, such development will be slow and evolutionary, so it is likely that the labour position will be self-adapting. Craftsman labour is in short supply at present anyway.

Labour Redundancy in the Clerical Field. The long-threatened labour redundancy in the clerical field has not so far appreciably materialized because automated clerical procedures and systems are still only in their infancy. A second fact is that such equipment has been very expensive, and could only be afforded by large and forward-looking firms. However, we are now at about the end of the proving phase of these techniques, and there appears to be no doubt that they will be wholeheartedly adopted by most firms in the future. The computer suppliers have now got their businesses off the ground, and can begin to put their prices at lower and more attractive levels. For example, the I.B.M. organization now offers a cheap data-processing system which can be hired for as little as about £1,500 per annum, and this is coming within the range of the very small man. So rapid acceleration may be expected in the use of automatic data-processing and it appears inevitable that this will lead to redundancy of clerical staff in such operations as banking and insurance, and in all business and clerical procedures in industry, such as works accounting and stores and production control. From the national point of view this reduction in clerical overheads by automation must be to the good, and it will allow sharp increases in efficiency to be made. But it may raise an acute problem among employees who may not be as versatile as the productive workers in factories.

We must, of course, hope that the evolutionary nature of these changes, and the good sense of the managements and trade unions involved, will work out a satisfactory redeployment of labour, but this will require some degree of labour adaptability.

LABOUR ADAPTABILITY AND THE TRADE UNIONS

Whilst automation should increase the net prosperity of a nation, its industries, and the workers employed, there is likely to be some local discomfort and redundancy even when the most has been done for reabsorption of labour within a given firm.

The general effect of automation should not be to change workers into mere morons tending a robot: but there is a particular challenge involved. This is a challenge to the technical men and engineers, who have to become even more intelligent and knowledgeable than they are now in order to cope with the problems of progress.

To some extent *all* workers will require an understanding of the subject, and the ability to upgrade themselves to meet the new needs. The awful thing would be if the general advance created a division between an "automation *elite*" and "the others." There is certainly some danger of this. I have witnessed it at first hand in Russia, where automation is a national policy. The small percentage of people selected to run the operation are given the best of everything, but "the workers" tend to be left out of the picture.

The challenge is, therefore, also to "the others," to make the effort to understand what this automation business is about. It also involves many organizations which have propaganda facilities. They must themselves understand the subject fully and do their part in putting it across to the workers. Outstandingly, this would appear to involve the Ministry of Education and the trade unions.

I propose to deal later in this book with the steps which should be taken by the Government on these lines, but one thing is clear, and that is that the unions have a major part to play in this operation. They must be as thoroughly in the picture as they are in the United States. All the evidence at the present time is that they are concerned with the problem, and making most intelligent efforts to understand automation and its consequences. Sometimes, I am afraid, they are making more effort than managers and managerial organizations.

Automation is going to call for great breadth of mind on the part of the unions. They may be faced with considerable problems in certain sectors. "Workers" and "labour" could be disappearing concepts, to be replaced by a broader concept of a class of people who earn their livings up to a certain wage level. The new concept is already growing, and the union structure to cope with "wage-earners" at large may have to be considerably modified and made more adaptable. To some extent the concept of "labour" was outmoded when workers were provided with power tools, and the term "worker" was a better new description. Now we are moving to a stage where power tools will be replaced by push-buttons, and many workers will become supervisors. The situation calls for more education for all concerned, and for more versatility and adaptability.

PAINLESS AUTOMATION AS A MANAGERIAL RESPONSIBILITY

Under no circumstances should the management in a firm work secretly on a major automation project, install it rapidly in a factory, and suddenly give 500 workers their notice. This is what I should call "acting unintelligently." It may be desirable for the first tentative surveys of automation possibilities in a firm to be carried out secretly —if the result of such a survey could be a decision *against* automation: there is no point in causing unnecessary anxiety to workers. However, as soon as management is becoming clear in its mind about the direction of increased automation in which it wishes to move, it should carefully prepare and state its case to its employees.

The management should first make clear *why* the firm wishes to automate further, and what the general advantages would be to the long-term prosperity of the firm as a whole. It should then give a broad indication of *how* it proposes to automate, and what will be the employment implications for different groups of workers. At this stage the management may be able to assure the workers that the net effect on the company will be to increase productivity and sales, and reassure them by undertaking that within a definite period nobody will be made redundant by the automation. The management may have to say that, as far as can be seen, the total number of workers will be unaffected, but the distribution of duties will be different: and when the new scheme comes into operation it will offer thorough and well-organized training for redeplyoment within the works for any employee who wishes it.

Should redundancy be unavoidable, the management must make its policy and intentions perfectly clear, agreeing with the unions concerned the amount of notice and compensation that will be given. In some cases automation may involve redundancy in an area where there is a labour shortage, and then it is up to the personnel officer to work out a progressive transfer scheme between the automating firm, the local employment office, and other firms, with the local unions seeing that no individual is worse off for transfer. The important thing is that all this should be forecast, organized, and thoroughly agreed with the unions and workers.

ROLE OF THE GOVERNMENT

Britain has come a long way from the days when a die-hard government could sit back and watch industrial discomfort without taking a hand. The initiative for automation must come from management, but the discomfort will be felt by certain workers. Whilst local goodwill, and intelligent behaviour on the part of local management, workers and unions, can do much to alleviate the discomfort, there may also be a part to be played by the Government. In my view this should come under two main headings—

(a) A co-ordinated plan for general education in the field of automation, with the initiative coming from the Ministry of Education.

(b) The setting-up of a national advisory council on automation to co-ordinate all the interests concerned and act as a steering organization.

I shall deal with the detailed implications and possibilities of the above in the last chapter of this book. In general, one may conclude that although the effect of automation on labour is not yet severe in Britain, now is the time to give full consideration to the problems, so that when they assume significant proportions we do not have to revert to our traditional policy of muddling through.

CHAPTER 23

THE AUTOMATIC FACTORY

A FEW years ago the British Institution of Production Engineers held a memorable conference under the title *The Automatic Factory— What does it Mean*? Every once in a while it may be useful to measure automation progress against that ultimate automation concept— the automatic factory.

There are already many production units that are highly automatic. They employ very little labour relative to the total value of production. Reduction of manpower is probably at its most advanced in an oil refinery. I was once told that eight men controlled the production of 30 per cent of Britain's petrol. There are also other factories, such as those in the biscuit-making industry, which employ astonishingly few productive workers considering the size of the factories and the high daily value of the throughput.

But, somehow, this is not quite the automatic factory concept. These highly automatic processes are able to grind out their product with very few because they are continuous processes, making a relatively standardized product.

In my view the real measure of progress towards an automatic factory will be how far any particular factory in a particular industry has progressed towards the ultimate *possible* position. This *possible* position will be different for different factories. The goal for factories employed in continuous chemical processing might be to have only one or two people left on the plant for essential maintenance. A toolmaking firm might be considered highly automated if it still employed many craftsmen for certain finishing operations, but had substituted data-programming for much of the craftsmanship formerly required.

Thus progress towards the automatic factory has to be measured in terms of the present position and reasonable possibilities. The aim is not to be considered as achieved simply when the last human being puts on his coat, walks out of the place, and leaves the whole operation to run itself. The problem is to define the nature of an automatic factory in some more general way, so that the definition holds for any type of production operation. The form of such a definition is now becoming increasingly clear. The approach is on the following lines.

All factories have three major functions—

1. The direct productive process.

2. Movement and storage of all materials.
3. The overheads structure of the business, with all its white-collar ramifications.

Let us call these three aspects of a factory by the short names of *production, handling* and *clerking*. Now we have seen in the practical chapters of this book that very great strides have been made towards the automation of the first two functions—production and handling (for example, data-controlled machine-tools and automatic storage systems). So, very broadly, we begin to realize that these two major aspects of a physical process can gradually come under data control from such devices as punched cards or magnetic tapes. We also know that "automatic data-processing" by business machines, electronic calculators and computers is steadily revolutionizing clerical procedures. So we are already at the position where all the three main factory functions of production, handling and clerking are being partly performed by automatic data-processing techniques of one sort or another, although up to the present time these operations have tended to be kept in separate compartments.

INTEGRATED DATA PROCESSING AS THE KEY TO THE AUTOMATIC FACTORY

Some progress has already been made, as shown in Fig. 23.1, towards the progressive control of production, handling, and clerking by

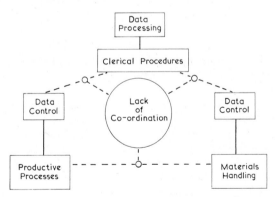

FIG. 23.1.   THREE ASPECTS OF DATA PROCESSING AND CONTROL

data-processing techniques, but the problem is how to integrate all these together so that they operate as an organic whole. The technique for doing this is clearly to integrate the factor common to the three functions, i.e. the data-control systems, and this leads to the concept shown in Fig. 23.2. There all three functions of production, handling, and clerking are manipulated by a single data-processing system. This concept is usually referred to as that of *integrated data-processing*.

So the concept of the "automatic factory" has changed greatly from what it might have been thirty years ago. At that time an automatic factory would probably have been conceived as some extremely complicated and integrated mechanism full of gear-wheels and conveyor belts. The prime feature now required is integration of all the unseen activity of thinking and calculation, resulting in automatic programming and automatic quality control.

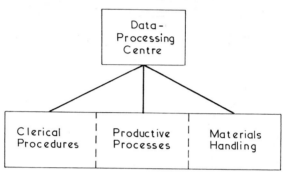

FIG. 23.2.   INTEGRATED DATA-PROCESSING AND CONTROL

This throws a new light on the apparently automatic oil-refinery. One can now ask much more penetrating questions, like: "Is it run on the highest possible load-factor to make the best use of the capital invested?" Or: "Is it making exactly the balance of products required to satisfy the market demand without making unnecessary stocks of some unwanted fraction?"

These questions are not a matter of how few people are employed as operators, but how well the planning and programming is being done, and it may well be that the oil refinery comes off rather badly when investigated on the qualitative results of its total data-processing.

This newer concept of an automatic factory, with its emphasis on well conceived data-processing and control, is in line with the original definition of automation in Chapter 1 as "development into data-controlled process," and the measure of progress is to be seen in the extent to which a factory is under the control of automatic and integrated data-processing techniques.

I was once asked, "what would an automated factory look like?" I answered that "it would look very much like any existing factory, but the people in it would not appear to be very worried or working very hard." The real key is in the automatic organization going on behind the scenes in a small data-processing centre, making sure that the factory is loaded in the best way, that it is being automatically progressed, and that instructions are being prepared and sent out to various production and handling processes.

THE GENERAL FORM OF INTEGRATED-DATA-PROCESSING AUTOMATION

The general form of a factory automated by means of integrated data-processing is shown in Fig. 23.3. In this highly simplified schematic diagram you will note the following principal features—

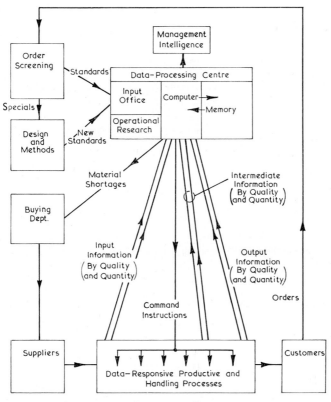

FIG. 23.3. THE AUTOMATED FACTORY

The Computer. A data-processing centre is based on a digital rather than an analogue computer because (*a*) only digital computers can maintain that accuracy over many successive calculations which is essential for accounting, and (*b*) data-processing centres require a large storage capacity or "memory," and this is very difficult to arrange with analogue computers.

A typical computer in a modern data-processing centre simply receives data in the form of punched tapes, magnetic tapes and punched cards. The data consist either of facts or of procedural programs to operate on facts. The output of the centre is a similar set of punched tapes, magnetic tapes or punched cards, carrying transformed data.

The Data-processing Office. Computers use highly coded information, but must have effective power of communication with the world outside the data-processing centre. The method of dealing with this "language" problem varies. Data-controlled machine-tools may often be able to use data directly, in the form of a magnetic or punched tape, with no intermediate translation. On the other hand, an incoming order from a customer may require manual translation onto a punched card.

Thus an essential auxiliary of the data-processing centre is a data-processing office equipped with coding typewriters for input translation. Human translation from punched-hole code into ordinary language is not normally required since the computer's automatic "print-out" typewriters will do the job. The data-processing office will normally require the services of one or two operational research specialists constantly to study how the data-processing centre can be put to increasing use in all aspects of the factory operation.

Order Input—Standardization Screening. The data-processing centre will contain in its records a great deal of standard information on the product. Such records will involve standard manufacturing procedures, standard material quantities, etc. But it is no use putting incoming customers' orders into the data-processing centre for processing unless one is sure that the centre contains all information required for dealing with the particular product. It is necessary to screen all incoming offers, and divert to a methods department all orders with non-standard features, so that new standards can be devised for the irregular products and their manufacture under data-control.

Methods and Design Department. Examples of design techniques using automatic-data processing methods have been described in Chapters 9, 10 and 18. Very broadly, one can say that the methods and design department in the automated factory of the future will convert both product design and production technique into a form which can be digested by data-controlled processes. The scope may vary widely, from translation into tables from blueprints for mechanical parts, to translation of a batch chemical proces into a punched-tape procedure. In certain cases, for example with data-controlled machine tools, the design department may use the data-processing centre for intermediate calculations before finalizing its specifications.

The Factory Area. Shop-floor processes should as far as practicable be arranged to operate directly from such data-program devices as punched cards, punched tapes and magnetic tapes. You have seen in the practical chapters in this book how many machine tools, chemical processes and automatic materials-handling and storage systems, equipped to operate in this way, are now becoming available. This is the *command* aspect of automation. But also necessary are a range of data-originated responses from the shop floor to the data-processing centre. These will include—

Input materials analysis by quantity and quality.

Intermediate materials analysis by quantity and quality to provide both quality control information, progress and stocks information.

Final product testing and inventory for shipment customer billing, and quality control information.

Management Intelligence. An automated factory run on these lines has marked advantages in management control, perhaps particularly in the provision of accurate, digested and up-to-date information. For example—

Information on the optimum loading of the factory and forecasts of order requirements.

Up-to-date job-costing figures.

Rapid job-tendering information.

Stock levels.

Total financial results of the factory.

Job progress information.

Not only can this information be produced extremely quickly, but it can be automatically digested to give figures showing deviation from budgets and production targets, and it can also be automatically plotted in graphical form to show trends.

Buying Information. Material-availability information from the shop floor and storage, taken together with data on advance stock allocations for jobs and orders in hand, can be automatically compared with maximum/minimum stock targets to give purchasing information. At the same time the data can be compared with production schedules to give forecast shortage lists for chasing action.

Production Progressing. Data provided automatically from the shop floor, as described in Chapter 17, can be compared with targets to give warning signals and to satisfy customers' progress inquiries.

Stock Levels. The value of work in progress may be ascertained from production progress data and taken together with total stock values to give information on capital tied up, with the possibility of quick management decision on future stock policy.

Quality Information. Quality information from the shop floor can be processed for direct modification of automatic instructions to the process, or for design-department information.

IMPLICATIONS FOR MANAGEMENT

A great deal of the time of top management, under existing un-automated conditions, is taken up in solving problems of "the system." Most factories are under constant re-organization in attempts to remedy the more glaring weaknesses of "the system," and that is why industry is such a happy ground for management consulting firms.

But an organization under integrated-data-processing control cannot be constantly re-organized on a piecemeal pasis. In the first place, when such control is installed there must be a major jump of organization. A great deal of thought will have been put into the system, and after that it has to be allowed to run. This is not to say that a plant with integrated data-processing cannot be developed, but it is rather like a machine constructed from gear wheels: either all the gear wheels exactly mesh together and operate correctly and consistently, or the mechanism does not work at all. A change in the system can be carefully planned and then introduced overnight. If the modifications have been correctly conceived, the machine will function accurately on the new basis.

All this means that a new management emphasis has to be placed on the importance of the data-processing system, considered as a single entity, since almost all the "system problems" will be focused in this sector of the business. We may expect to see companies appoint "directors of data-processing," and the importance of certain in-dividuals (such as chief accountants) diminish. The general effect will be to put the reins of a business much more firmly in the hands of top management, and greatly to reduce the number of day-to-day decisions required: very many of the decisions will be made auto-matically by the data-processing centre. Some people have the mistaken idea that computers are "stupid" and cannot make effective decisions. This is entirely erroneous. If there is one thing that a computer can do well, it is to make decisions: and it can do this on an amount of data which an average company director would find quite indigestible. So, more and more, the data-processing centre will relieve management of complex decisions and free it to concentrate more on policy problems, for which the computer will have prepared some very elegant paper-work.

IMPLICATIONS FOR PRODUCT POLICY

A highly automated factory should be capable of making any product for which its machinery and plant are suitable, and it should allow highly complicated and mixed programs to be dealt with in a very efficient fashion. The basic idea of data-programming is automatic and rapid adaptability. All this gives prospects of securing far higher factory-loading on a mixed bag of product.

But the contents of the mixed bag must all pass one sort of test: the manufacturing method required should comprise standard procedures. A new feature of a product should not be beyond the scope of the data-processing system. This implies a certain restriction upon product *design* rather than upon product *variety*. If a manufacturer has installed data-controlled machine-tools which can only interpolate hyperbolic or circular arcs, then every product of the factory must be designed with one or the other of these two kinds of curve. Although some restriction is therefore imposed on design, if the data-processing rules are obeyed it should be possible to handle an even greater variety of small-quantity orders than is efficiently possible with existing methods.

THE ULTIMATE—THE AUTOMATED
MANUFACTURING GROUP

So far we have considered integrated data-processing for automation of a single factory in one location. But there are many larger companies that may have numerous factories, offices and warehouses in different localities, and they may wish to operate the whole as a single automated system. This does not really involve any new principle. It simply requires that inter-factory communication be by automatic transmission of data. Such developments are already under way in the United States. Perhaps the most dramatic examples are in automatic airline-seat-booking systems, but the concept is making inroads into industry at large.

One version of this system, by the Radio Corporation of America, consists of data-processing equipment of various kinds in different localities, with telephone-wire connexions to transmit data at high speed. This so-called "Da-Span" system, which is only one of six now available in the U.S.A., is a digital communication system which can operate at up to a hundred characters a second. The "Da-Span" system is fed by punched paper tape and converts this into a code suitable for long-distance telephone-transmission. At the far end the message is decoded into a corresponding punched-tape output. Owing to the high speed of transmission, a great deal of information can be dispatched in a very short time, so there is no need to employ expensive tied telephone lines.

AUTOMATING ORGANIZATION

The direction of development is towards integrated data-processing tied to all aspects of the factory floor. This should not surprise anyone. Running a factory presents primarily a problem of good organization, and the integrated data-processing technique is aimed at *automating good organization*. The automated factory of the future will still have quite a few people on the shop floor, but there may be very noticeable absentees in the overhead and office structure.

CHAPTER 24

ATTITUDES TO AUTOMATION IN RUSSIA AND AMERICA

THE two largest industrial nations in the world, Russia and America, are both fully committed to a policy of progressive automation as their principal means for achieving and maintaining economic prosperity. Their reasons for this policy are not the same by any means. The American urge stems directly from the high cost of labour in that country, a result of the general evolutionary pattern over the last fifty years, which has made the American standard of living the highest there is. The causes of this high standard of living are manifold: inheritance of mixed pioneering European stock appears to make the average American energetic, enterprising, and progressive in outlook: the size of the country raised original difficulties which forced the rapid development of transport in general and the mass-produced motor-car in particular: the country is richly endowed with raw materials.

The net effect has been to raise wage rates to a level some three times as high as in most other industrialized countries, so American industry has to treat labour as a very expensive commodity, and make every possible attempt to use machines rather than men.

The American urge to automate stems from present prosperity, but in Russia labour is cheap because the standard of living is low. Over the last fifty years Russia has not had the same strong industrial development as America, and this has left Russia relatively weak in industrial skills, management, and organizing capacity. But Russia must compete in the economic race if she is to play her part in giving aid, from whatever motive, to the backward economic areas of the earth.

Indeed, in both America and Russia, the urge to automate may be part of the struggle for surplus wealth to distribute to the uncommitted nations, whether from compassionate or political motives.

At the present time America leads all nations in productivity, and by a wide margin. The problem for Russia is how to make up this leeway when she is inherently deficient in organizing and technical skills at all levels. The Russian answer to this problem is to press on with automation, but to be highly selective, dealing with one industry after another in order of priority. By this means she can acquire highly efficient manufacturing facilities requiring the minimum of supervisory skills, and, with luck, she may even be able to leapfrog the west.

AUTOMATION IN RUSSIA

Information on progress in Russian automation is becoming increasingly reliable. There have been many technical missions from Britain to Russia over the last six years, and these have made very adequate reports, many of which are available for inspection at the information library of the Department of Scientific and Industrial Research. I myself visited Russia in 1960 and formed certain impressions. Increased trade between Russia and Britain, especially in the field of automated-factory projects, also gives us a fairly clear idea of progress.

Official Policy in Russia

One of the most authoritative statements concerning the Russian attitude to automation was made by V. A. Trapeznikov in June 1960, in his speech to the International Federation of Automatic Control in Moscow. He took as his title *Automation and Mankind.* You may think it worth while to consider the following substantial extracts from his speech.

> It is pertinent to ask what the overall goal of automation is? What can automation give humanity? Before we can answer this question, let us picture to ourselves the likely fruits of automation and trace the effects of automation on man in the foreseeable future.
>
> First and foremost, automation spells a steep rise in labour productivity. Of course, automation is by no means the only factor contributing to scientific and technological progress which results in higher labour productivity and expanded production of the good things in life. A big role here will be played by advances in controlled fusion, synthesis of man-made organic substances including foods, and in the multitude of other sciences and branches of technology. However, all departments of knowledge today are knitted together closer than ever before, and their further headway is inconceivable without automation. To cite but a few examples, a man owes to automation his space prowess, photographs of the moon's reverse side, and the very existence of powerful means of research like the proton synchrotron.
>
> But automation is still an infant. It will rise to maturity in the life-span of generations to come. What we can therefore do now is to outline its benefits for man in general terms only.
>
> Automation will bring in its wake a big leap in productivity not only because man will not have to operate machines by hand, and a single operator will be able to attend to many automatic units at a time. What is more important is that the expansion of production will no longer be constrained by the human factor of process control.
>
> In many cases today, the rate of industrial processes is restricted by the potentialities of control. Man's response to environmental changes is rather slow. This is why we can only use slow processes.

Automation will revolutionize the majority of manufacturing techniques, as it will provide for control of industrial processes which occur at extremely high rates and on a large scale. While our practice to date has been confined to stable processes, automatic control will place unstable processes at man's disposal as well. Man will be able to control both the outcome and kinematics of reactions.

Atomic energy is but one example of how an effective control system has enabled man to utilize extremely dangerous phenomena to the best advantage. With absolute confidence in automatic instrumentation, it will be possible to maintain processes as close as possible to critical operating conditions. As a result, use will be made of the processes which seem to be beyond man's control today.

The goals of automation can only be achieved when all steps of the industrial process have been automated in all basic industries, transport and building, including the assembly, adjustment, inspection, shipment and distribution of the finished product, that is, when comprehensive automation has been realized to cover ramified remote-control systems widely using computers.

It stands to reason man cannot possibly be excluded from this process entirely. Supervision, maintenance, research and development will always call for his more or less regular attendance. It is beyond any shadow of doubt that man's potentialities in the field of control are great indeed and will never, it appears, be fully surpassed by machines. Therefore, it is the foremost and noble task of scientists in the field of automatic control theory, physiology, psychology and technology to find the best possible uses for man in control systems and to create the best possible conditions for man's activity in process control.

Not only will automation raise productivity, but it will also radically change the very nature of labour. Already now a number of arduous and hazardous occupations have almost completely been done away with, and the trend will continue. In many cases you can no longer see the stoker doing his exhausting job, while those of the steelmaker and blast-furnace operator have become appreciably easier to do. Looking farther out into the future, automation will completely take over jobs involving elevated temperatures and pressures, contaminated or harmful atmospheres. Automation will help turn manual labour more and more into mental work, thus removing the difference between them, so that man's energy and vital strength directly involved in production may be utilized to an ever greater degree, not for process control or—less so—for manual labour, but to produce and realize novel engineering ideas, such as would further relieve man of direct participation in production and would give him abundant life and more leisure.

The higher labour productivity and expanded material production stimulated by automation will sharply improve the standards of living and reduce the working day to but a few hours in the near future.

The full utilization of the benefits arising out of automation, however, is only possible in a rationally organized society, where the manpower made redundant due to automation in one field is easily absorbed in others. Our firm conviction—which we do not, of course, impose on anybody—is that this possibility is offered by the socialist system.

With increasingly more material benefits available due to automation, a smaller proportion of people will be needed in production. A larger number of them will be concerned with research and development, public health and the arts, making our communities better places to live in by laying out parks and gardens, decorating public buildings, and so on.

With more leisure time, means and possibilities at his disposal, man will be able—for the first time in history—to devote to himself the attention he rightly deserves. An era will set in of a scientific approach to human health, with emphasis on balanced daily regimen and diet, sports and prophylaxis. Medical and biological sciences will be given priority to the point where the main duty of the physician will be that of prophylaxis and every case of disease will be regarded as an emergency. Automation's important contribution to medicine will be automatic and semi-automatic apparatus to watch the patient's health, keep his case history, diagnose and treat his ailments . . .

Automation is changing the forms and techniques of research in many departments of science and technology. The very process of cognition is being speeded up. Our knowledge is growing in a kind of chain reaction. The more we learn, the wider the horizons and prospects in front of us, the ampler the opportunities for further progress of research, discoveries and knowledge. This, however, poses further difficulties. For one thing, it is becoming increasingly difficult to store the huge wealth of information and to transmit it in concise, condensed form. On the other hand, it is becoming increasingly difficult to glean new data, to carry on new studies, as science is ramifying at a high pace. Whatever we look at—numerous experiments on alternative chemical reactions made to find unknown properties of chemical substances; studies into the living cell; investigations into conditioned reflexes; research into economic and other complex problems—all this takes a heavy toll of human effort, and of skilled effort, for that matter. In the future, human work will be substantially supplemented and partially supplanted by automatic machines. Automatic systems, with minimum *a priori* information put into them by the designer, will collect information in new fields of knowledge. Already now the researcher is equipped with a variety of measuring, recording, computing machines. In the future a veritable research industry will emerge, based on specialization, co-operation, and use of machines . . .

Machine translation and programming of problems which would seem to belong to the human brain, such as chess problems, have convinced many that formal logic, that is, thinking which can be programmed, is much wider in scope and plays a far bigger role that it was customary to believe. Where do the limits of such possibilities lie? How wide is the field of brainwork which can be handled by automatic machines? Is this field limited to processes which can be reduced to an algorithm, or does it extend far beyond? We take an optimistic view of such things, and hope that automation holds an unlimited promise as a helper of man in his mental activity. In effect, automation plays a noble role here, for it is relieving the human brain of routine work on an ever larger scale, to offer man inexhaustible opportunities for creation and aesthetic endeavour.

The goal of automation is a noble one. It is realistic and feasible. But there is a number of obstacles to clear and a number of formidable problems to solve before it can be achieved . . .

It is also essential to study the principles governing the design of automatic machines which supplement or supplant the human design engineer.

It is often the case that man fails to produce the best possible result, if any, when a given design problem involves mechanical structures with a large number of elements. This is where the automatic machine may play a key role. Unfortunately, the theory covering this field is still in embryo, and there is even lack of understanding of relevant design principles. Perhaps, much support here may come from co-operation with physiologists and psychologists and from studies into the manner man handles similar problems. Though rather inaccurate and slow, these methods are remarkable—compared to the existing automatic machines—for flexibility and adaptability to most varying problems, for their "intuition", "imagination" and the faculty of analogy and generalization. It is in this field that automatic control theory comes closest to cybernetics, of which it is, strictly speaking, the engineering branch. The possible theory in this new and intriguing field of complex automata may crystallize into a unique alloy of theoretical logic, statistics and perhaps calculus of variations. It is not unlikely that entirely new approaches will emerge to the treatment and solution of problems. Our duty is to speed up progress in these directions in every possible way.

In the Soviet Union, there is a large number of investigators working in this field. A whole range of devices has been developed for the automatic synthesis of optimal control systems, as well as a machine for relay system analysis . . .

No progress of automatic control theory and engineering, however, is possible without commensurate advances in automation hardware. It has always been that every new device and every new physical principle embodied in its structure has given rise to quantitative changes, to further headway of automatic control theory. This can be exemplified by the impact the advent of electronic computers, both analogue and digital, has had on automation and automatic control theory . . .

Another crucial problem in the field of automation hardware is that of unitized control systems, which can be combined into various packages suitable for a given plant. This technique simplifies the design, manufacture and operation of automatic control systems and reduces the overall cost of automation . . .

Organization for Automation in Russia

The above extract makes it clear that the sky is the limit for automation in Russia. But objectives are one thing, and achievements—and the organization for future achievements—could be another. This does not appear to be the case in Russia. All the indications are that the country is being organized to reach the high targets set in Trapeznikov's speech, and in speeches by other Russians, including Krushchev himself.

The D.S.I.R. team which visited Russia in 1959 reported that a great potential was being built up in Russia in the automation research institutions, and that there was a program to train the many thousands of control engineers required for their staffing. At the Central Institute for Automation in Kiev it is intended to house over 4,000 employees, and there are four or five other major institutional activities, most of which are provided with pilot process plants for experiment.

The existing effort in Russia already far exceeds the capacity for similar work in Britain. My own impression in Russia was that the work on automation was somewhat overbalanced on the theoretical side, but it must be remembered that there is also a great deal of work in the field, directly attached to local industries. It is noteworthy that British investigators in specific industries such as mining and steel have come back with the firm view that the Russians are forging ahead in practical automation in the heavier industries, and have repeatedly warned Britain against complacency.

The general conclusion from all this is that the official adoption of automation as perhaps the major plank in Russian economic policy, backed up by adequate development facilities and a remarkable training program for young engineers, is bound to produce quite remarkable results. Everywhere there is enthusiasm, a great desire to learn from the west whenever the west have something to give, and unbounded confidence in future success. Experience in Britain has shown that whenever enthusiastic young people are given worthy aims and adequate facilities they always pull things off. There is no reason to suppose that this will not happen with automation in Russia.

There is plenty of published information on Russian automated establishments, such as the well-known ball-bearing plant and piston factories, but I have deliberately omitted them from this chapter because they do not represent advances on technique in the west. The real significance of automation in Russia is *the organized potential for the future, combined with official policy backing*. It is this we have to watch, rather than current achievements.

From all the information in my possession it would appear that the average state of industry in Russia is well behind that of average industry in the west, and a long way behind the American position with regard to automation achieved. In certain sectors of heavy industry, particularly steel, Russia may already be ahead of Britain and level with the States. But in *rate* of progress Russia appears to lead the world, and this appears to mean that one day she will turn an average lag into an average lead. When this will occur is difficult to forecast, since some of the Russian standard-of-living objectives do not coincide with our own. She appears to have no particular plans for the widespread ownership of refrigerators and motor-cars, but she may well create a new sort of civilization, a civilization of very high average mental power and artistic achievement.

AUTOMATION IN THE U.S.A.

Between 1958 and 1962 I have toured the U.S.A. four times, to evaluate generally the development of automation in that country. The first impression an Englishman receives on surveying the scene is that the attitude of management is totally different. American management does not need to be sold on the mere idea of automation. They have been used to the concept for many years, and the only problem is simply the economic question—will it save costs?

It appears to be a simple fact that, on average, the U.S.A. leads the world in automation by a margin of several years. This is simply due to the much higher labour costs—management is constantly on the watch for machines that will replace workers.

Practical Automation in the U.S.A.

The U.S.A. has been responsible for the effective pioneering of two particular branches of automation.

The first is data processing, following the inventions of Hollerith, and she has continued to lead in the development and application of business machines of all sorts. Complete familiarity with punched cards and their manipulation leads the American, naturally, to expect the extension of these techniques to the control of production and distributive processes. In particular, the U.S.A. is highly prepared for the concept of the integrated data-processing system which will combine the automatic handling of all paper work with the automatic control of production and distribution. But the preparatory work for realization of such concepts requires first the mechanization and then the data control of the individual productive processes, and it is in this down-to-earth sector that the U.S.A. is so advanced.

The second branch of automation in which the U.S.A. has done much pioneering work stems originally from Ford's mass-production developments of thirty to forty years ago. These, it will be recalled, emphasized the design of productive equipment capable of new standards of accuracy, so that the items made could be assembled to precision fits without need for laborious hand-fitting. This concentration upon a greatly increased standard of accuracy for mass production was a tremendous step forward, but twenty years or so ago it was realized that even these techniques were not adequate to meet the requirements of precision in mass production.

The latest developments in automation in the U.S.A. have, therefore, been much concerned with the development of selective assembly techniques, based on the use of automatic grading machines as described in some detail in Chapter 11. The natural development of such techniques is the *automatic* selective assembler, and it is my view that this will represent one of the major sectors of advance in the U.S.A. The process has already started in parts of the ball-bearing and motor-car industry, and rapid further developments may be expected.

Perhaps the major development at the present time is the move to automate materials-handling systems. The American philosophy is a philosophy of service and speed of service, and once an article is made the Americans get it into the customer's hands as soon as possible, in order to reduce space and capital tied up in static stocks.

K*

Most of the practical examples of American automation described in this book are either in the Mid-West, the centre of the heavier industries, or on the West Coast, where the cross fertilization between military electronics and commercial applications is beginning to bear fruit.

The Implications of Missile and Space Research

The effort being put into automation technique and data-processing as part of the military effort on the West Coast of the U.S.A. is a unique phenomenon.

Whilst this fantastic expenditure is considerably stretching the American economy, and many might consider that the effort has merely military significance, the fact is that many new techniques of materials, miniaturization, systems and instrumental accuracy are emerging which have profound significance for the automated future. When one realizes that, in Britain, most major steps forward in technique and in the application of science to technology have taken place under the stress of war, it is not to be wondered that the cold-war military effort in the U.S.A. is producing similar results. It is too early to forecast just what the results will be, but already there are commercial developments in automatic assembling machines, automatic inspection and testing systems, and identification techniques, which are directly the outcome of military contracts. Another powerful line is the increased accuracy of instrumentation, e.g. in such products as strain gauges, load cells, and similar measuring devices.

One has to realize that a guided missile or a space vehicle represents the very highest level of automation, just as aircraft engineering represents the highest level of mechanical engineering. To take a photograph of the back of the moon, an exploit accomplished by the Russians, involves just about all the automation technique one can imagine, and all this miniaturized and raised to new levels of reliability.

Automation Technique in the U.S.A.

Although many new and sophisticated techniques are emerging in the U.S.A., this does not represent the general current picture in U.S. automation practice. American applied automation is very practical, and above all very economic, and installations often use techniques which might be considered antiquated in Britain. For example, so far, there is very little use of solid-state devices, and most automation in the manufacturing industries is based on well-tried telephone hardware like uniselectors and relays.

Furthermore, although the average American welcomes the automated approach, he likes devices which he can understand and see working, and there is still considerable resistance to the use of electronics in industry. Thus the suppliers of automation equipment in the U.S.A. have quite a problem of education on their hands. They have to persuade industry to use modern electronic technique, and they go to some lengths to bridge the educational gap. As an example, the Sheffield Corporation at Dayton, Ohio, has recently introduced electronics into its automatic inspection equipment, and it has a well-equipped demonstration laboratory and school to which customers' operatives can go for a thorough course of instruction on the working and maintenance of these new systems.

The "Do-it-yourself" Tendency in American Automation

In order to automate a process it is necessary to know a great deal about the process itself. Such knowledge is possessed by the industries which are customers for automation. But the techniques of automation are data-processing techniques, and belong to a different group of industries. How does one bridge the know-how gap between the two sorts of industry?

Over the last few years the larger users have exercised initiative in the matter and have built up teams of electronics and other experts to work internally on automation projects. This is particularly true of the automotive industry in Detroit. The result is some very effective "do-it-yourself" automation of a very practical kind, if with rather antiquated technique. The larger electronics firms have always been very eager to penetrate these markets, but many have not had sufficient process know-how to make economic propositions. Even the American machine-tool industry has tended to keep overmuch to the supply of standard tools, although the user has demanded "specials" and has particularly demanded "specials" for highly automated processes.

Up to recent times this dilemma had not been satisfactorily resolved in many instances, but there is now a new move which may well be very successful. Large electrical and electronics firms, such as General Electric and Radio Corporation of America, are getting down to automating their own very substantial factories, on the basis that "automation begins at home" and that the automation know-how so gained will duly become a saleable commodity. This process now appears to be about to pay off, and the work which General Electric has put into data-processed machine-tools, automatic stores systems and other projects is now beginning to come on to the market. A very similar operation by Radio Corporation of America also seems about to bear fruit.

Automation Specialization in the U.S.A.

One of the surprising impressions of visiting some American automation supply companies is how small they are, considering that they often have a world-wide reputation. This is due to specialization to a degree far beyond that encountered in Europe. These firms are almost always situated close to the principal users of the specialized processes concerned: Detroit for vehicles, Pittsburgh for steel, etc.

COMPARISON BETWEEN RUSSIA AND AMERICA

Russian automation is mainly a matter for the future, but the very considerable education and institutional efforts on the subject would appear bound to pay off in due course. Already considerable progress has been made, particularly in the steel industry. Practical effects are being felt from the automation that is being supplied to Russia by foreign firms in packaged factories.

American automation is already very practical, with many advanced installations and devices, as described in the various chapters of this book. There is a very strong new effort coming from the larger American electrical and electronics companies, which will almost certainly cause a big surge-forward in technique and in the realization of integrated-data-processing systems.

American automation leads the world on the average by several years, but the *rate* of progress in Russia is probably greater than anywhere else. Unless other nations look to their laurels, these two nations appear likely to walk away from the rest of the world.

CHAPTER 25

THE FUTURE OF AUTOMATION IN BRITAIN

HISTORICAL ROLE OF BRITAIN IN INDUSTRIAL PROGRESS

THE foundations of modern industry were laid mainly by a few Britons in the seventeenth century. Outstandingly, the establishment of the mathematical basis of mechanics by Sir Isaac Newton created the possibility of rapid progress in the design of all sorts of machines. Sir Robert Boyle, with the Frenchman Charles, established the gas laws: these are the bedrock of thermodynamics, and they opened the way for the development of power engineering. On this seventeenth-century base has been erected the great pyramid of power mechanics, which is the essence of mechanized industry as we know it today. The British contribution to this historical growth has been immense, and has included such inventions as the steam engine by Watt, the earliest development of electrodynamic machinery by Faraday, and countless other major milestones in the fields of mechanics, power, and process engineering.

By the end of the nineteenth century Britain was established as the workshop of the world, and led all nations in industrial activity. But over the last sixty years this country has seen her industrial leadership wrested from her by the Americans, and more recently there has been the unexpected emergence of the Russians as a major industrial power. At the present time Britain is about third or fourth in this industrial league-table, along with other nations such as Germany, Japan, France and Italy. And the new European Economic Community of six European nations bids fair to place the U.K. as a complete "also-ran." How has this decline come about?

REASONS FOR RELATIVE BRITISH DECLINE

A main reason for the decline appears to be the smallness of the British home market. It was a large home market that first enabled America to get ahead with mass production. This led to great prosperity in the U.S.A., and an effective total buying power probably about six times as great as the British. Russia is following the American pattern, but is concentrating on its capital goods industry before making an immense mass-production effort.

On the whole, Britain in 1962 is not so far behind other European countries—taken individually—but the European Economic Community is a threat of the first order. This will establish a third industrial competitor with the basic advantage of a large and compact home market.

Now this picture is *far blacker* than the current balance of trade indicates. So far Britain has been a little protected from American competition by the high wages ruling in the U.S.A., but this should not blind anybody to the fact that American productivity, in real goods per worker, is the highest in the world. Both Russia and the European Economic Community are still in low gear, but as they continue to change up Britain will encounter increasingly formidable competition. The country is going to be in real trouble, because non-self-sufficiency in raw materials means that we must export merely to live, and cannot withdraw into a self-contained economic unit satisfied with whatever standard of living we can maintain on our own.

STABLE FEATURES OF BRITISH EXPORTS

If one examines the record of British export for stability and growth, one does not find them in consumer goods such as motor-cars. These goods are very valuable exports, but they are subject to very serious periodical fluctuations. On balance, the trade figures show that the stable and growing export lines are capital goods, and industrial products like trucks, jet engines and tractors. Specifically, the British problem is to outsell Continental countries in the world's markets. It does not appear possible to do this on the basis of lower prices alone.

The outstanding possibility for the future is to sell on *specification* and *quality*, backed up by adequate servicing arrangements.

EXPORT RULE 1: UNIQUE DESIGN AND QUALITY

You may wonder what all this has to do with automation, but if you will bear with me a little longer you will find that automation is fundamental to Britain's future prosperity as an exporting nation.

So far I have touched upon facts and arguments which are well known to all who have to do with our export trade. They can be summed up by saying Britain can only hold her own in the future by upgrading product quality and design. In practice this adds up to two things: to (1) know exactly what is being offered throughout the world, and (2) be five years ahead in what Britain offers.

The major question is—how to be ahead technically? It is not enough simply to *wish* to be ahead: product designers all over the world have the same wish. There must be a method. We can easily see what this method is if we examine firms that are consistently successful in the export market. Certainly I.C.I. and Rolls Royce are two shining stars in the export heavens, and they have won their position by *research*. The day of unaided craftsmanship has passed: the future of industrial strength is contained in the laboratory, in the effort to find quite new, scientific, ways of doing things, and incorporating the experience in export products.

Britain's future depends on exports of advanced design and quality, and these depend upon applied scientific research.

AUTOMATION AS THE MAIN NEW SCIENTIFIC FIELD

The data-processing techniques of electronics are highly scientific, and they occupy a unique position relative to industry and production. When these techniques are applied to such a process as a factory the result is called "automation." Now automation is the *only* scientific field which is relevant to *all* branches of industry. What is the significance of this for export? Here are some of the answers—

1. There is a world demand for automated factories and equipment.

2. An automated factory should make cheaper products than a manual plant, mainly because it increases the effective utilization of capital employed.

3. An automated plant should make the highest possible quality of product. Not only does it exercise ceaseless control over product quality, but it can optimize that quality in a manner beyond the powers of normal human control.

4. Automated design procedures facilitate most-economic-product design.

5. Automated intelligence systems enable management to short-circuit out-of-date information. Valid current decisions can be taken on all aspects of business. One of the main practical export implications is the ability to give accurate quotations at short notice.

Altogether, can you doubt but that these major benefits of automation are of the highest significance for Britain's industrial position?

THE UNIQUE BRITISH SCIENTIFIC POSITION

Britain's ability to export turns on the extent to which she applies science to industry, particularly by automation. Is British industry strong enough for the purpose?

In fact, Britain has a really unique industrial and scientific position in the world today. She is steeped in the rigorous scientific tradition of her universities, which are still prolific in fundamental thought and work. Indeed, this alone gives Britain a highly respected position in the world of science.

But in addition there is a most unusual organized system of industrial scientific investigation in the Department of Scientific and Industrial Research (D.S.I.R.). This Government Department had its origin in the middle of the first world war, when it was realized that the war effort did not have an adequate scientific background, and that special steps would have to be taken to organize more science into British industrial activity.

In the early twenties this Department was officially established with the object of setting up industrial research laboratories of two kinds. First there were to be establishments such as the National Physical Laboratory, wholly financed by the state but essentially for the benefit of British industry, and covering subjects so general that no particular sector of British industry could be expected to finance research on them. There are now about twelve of these general industrial laboratories, wholly financed by the Government. The second group of D.S.I.R. laboratories is concerned with well-defined sectors of British industry. These organizations have been formed as a result of the initiative of each industry, with financial aid from the Government. There are now about sixty of these laboratories, covering such industries as steel, paint, pottery, etc. They tend to concentrate on fundamental problems in their industries. This is very important for automation, since the more basic knowledge there is about a process, especially as to its mathematics, the easier it is to design an automatic system to control it. Most industrial research associations are now working on automation, and all are aware of its importance.

A second unique British organization is the National Research Development Corporation (N.R.D.C.), which was formed to ensure that good ideas and inventions which were premature for industrial development would receive financial backing. The outstanding project so far backed by this government body has been the development of digital computers. The present healthy position in this sector of British technique is largely due to the N.R.D.C. In due course that body may be expected to help pioneer other embryo techniques in automation.

The third Government effort relevant to the development of automation in Britain is the result of the military electronics program. It might be a little embarrassing to know the percentage of the British professional electronics industry that is supported by Government military projects, but it is clearly very high indeed. These projects have permitted many electronic techniques to be pioneered and they will ultimately be of value to industrial automation.

Basically, then, the British scientific effort in industrial fields is well placed and highly organized. If it were a little more specifically directed towards automation it could put Britain in a very strong position.

BRITISH TECHNIQUE IN AUTOMATION

From my own travels about the world, examining automation *technique* (as distinct from applications), there appears no doubt that British technique is fully as advanced as any. This is partly because of the general strength of Britain's electronics industry, but perhaps even more because of the atomic power-station program. The British atomic-power-station program is the most progressive of any in the world, and the control requirements for such power stations are very stringent indeed. They have caused a number of British electronics firms to carry out special electronic development, particularly of various solid-state electronics devices with high reliability. Although in 1962 it is by no means clear that the atomic-power-station program will be economically successful, the side implications in control electronics have been considerable.

Every important automation *technique* is to hand in Britain, and the trouble is simply that industry is *not applying* these techniques to anything like the possible extent.

BRITISH APPLICATIONS

Practical automation in Britain is sadly below the level achieved in American industry. In several chapters in this book describing practical applications, I have had to draw almost exclusively from American sources. None of these applications represents very advanced practice. All could have been realized years ago on the basis of British technique.

WHY BRITAIN LAGS IN AUTOMATION

If British electronics technique is so advanced, why is application lagging? There appear to be six basic reasons. Let me state them briefly and then deal at some length with each in turn.

1. British labour rates are not sufficiently high to create automation incentives at the American rate.
2. British mass-production throughputs are so much lower than in the U.S. that certain automation (such as automatic inspection) is on the economic borderline.
3. Britain as a whole is still very insular. Britons do not travel about sufficiently to see what is happening in other countries. A visit to America or Russia is still looked upon as something of an adventure instead of an afternoon flip.
4. British user industry, the customer for automation, does not sufficiently understand the potential of electronic automation.

5. The British electronics industry has been mainly concerned with the communications, entertainment and military fields, and does not fully understand industrial requirements.

6. I have defined automation as "development into data-controlled process." This is a single concept involving mainly the *integration* of electronics and industrial processes. Britain has no technical or educational structure corresponding to this integrated concept, so the whole subject is out of focus.

British Problem No. 1: Labour Rates

The high American labour rate is a powerful incentive to automate in order to reduce labour costs, but it is a great mistake, as we saw in Chapter 21, to consider that only labour savings justify automation. Unfortunately, British industry at large is under the illusion that only labour savings can justify capital expenditure on automation. This illusion is a major factor impeding progress. If British industrialists, visited the U.S.S.R. they would observe (*cf.* Chapter 24) that the Russians are automating in an atmosphere of very low labour rates, because they realize that an automated plant has the advantages of increased utilization and improved product quality.

It would be a fatal mistake for British industry to wait for labour rates to inflate to American levels and then be forced into some increased automation. Basic rethinking is required.

British Problem No. 2: Low Mass-production Volumes

The motor-vehicle industry has pioneered the application of mass production since the time of Henry Ford. The modern developments of automation in this industry are directed towards automatic assembly, inspection and testing. This is very expensive, and the economic equation is only favourable to automation if throughput is very high, probably not less than a million parts a year. Many British factories are running at only a very small fraction of the output of their American opposite numbers, and the corresponding capital-investment "break even" is unfavourable to Britain in certain sectors. This implies that Britain must not copy American methods but must develop much more adaptable automation equipment capable of rapid resetting for different products. Whilst the Americans can afford to use (for example) *highly specialized* automatic inspection machines, Britain must make *highly adaptable* automatic inspection machines, for use on a considerable variety of products.

British Problem No. 3: Insularity

Very few people in Britain have any idea of what is happening abroad in automation development. Average British management does not realize how important it is to see these things, and it is notoriously parsimonious in providing look-see travel expenses for its younger employees. Even the technical directors of some British firms find it hard to justify the costs of a month's visit to the States—foreign visits and travel are still considered to be something of a spree by everyone except those who have to go. Although over the last few years the position has been getting better, there still appear to be special British genes which inhibit desire for foreign travel. Sometimes this leads to ludicrous situations: British managements will hold forth on the superiority of British Craftsmanship, etc., without ever having seen for themselves what is really happening abroad. This leads to one particular fallacy: "The Americans can't teach us anything." The fact is that the Americans can teach Britain a lot in almost all branches of industry. And not only the Americans, but also the Russians, the Italians, the French, the Japanese, the Dutch, the Germans—all can teach Britain plenty. This complacency, based on insularity, is very serious—perhaps the necessary waking-up shock can only be administered if the country runs into a really disastrous export situation. It might well pay British industry to allocate 1 per cent of its total turnover to foreign technical travel and investigation, to ensure that its own products and productive techniques were highly competitive in the world. There are a few firms that do this, and the results are astonishing.

British Problem No. 4: British User Ignorance of Electronics

It is no use mincing words. By and large, British industry is lamentably ignorant of the fundamental significance of electronics for industrial progress or "automation." This is because industry looks upon electronics as a sort of mysterious gadgetry, with horrible complications of the sort one sees in the back of a faulty television set. It is true that the only thing to be done in such circumstances is to replace the back cover hastily and telephone the experts. Indeed, the rapid growth of television rental services is a precise measure of the average man's suspicion of electronics and all its works. This common experience with entertainment electronics is not lost on the industrialist, and it is probably the major reason why he is "not having any of that damned nonsense running my factory."

The correct answer is to kick in those television screens, stop the moronizing rot, and use electronics in industry where it can *work* for us.

But the British industrialist simply does not know *how* to make electronics work for him. He has not mastered the philosophy of data-processing. He simply has not realized that the data-processing techniques of electronics, which have so transformed his private life through television, are going to have just the same powerful effect on his business in due course.

Owing to this ignorance, many British industrialists have taken up the same attitude and position as King Canute. They defy the electronic sea to come in. And they are going to get very wet.

British Problem No. 5: Ignorance of Electronics Industry about Processes

Just occasionally a representative of the British electronics industry penetrates to the boardroom of a British industrialist. The following is a typical experience.

The scene is set in a "where-there's-muck-there's-brass" locality, such as Leeds or Birmingham. The conversation will open from the electronics side something like this: "We would like to apply electronics to your industry, and if you can tell us your problems I am sure we can solve them for you by electronic automation. We have had a great deal of experience at the Government's expense in automated rocket ranges, experimental atomic reactors, and aircraft navigation systems, and I am sure these will be of great value to you."

The point about the Government having already paid for the development of all these wonders is not lost on the canny industrialist, and he willingly unburdens himself about some of his practical manufacturing problems, such as "colour matching," "reducing work in progress," "casting blow-holes," or whatever is his principal expensive bottleneck.

Now these *real* problems, which the industrialist would like to see automated away, throw the electronics man into a complete panic. He has never heard of such problems before, and he desperately searches for any gleam of a solution. At this point, if he has any sense, he will play for time and suggest that he should be shown round the works to see "exactly the nature of the problem," but the result of his tour will be to complete his bewilderment, and when he returns to the boardroom and is asked what he thinks about the prospects he will have no choice but to relapse into gobbledygook. This gobbledygook will consist of the Queen's English, but all the nouns and verbs will sound like something out of Lewis Carroll's "Twas brillig and the slithy tove." He will begin by using the words "data-processing" as a twilight departure from effective communication, and will then really warm up to "transistors," "operational amplifiers," "flip-flops," "analogue logic," and, in general give the full esoteric treatment. At the point where he has arrived at a description about "probability coefficients" the appearance of the industrialist will be indistinguishable from that of a rabbit faced by a weasel.

During all this time the electronics man will have the misguided impression that he is securing a commercial triumph of the first magnitude. Now is the time tentatively to propose a "study contract!"

He mentions a sum of money in units of tens of thousands of pounds. At this point the industrialist, after pinching himself to make sure it is not all a dream, staggers out of the door towards an unusually alcoholic lunch. In passing he warns his secretary of the dire consequences to her prospects if she "ever again lets that chap get within a hundred miles of this factory."

You may consider this story an exaggeration, but the electronics man knows that it is too true to be funny.

Not only does the electronics industry not understand the practical problems of general industry—it does not even talk the same language, and certainly it does not understand industrial economics. This latter point is not unrelated to years of working on Government-costed military contracts.

British Problem No. 6: Lack of Integration

The fact that the electronics industry and general industry do not speak the same sort of language is itself indicative of some lack of integration in the subject of automation. But the problem is more fundamental than this.

Industry is subdivided into two main categories—

> *Vertical Industries*, each concerned with some speciality which does not appreciably overlap other industries. Such industries are food, chemicals, leather, pottery, etc.
>
> *Horizontal Industries*, which are really services providing products that are common to a wide range of industries. Typical examples are the electronics and the engineering industries. Very largely, such industries are concerned with the supply of process plant and machines to the vertical industries, and they are mainly involved with capital goods.

Automation is much more closely associated with the outlook of horizontal than vertical industries, and itself consists of aspects of all these horizontal industries plus certain scientific techniques, such as mathematics and information theory. To deal adequately with the problems of automating a chemical plant one may well have to consider problems of—

> The special process concerned.
> A mathematical evaluation of the process.
> Chemical, electrical and mechanical engineering.
> Electronics and data-processing.

The problem of automation is not to be simply and quickly resolved by bringing together electronics and general industry. It is true that this is the essential starting point, but afterwards they have to work together for many years to evolve something new, i.e. a data-controlled process considered as an integrated entity. A long evolutionary partnership is required, which will create something greater than the sum of the two parts.

It is a great mistake to think of electronics as something merely to be superimposed upon the established processes of industry. What is needed is a great cross-fertilization of ideas. Thus electronics may well change the existing production processes themselves, and the partnership may call for some new forms of electronic technique not yet available. Some of these developments will come from purely economic considerations. A process might call for the application of a computer, but available computers that could do the job might cost £20,000. If industry became vocal and stated that it would use computers for such and such an application *if* the computer only cost £2,000, then electronics industry would find a way to meet the need.

The real problem is how to get all the various interests together so that they begin to speak a common language, and begin to seek together for really economic automation. A small beginning has been made in this direction in the setting up of the British Conference on Automation and Computation (B.C.A.C.), which is representative of almost all British professional technical institutions. Although a praiseworthy start, this organization does not really meet the need.

GENERAL SOLUTION OF THE SIX-SIDED PROBLEM

The above analysis shows two factors which are out of the country's control, and four factors about which something can be done.

The first two factors are: (1) labour rates that are low compared with the American, and thus lower natural incentive to automate, and (2) production volumes that are low compared with those in America, Russia and the European Six. These two factors are, however, both good reasons why Britain *should* do all she can to automate, since they will otherwise count against her in her fight to win the export battles of the future.

The other four factors are problems of ignorance. The electronics industry lacks knowledge about general industry, and *vice versa*; both the electronics and general industry lack knowledge about what is happening overseas.

One of the paradoxical features of the situation is that there is so *much* information being published in periodicals that no-one can make the effort to keep up with it all. There are now something like 50,000 technical periodicals in the world, all occasionally containing snippets about automation—but how can one attempt to read even a small part of all this?

It is a unique problem: how to distil the essence of the subject of automation and how to put this concentrated knowledge across to the whole of British industry.

The Heart of the Problem—Education for Automation

From time to time a country is faced by the necessity of learning the essentials of a new subject quickly. The training of soldiers and fighting specialists when a war breaks out is one example. Many present-day electronics experts were drapers and clerks before the last war, but the rapid training they were given in telecommunications and radar gave them effective know-how. A second, equally striking, example is atomic power, which was unknown to the general public at the end of the war. Nowadays, industry has a great number of experts in the subject, and most schoolboys know how a reactor works.

The country needs some very similar educational effort in automation at the present time. The lesson of the war and atomic power is that such education must be organized.

There appear to be two ways of tackling the problem: (1) through a conventional educational program aimed at various levels of the community, and no doubt organized by the Ministry of Education under the advice of an expert committee: and (2) by the establishment of some sort of Automation Centre, where people could get answers to their questions.

Both types of effort seem to be required.

ORGANIZATION OF GENERAL EDUCATION FOR AUTOMATION

Any comprehensive scheme for automation education must cover university graduates, technicians involved in either operation or maintenance, supervisors, and management.

Graduate education. From the contents of this book it will be clear that the practical design of automated systems requires the employment of men and women of university-graduate level. At present the nearest suitable type of graduate for this work would be one who had taken an engineering degree including electronics. Existing courses do not embrace the sort of knowledge given in this book. Some kind of automation teaching should be sandwiched into existing engineering courses, in order to give the broad background.

The detailed science of automation is commonly called "control engineering." A good start has already been made in teaching this to British graduates, and there are now post-graduate one-year courses in control engineering at Cambridge, Imperial College, Manchester College of Science and Technology, Northampton and Loughborough Colleges of Advanced Technology and Cranfield College of Aeronautics. It is very important to discriminate between automation as a science, i.e. "control engineering," and practical automation. Only the latter, I suggest should be incorporated in general-engineering-degree courses, the former being matter for post-graduate studies. Perhaps the main problem is to find a sufficient number of teachers with the necessary practical experience. There are a very few persons in industry with the necessary breadth of outlook and experience, but the universities might do worse than to recruit such people to teach.

Automation technicians. The Society of Instrument Technology has made a strenuous effort to get something done about the education of automation technicians, who they consider should be qualified to the level of Ordinary and Higher National Certificate. At present the general syllabuses are not suitable for the training of automation technicians, but one or two technical colleges, notably the Northampton College of Advanced Technology, have taken steps to incorporate this type of teaching in their National Certificate Courses. The incorporation of automation in National Certificates places a particular strain upon students doing these courses in their spare time, since they already have to cover many other subjects in order that their certificate be recognized by the British professional institutions. There is a move by the Society of Instrument Technology to obtain recognition for a form of the Certificate that will place greater emphasis on automation, even though this be at some expense to the other subjects normally taken.

Education for management and supervision. In my view, automation education for management and various levels of supervision is not a matter for formal courses organized by the Ministry of Education. The education requirement for such people would vary greatly. Top management may require a broad view of all possibilities in the industry concerned, whereas a process foreman may only need a narrow training, probably best arranged at his own works. There is, however, a need for a "come-and-get-it" arrangement for anyone who needs to know something about automation quickly.

The National Automation Centre Proposal

The idea of setting up a National Automation Centre was first proposed by the Engineering Industries Association in 1959. The prime objective of such a Centre would be to act as a national focus for automation information. It should be an integral part of the Department of Scientific and Industrial Research, most conveniently located in London.

It is not suggested that the Centre would carry out any research work. It would be something of a cross between the Building Centre, which is a permanent exhibition, and the Harwell Reactor School, which holds short courses and has access to experts. The principal features of the proposed National Automation Centre would be—

1. A permanent exhibition of automation techniques and practice on a classified basis, to include such subjects as control of continuous chemical processes, control of batch processes, data-controlled tools, automatic inspection and testing, automatic assembly, automatic mechanical handling, automatic storage, integrated data-processing, etc. In addition to exhibits classified by automated-system practice (as above), there would be a complementary set of exhibits related to technique, such as digital computing, analogue computing, general data-processing "black boxes," programming devices, data-controlled actuators, etc.

2. A reference office. This would deal with any questions, and would obtain its information partly from classified literature surveys and commercial information.

3. A library, rather on the lines of the Patent Office Library, where one could buy photostatic copies of interesting articles.

4. A small resident "brains trust," seen by appointment, covering a few very important sectors such as computers, automation in manufacturing industry, and automation in process industry. This brains trust would supplement the reference office, and its job would be to explain obscurities.

5. A lecture theatre or conference hall, in which general courses on automation would be given, lasting a few days for industrial supervision and perhaps one day for management. Films would be available of all the important automated installations in the world.

In addition to the above, such a Centre could also usefully house the secretariat of the British Conference on Automation and Computation, and possibly other national committees yet to be formed, and so become a focal point for many lines of activity.

The essential purpose of the National Automation Centre would be to induce general familiarity with the subject, whether the visitor were a schoolboy or a managing director, and in this it would be unique in the world. Compared with the benefits that would accrue the costs would be negligible.

National Organization

Whilst the two steps of strengthening education through the Ministry of Education's normal channels and a new National Automation Centre would go far to solve the problem of education for automation, there is one other matter that requires attention. Which body is to be responsible for national policy, and which Minister of the Crown is to be responsible for co-ordinating action?

Since we already have a Government-subsidized body for general productivity, The Productivity Council, it would appear that this body could pay more specific attention to automation. But, unfortunately, automation is a wider subject than mere productivity. It includes such matters as traffic signalling, automatic stores, automatic shops, etc. Something is to be said for setting up a National

Automation Council or Committee, representative of industrial trade associations, the Productivity Council, professional bodies such as the B.C.A.C., trade unions and Government departments. Its first job would be to press for and organize towards the two objectives described, more education and the National Automation Centre.

As to which Minister should be reponsible, this would appear to be a matter of timing. In the first instance, as there is no Minister of or for Industry, the responsibility would appear to fall squarely on the shoulders of the Minister for Science.

INDEX